D1073988

Workshop Report
VLSI AND SOFTWARE ENGINEERING WORKSHOP

RYE TOWN HILTON, PORT CHESTER, NEW YORK

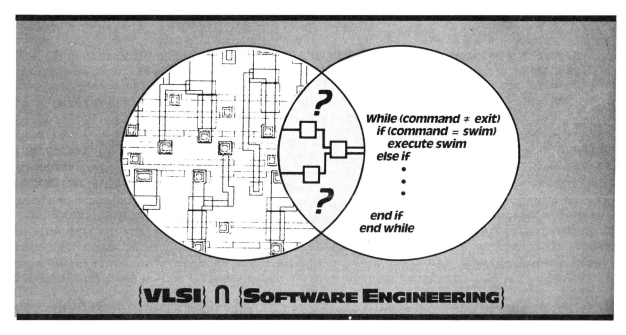

{VLSI} ∩ {SOFTWARE ENGINEERING}

ISBN 0-8186-0493-X
IEEE CATALOG NO. 82CH1815-0
LIBRARY OF CONGRESS NO. 82-82340
IEEE COMPUTER SOCIETY ORDER NO. 493

IEEE
COMPUTER
SOCIETY
PRESS

 IEEE COMPUTER SOCIETY

 THE INSTITUTE OF ELECTRICAL AND ELECTRONICS ENGINEERS, INC.

Published by IEEE Computer Society Press
1109 Spring Street
Suite 300
Silver Spring, MD 20910

ISBN 0-8186-0493-X (paper)
ISBN 0-8186-4493-1 (microfiche)
ISBN 0-8186-8493-3 (casebound)
Library of Congress No. 82-82340
IEEE Catalog No. 84CH1815-0
IEEE Computer Society Order No. 493

Order from: IEEE Computer Society   IEEE Service Center
            Post Office Box 80452   445 Hoes Lane
            Worldway Postal Center   Piscataway, NJ 08854
            Los Angeles, CA 90080

 The Institute of Electrical and Electronics Engineers, Inc.

Foreword

This new workshop was conceived to explore the intersection of two disciplines which have become increasingly interrelated in recent years. These disciplines are VLSI and Software Engineering. IEEE Computer Society Technical Committees exist for both disciplines and the workshop was sponsored by the two committees. There were 47 participants from six countries, 37 from the U.S. and ten from abroad.

The application of software engineering tools and techniques to VLSI and the application of VLSI tools ad techniques to software engineering was the theme of the workshop. As the line between software implementations and hardware implementations blurs, and as both software designs and VLSI designs become increasingly complex, ti is appropriate for practitioners of both disciplines to exchange information so as to increase intellectual leverage.

The workshop began with an incisive keynote address by Richard P. Case, Vice President of IBM's General Technology Division. Then, over the next 2 1/2 days, the participants conferred in five different working groups, each group discussing a different topic and each group presenting the results of its discussions to the combined workshop on the last day. In addition, interspersed among the discussion sessions were six formal talks, covering such topics as silicon compilers, design verification techniques, and comparisons of VLSI and software design processes.

The discussions and writings of the working groups represent the main contribution of the workshop. Each working group explored the fundamental similarities and differences between VLSI and software engineering with respect to a particular area. The five areas which were explored are: (1) design methodology; (2) design synthesis and measurement; (3) verification and testing; (4) design environments; and (5) hardware description languages. At the workshop, each group agreed to produce a white pape and selected and editor to coordinate the writings of the group. These white papers, which took several months to produce, appear as Part I.

Part II contains 15 papers contributed by the workshop attendees. These papers are not refereed and should be considered as working papers. Versions of some of these have been submitted elsewhere. In particular, several will appear in a special issue of the Journal of Systems and Software toward the end of 1983, along with a few papers which do not appear here.

Part III contains reprints of three papers from COMPCON Spring 83 which were generated as a result of the workshop.

Part IV contains the names and addresses of the participants of the five working groups.

The success of this workshop is due to the dedicated efforts of the program committee, whose names are listed on the next page. Deserving particular mention are Les Belady who first conceived of the workshop, and Mel Cutler who assisted me in many ways.

Jock A. Rader
Chairman
VLSI and Software Engineering Workshop

WORKSHOP COMMITTEE

Chairperson

Jock A. Rader
Hughes Aircraft Company

European Representative

Jean-Claude Rault
Agence de l'Informatique

Treasurer

Mel Cutler
Aerospace Corporation

Duane Adams
DARPA/IPTO

Howard Baller
Hughes Aircraft Company

Les Belady
IBM

John Darringer
IBM

H. Mark Grove
OUSDRE

Local Arrangements

Guy Rabbat
IBM

IEEE Computer Society

Chip Stockton
Harry Hayman

Table of Contents

Foreword iii

Workshop Committee iv

Part I: Workshop Working Group White Papers
VLSI/Software Engineering Design Methodology 3
    H.H. Baller
Design Synthesis and Measurement 6
    R. Cuykendall, A. Domic, W.H. Joyner,
    S.C. Johnson, S. Kelem, D. McBride,
    J. Mostow, J.E. Savage, and G. Saucier
The Intersection of VLSI and Software Engineering for
Testing and Verification 10
    Z. Kishimoto, D. Lubzens, E. Miller,
    W. Overman, V. Pitchumani, R. Ramseyer,
    and J.-C. Rault
Development Environments for VLSI and
Software Engineering 50
    R. Katz, W. Scacchi, and P. Subrahmanyam
The Relationship between HDLs and
Programming Languages 64
    G.M. Baudet, M. Cutler, M. Davio,
    A.M. Peskin, and F.J. Rammig

Part II: Submitted Papers and Abstracts

Parallels between Software Engineering and VLSI Engineering
The Revolution in VLSI Design: Parallels between
Software and VLSI Engineering 75
    S. Hirschhorn and A.M. Davis
A Comparison of Design Strategies for
Software and for VLSI 85
    C.U. Smith and J.A. Dallen
Software Engineering Lessons for VLSI
Design Methodology 86
    W.R. Franklin
Transformation Systems for Software-Hardware
Design: Language and System Design Issues 90
    P.A. Subrahmanyam
Software Metrics and Lower Bounds 97
    R. Cuykendall
A Language-Independent Environment for
Software Engineering 99
    W. Scacchi

VLSI Design and Engineering
Intelligent Assistance for Top-Down Design
of VLSI Circuits 107
    G. Saucier and G. Serrero
Hierarchical Modular Description of
VLSI Systems 112
    F.J. Rammig

A Decision-Based Framework for Understanding
Hardware Compilers 117
    J. Mostow
A Program-Transformation Approach to
VLSI Design. 126
    J. Mostow and B. Balzer
Compilation Techniques in Logic Symbols. 134
    W.H. Joyner, Jr.
Tools for System Level Design, Test,
and Prototyping. 135
    R.H. Katz
An Inductive Assertion Method for Hardware
Design Verification. 138
    V. Pitchumani and E.P. Stabler
Symbolic Execution for VLSI Design Verification. 140
    Z. Kishimoto and K. Son

VLSI Computer Aided Design
Integration of Design Automation Tools
for the Custom VLSI Capability of a
Systems Firm 149
    J.S. Thomas

Part III: Reprints from COMPCON Spring 83
An Overview of VLSI Intersected with Software
Engineering. 157
    M. Cutler
A Comparison of Design Strategies for
Software and for VLSI. 160
    C.U. Smith and J.A. Dallen
Formal Verification of VLSI Designs. 169
    R.E. Shostak

Part IV: List of Working Groups

Author Index 176

Part I: Workshop Working Group White Papers

VLSI/SOFTWARE ENGINEERING DESIGN METHODOLOGY

H. H. Baller, Editor

Hughes Aircraft Company
Radar Systems Group

The intersection of software engineering and VLSI and the choice of a design methodology appropriate to the current state-of-the-art in these two rapidly developing disciplines was the subject of keen discussion at the recent workshop. In the course of the effort to define design methodology, two types of requirements emerged: (1) the need to apply past lessons learned by painful experience in the development of software engineering design methodology to the automatic, software controlled design of VLSI chips, and (2) the need to improve the methodology of computer system architectural design to utilize the new VLSI devices effectively, particularly to make proper choices for the functions to be incorporated in chips of enormous complexity[1].

Definition of Design Methodology

We can define a design methodology as a set of codified techniques, broadly applicable, that facilitate the creation of designs that are functionally correct, qualitatively acceptable (i.e., having acceptable space/time characteristics), are easily understood, and are easily modified.

The usefulness of a methodology is improved when designs are expressible in progressive levels of abstraction which by formal or informal means can be shown to be equivalent. Irrelevant details at each level of abstraction can be omitted. Designs are "structured," i.e., they are developed from a limited set of forms to provide an intellectual partitioning of the overall function.

In order to transfer software design methodology to VLSI, individual devices and subsystem elements, the design rules must be expressed in digital terminology, allowing not only for the various logic states, but also for finite time delays in clock and logic signal propagation. Aspects of software engineering methodology which may be applicable to VLSI devices and VLSI-based computer systems include (1) design models, (2) top-down design procedures, (3) bottom-up design, and (4) simulation. The design models may be represented as a network of asynchronous "modules," each a representation of a finite state machine (or equivalently, a data abstraction). Modules, as illustrated in Figure 1, are packages of state data and data transformers. State data is directly

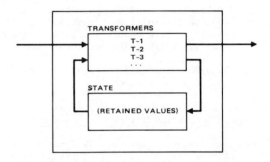

Figure 1

accessible only by the local data transformers. Communication between modules is constrained to narrow bandwidth links with clearly defined interfaces. No time dependencies are assumed between modules: a module fires only when a data signal (from a different module) and an appropriate (local) clock signal are both available.

The manner in which these four components of a design methodology might interact is illustrated in Figure 2.

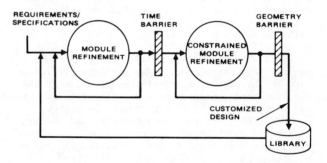

Figure 2

1. An initial design objective is expressed as an abstract module. Guided by the availability of earlier designs, the new design is refined by successively replacing modules described with abstract data and transformations into networks of modules with more concrete representations of

data, and more concrete descriptions of transformations.

2. When the design reaches the level of detail when clock signal delays become relevant, design rules are employed, permitting the refinement process to continue, albeit with additional constraints.

3. When the design reaches the level of detail when geometric characteristics of the design become relevant, assuming that previously executed designs are not available, the design proceeds in essentially a customized fashion, (using generally accepted design guidelines such as regularity, two-phased clocks, orthogonal data flow and control flow lines, etc.). The results of such customized designs are retained in libraries for future use.

4. Throughout the design period, designs are simulated to predict behavior.

Application of Design Methodology to Chip Design and System Configuration

Past experience in software development has demonstrated the need for a logical methodology. Requirements for software testability, defensive programming, and block modularity are still ignored, even though billions of dollars have been spent and much of that investment wasted[2]. These painful lessons point to the opportunity to avoid much of this wasted effort in VLSI design, particularly by recognizing and satisfying the need for dissemination of existing tools, the need for standardization, and the differences in economics and technical performance desired by users as compared to manufacturers.

There seems to be a need for a specific organization with assigned responsibility to acquire research-quality software used in VLSI development and design, which has demonstrated general usefulness, and to prepare and support it for public distribution.

This has not been accomplished in software engineering, where there is an enormous difference between the current state-of-the-art and what the average working programmer uses. The dissemination and usage of very high level languages such as LISP and SMALLTALK, interactive debuggers, and abstract data bases has been unfortunately slow. By comparison, in the commercial computer field, IBM Assembly Language is one of the most widely used languages in the USA, and many people still debug programs in batch mode with hexadecimal core dumps. Motivation for preparation of software tools available for public use must arise from profit or financial incentives. A program suitable for research use must be supplemented for general use by error checking for invalid inputs, user documentation, ergonomic features, test programs, and well prepared manuals. These additions usually increase the cost of software by a substantial amount[3].

Several past attempts to provide public usage software have been unsuccessful,[4,5] primarily because of the lack of support available on a volunteer basis.

The need for standardization in data structures and program interfaces is evident. While existing widely used programs, such as CIF, are already proliferating assorted dialects, major efforts to provide compatibility in graphics and CAP systems have been initiated. The Department of Defense VHSIC program is planned to have multiple source manufacturing capability by virtue of CAD/CAM/CAT exchange. Other projects include SIGGRAPH[6] and GKS[7] for graphics standardization, and IGES[8] for CAD. All of these rules concerning graphics and CAD can be applied in similar fashion to VLSI.

The differing, and sometimes contradictory, motives of users and manufacturers have led to damaging contention in software and graphics. There have been nonstandard accretions to standard languages, as well as program implementations of only a portion of a higher order language, such as FORTRAN. Even some of the new compilers for ADA are being offered in simplified form, which may nullify inherent and well advertised features of the language. Manufacturers have also promoted proprietary features in operating systems as a means of business, competitive advantage, although designs which are inherently portable (and well conceived) such as UNIX(R) have come into widespread use because of the ease of application to systems other than the original target.

Other user-manufacture factors which strongly influence system architecture are beyond the realm of design methodology as defined above. A manufacturer faces changing demands of a market, which compel him to redefine the performance requirements originally defined for a system. The rapid evolution of technology may cause re-evaluation of the choice of devices before the ideal process of design can be completed. The manufacturer may not only have to adjust to external competition, but may delay the introduction of a new design in order to optimize his total market for older existing systems along with new configurations. Consequently, the uncontrollable environment of device technology, competitive manufactured offerings, plus the beliefs and superstitions of the user community serve to erode the clarity and stability of any idealized design methodology.

The application of intelligent software engineering principles to VLSI components and to computer system design will undoubtedly be profound, although determined efforts from the software/semiconductor community will be required to achieve better success than has been evident in software engineering methodology thus far.

References

1. Carlos H. Seguin, Caltech Conference on
   VLSI, 1979. Architecture Session.

2. B. W. Boehm, "Software Engineering - As It
   Is," Fourth International Conference on
   Software Engineering, Munich 1979, spon-
   sored by IEEE and ACM, 11-21.

3. F. Brooks, "The Mythical Man-Month," published by Addison Wesley, 1975.

4. D. Scherrer, "Editorials," Software Tools
   Communications, 7, Newsletter, Lawrence
   Berkeley Lab, CSAM 50B/3238, University of
   California at Berkeley, November 1981.

5. B. W. Keningham and P. J. Plauger, Software Tools, Addison Wesley, published
   1976.

6. ACM, "Status Report of Graphics Standards
   Planning Committee," from "Computer
   Graphics," Quarterly Report SIGGRAPH
   ACM-13, March 1979.

7. H. K. Quigley, Jr., "Standardization of
   Computer Graphics," Computer Graphics
   News 2, 4, November 1982.

8. IGES Y14.26M, Response Committee, Final
   Draft Sections 1, 2, 3, and 4. Proposed
   American National Standard Approved,
   September 1981, published 1982.

DESIGN SYNTHESIS AND MEASUREMENT

Robert Cuykendall, Jet Propulsion Laboratory
Anton Domic, Lincoln Laboratory
William H. Joyner, IBM Thomas J. Watson Research Center
Steve C. Johnson, Bell Laboratories
Steve Kelem, The Aerospace Corp. M1-102
Dennis McBride, IBM Thomas J. Watson Research Center
Jack Mostow, USC-ISI
John E. Savage, Brown University†
Gabriele Saucier, Laboratoire IMAG

ABSTRACT

In this paper we present the results of the Working Group on Design Synthesis and Measurement on the issues that separate and bind software engineering and VLSI design. We examine design views and tradeoffs in design, levels of abstraction and their importance in the design process, methodologies, their support for design and the types of design decisions that are often made. We also examine the types of support environments needed to facilitate design in both spheres, and we examine the state of the art of silicon compilation today and the types of problems that are suited to such compilation.

Introduction

Design synthesis in the area of VLSI has much in common with that in Software Engineering. In the following sections we detail some of the common aspects and discuss the problems that are peculiar to VLSI and to the production of chips.

Systems Design

There are many views of a system. From a user's point of view, a complex real-world system is seen as a whole. It is a matter of indifference if the system is realized in dedicated hardware, microcode, compiled code, or interpreted code, as long as the performance is correct and the price is reasonable.

From an implementor's point of view, however, the barriers between these implementation methods are dramatic; it is a rare designer who is familiar with more than one or two of these methods, and such tradeoffs as are made are usually done by intuition rather than being supported by a consistent methodology and effective design aids.

From the system designer's point of view, a design is likely to be quite familiar and straightforward. It should be correct and satisfy the design constraints, and do so at reasonable cost. For example, in the hardware/software hierarchy, as we go from dedicated hardware to interpretive languages, we generally move towards slower, cheaper systems. It is the task of the system designer to choose the correct tradeoff between cost and performance.

Tradeoffs

How is the designer to make such tradeoffs? At the moment, this is extremely difficult. What is needed, and what we foresee, is a design system that allows the overall structure of the system to be specified, the interfaces to be laid out (and changed quickly where appropriate), and the time and dollar costs of each section to be estimated quickly. Once this is available, the decision as to what technology to use for each portion of the system can be quickly controlled and adapted, allowing convergence to systems that are likely to be more effective than many we have today.

These issues are illustrated by the selection of control strategies for computers. Typically a designer can choose from synchronous, distributed, dataflow, serial, parallel strategies, or a mixture of these. For example, two operations done in parallel may require more hardware for functionality, control, and communication, but offer a higher speed of execution. How a design decision is made is irrelevant to a user of a system, and ideally should be made based on global considerations.

Levels of Abstraction

The specification of VLSI chips has much in common with the specification of software. In fact, the first few levels of specification of software are very similar to the first few levels for VLSI. There are differences in that the algorithms specified for VLSI must reside on chips. In both environments, decisions at the higher levels have a larger scope than those at the lower levels. The higher levels tend to mask details at the lower levels and decisions at these levels can usually be made without much information from the higher levels.

Some of the levels of abstraction used in the systematic refinement of chip definitions are the following.

(1) Requirements: The specification of the overall performance, area, and I/O for the circuit.

(2) Abstract Algorithms: The behavior of the circuit without a binding for the actual operations and data types.

(3) Concrete Algorithms: The behavior of the circuit expressed in a machine-independent programming language. The operators and data types are made more explicit at this level.

(4) Programming: The machine language for the circuit if it is programmable. The algorithm described above would be programmed in this machine language.

(5) Register Transfer: The level at which behavior is described in terms of states, during which data is transferred between registers in the circuit.

---

†Scribe for the Working Group.

(6) Logic: The circuit is described in terms of logic components and their interconnections.

(7) Circuit: Logic functions are described in terms of transistors, resistors, capacitors, etc.

(8) Topology: A circuit in which physical dimensions are absent, but in which relative positioning is expressed.

(9) Masks: Transistors are defined by the intersections of polygonal areas on masks that are used in the fabrication process for integrated circuits.

Each level represents a class containing a large number of design choices. Since the total number of possible choices for a given system grows exponentially with the number of levels, means of dealing with the complexity have been developed. These include:

(1) The evolution of specialists familiar with the choices on one or a few of the levels.

(2) The use of a methodology that limits the number of choices at one or more of the levels.

(3) The use of a methodology that reduces or limits the number of levels of abstraction. This is similar to the previous method where only one choice is available at the merged or skipped levels.

Design Methodologies

A structured design methodology should be a combination of top-down refinement and bottom-up composition. In bottom-up composition, one constructs systems by combining existing primitives, connectives, and other systems defined in the same manner until the desired system is created. In top-down design, one partitions or refines a description of a system until it consists entirely of existing primitives, connectives, and systems. Useful design methodologies must combine both of these strategies. That way, the top-down partitioning is guided by the available primitives and the bottom-up composition is similarly guided by the overall system goals.

Software engineers usually do not use information from the abstraction levels below the programming level since they cannot change any of those levels. When they do use that information, it is only to define more clearly the behavior of the machine that is being used. However, software designers who do machine language programming may need to know details of the underlying microcode or register transfer models of their machine.

Top-down design in VLSI proceeds through stages. At the highest level a behavioral description is given that is further refined into a functional or algorithmic description and then translated into a structural description. The functional or algorithmic description is not complete until control and timing information is added to the picture. This then is used to further refine the description into a structural description that includes the logic and topological characterization.

LSI engineers typically work at the lower levels of abstraction. To handle the increasing complexity of VLSI circuits, VLSI engineers typically sacrifice the wide latitude of decisions available at the lower levels by limiting the number of design primitives used to the more conservative and robust. In return, the ability to make higher level decisions becomes feasible. This turns out to be not much of a sacrifice, since the low level decisions often have a factor of two or three effect on performance, whereas the higher level decisions may effect performance variations over several orders of magnitude.

By limiting the number of design decisions at the lower levels, the gap between software engineering and VLSI engineering can be bridged. If this can be done without too large a penalty on chip area and performance, then the gap will close.

Design Decisions

There are many types of design decisions that can be made at every level in the design process. Such decisions concern the allocation of a solution between hardware and software, and the meeting of performance criteria of various kinds. The first type of decision involves non-traditional compiler issues for which automation is very difficult to imagine at this time. The performance issues in VLSI are many faceted. They range from simple limits on the area, power dissipation and pin-out, to limits on path length, capacitative loads on gates and gate sizing. Complex relationships exist between even the more simply stated performance requirements.

At the highest level in the design process it is easy to state global requirements but difficult to translate these down to levels at which they can be realized. By contrast, decisions made at a low level have an impact on global requirements that are hard to predict. Decisions on the type of problem representation to be used, such as register transfer logic, can put major restrictions on the flexibility that is available in representation. Also, decisions on the layout technology to be used, such as gate arrays, can have a major impact on global parameters, such as area and chip speed. Another example at the logic level is given by the type of method used to convert Boolean equations from some standard notation, such as AND/OR/NOT, to a notation that is most naturally realized in the technology, such as NAND and NOR in NMOS. The conversion process should take into account such factors as the length of logic paths, since they affect speed, and the heat dissipation, since rearrangements of logical expressions can affect the number of active elements and power consumed.

Finally, it should be recognized that it is probably useful to permit the designer some freedom concerning the place in the design process at which decisions are made. We recognize that design decisions can be made *a priori*, that is, the design environment may embody a decision, e.g., by using a fixed target architecture for a machine, *in the input*, that is, the user may be required to incorporate the decision in the input to the system, *automatic*, that is, the system may make the decision based on the problem instance supplied, or *interactively*, that is, the system may request the user to supply a design decision. Each of these types of design has a place, based on the the degree to which one can acquire enough knowledge of a design to automate the design process.

The Design Environment

A principal objective of research in VLSI is to produce "silicon compilers" that will translate functional specifications into geometric layouts. For such systems to do this and meet reasonable design goals, much research is required.

It is perhaps too early to expect that such compilers can be constructed that are fully automatic since too little is known about the process of compiling functional descriptions into chip geometry. We do not fully understand the interactions between functional and geometric specifications, nor do we have adequate knowledge of the effect of various heuristics on the efficacy of placement and routing.

In the face of the uncertainty that prevails, it appears that the designer should be provided with explicit control over the heuristics used to produce a layout because of the complex interactions that result from their application. Since VLSI layouts are geometric, it is most reasonable that designers should be provided with interactive *visual* feedback on the effectiveness of individual heuristics and their interactions. This requires design environments that have high resolution displays, a window manager to provide multiple views of progress in the design, an interaction facility to provide input to the design process, and the computational power to compile specifications into layouts quickly for rapid viewing and interaction.

High resolution displays are necessary to display the large volume of data to which a designer must attend. For example, in a design, the length of paths is a factor in determining the speed of a chip, as is the load on gates [Dar81a]. Similarly, the power dissipation and area are important parameters. A designer will make surer progress if this type of information is available at all times. Since some of this information should be available simultaneously, multiple windows are desirable.

Given that a designer will use such a facility to interact with a layout, a means of interacting with the layout facility is needed. To facilitate this, it would be desirable to have a menu manager to display menus and associated actions, and a window manager that permits user and program control. Also, it is desirable to have a means of generating multiple views of the layout automatically, thus showing electrical and geometric parameters. In addition, to keep a record of a design and of past steps in a design to which a designer might want to retreat, it is useful to have a database management system integrated into the environment.

The type of facilities required for VLSI experimentation have great utility in software engineering. A principle difference is that the software engineer needs to have logical rather than physical views of a design. In this case, the connections between modules, their size and frequency of use are important variables, and not the geometry of the design. Such facilities would also permit the designer to obtain views that can be important in understanding the performance of the software being developed, perhaps by seeing it animated.

State of the Art of Silicon Layout

The state of the art of silicon layout is changing rapidly. Mead and Conway [Mea80a] give a good introduction to VLSI design from the architectural and geometric points of view. Below we provide a brief summary of developments in silicon layout. Another view of the state of the art in silicon compilation is given in [Wer82a].

Graphical Editors

Graphical editors have been developed for silicon layout at the cell level. Users are generally required to know the design rules of a technology and are responsible for placement and routing. Examples of such systems are ICARUS [Fai78a] and Caesar [Ous81a]. They both permit cell definitions to be used multiple times, while Caesar permits cells to be designed hierarchically. Usually design-rule check must be done after using such editors. Sticks [Wil78a] allows chips to be designed from a symbolic representation of components that are then expanded into rectangles.

Automatic Layout Systems

A technology has developed for the placement and routing of cells that began in the era of printed circuit boards [Bre72a]. The methods used consist of heuristics for cell placement that are designed to minimize wire length and board area, and methods for routing in channels between cells. Such methods have resulted in several different systems for the layout of cells in rows [Per77a, Shi80a]. Some of the algorithms used to place cells and route in these systems are cubic in the worst case, which is unacceptable for large chips.

Routing algorithms receive much attention in these methodologies and in VLSI layout systems. Maze routing methods [Lee61a, Sou80a] and channel routing methods [Hig69a]. are widely used.

Silicon Compilers

Silicon compilation is in its infancy. Currently this term refers to systems that translate a functional, behavioral or architectural (as opposed to geometric) description of a machine to a chip layout. Such systems understand the design rules of a technology and can translate such descriptions into component placement and wire routing.

Drawing the line between automatic layout systems and silicon compilers is sometimes difficult. Packages to produce programmed logic arrays (PLA's) are a primitive form of silicon compiler. Such packages understand the design rules of a technology. Weinberger arrays [Wei67a] are in the same class. They consist of linear arrangements of NOR gates connected by wires horizontally and vertically above and below the arrays. They also can be laid out automatically with simple algorithms and from a knowledge of design rules [Sou82a]. Both methods make much less efficient use of chip area for some problems than an unrestricted planar layout [Sav83a].

Much work must be done before true silicon compilers can be developed. However, recent developments point the way. Johannsen [Joh79a] has developed a system to place stretchable blocks with bristles on both ends in a fixed architectural framework. Rupp [Rup81a] has described another method to translate architectural descriptions into a target architecture. Siskind et al [Sis82a] describe a system that accepts descriptions of a bit-slice architecture and configures the descriptions into a layout consisting of a data path and a control unit. The layout of the control unit uses Weinberger arrays while the layout of the data path follows preset architectural constraints. Floyd and Ullman [Flo82a] have a method for the translation of regular expressions into a PLA layout with feedback.

Savage and Reiss have a highly interactive system called *SLAP* [Rei82a] that compiles Boolean equations (with or without feedback) into layouts without imposing architectural limitations and that permits a designer to select among layout heuristics. Johnson [Joh83a] describes a system to produce chips from Boolean equations that a designer partitions into collections that are laid out in a grid, similar to Weinberger arrays. It does automatic placement and routing.

We can hope that as our understanding of VLSI design improves, silicon compilers will come to resemble software compilers and require less experimentation and measurement. In the meantime, a closer software analog seems to be provided by knowledge-based compilers that make high-level implementation decisions like data structure selection by explicitly evaluating alternatives [Kan79a].

In the short term, the realization of high-performance VLSI designs will remain a combination of hand layouts aided by graphical editors and by semiautomatic means of analysis, such as design-rule verifiers and node extractors. An important factor in successful design of this kind is the creation of libraries of highly optimized functional blocks, to be used as stepping stones to complete designs. Today this is commonly done for the simple case of word width matching. For example, single bit width ALUs and registers are kept in a design library after being characterized by circuit simulation. Word width functions of other sizes are easily assembled by calling a program to establish a regular pitch and connect to proper signal lines across the replicated functional boundaries. It is possible to spin off variations of the same design for low power, small area, maximum performance, and so on.

<u>Tasks Suited to Automatic Hardware Compilation</u>

The working group has agreed that a certain class of design tasks is most likely to be suited to automatic compilation in the next 5-10 years. These tasks are either of low volume, not large enough to amortize intensive human design effort, or require fast turnaround, or high speed, and can have sub-optimal speed performance. This class of tasks is sometimes called "custom VLSI." Other factors cited in favor of VLSI implementation of such tasks include reliability, security, and speed-up due to elimination of software overhead, e.g., protection and memory management.

Two classes of tasks appear inappropriate for automatic compilation in the near future. These are low-speed tasks that can be more cheaply implemented by programming off-the-shelf processors, or production-quality chips that must be fully optimized to beat the competition -- a difference of 10% in performance can be critical. High volume justifies massive design effort to achieve this performance, which cannot yet be achieved automatically.

<u>References</u>

Dar81a.
C. A. Darringer, W. H. Joyner, Jr., C. L. Berman, and L. Trevillyan, "Logic Synthesis Through Local Transformations," *IBM J. of Research and Development* **25**(4) pp. 272-280 (July 1981).

Mea80a.
C. Mead and L. Conway, *Introduction to VLSI Systems*, Addison-Wesley (1980).

Wer82a.
J. Werner, "The Silicon Compiler: Panacea, Wishful Thinking, or Old Hat?," *VLSI Design*, pp. 46-52 (September/October 1982).

Fai78a.
D. G. Fairbairn and J. A. Rowson, "ICARUS: An Interactive Integrated Circuit Layout Program," *Proc. 15th Design Automation Conference*, pp. 188-192 IEEE, (June 1978).

Ous81a.
J. K. Ousterhout, "Caesar: An Interactive Editor for Layouts," *VLSI Design*, pp. 34-38 (4th Quarter, 1981).

Wil78a.
J. D. Williams, "STICKS - A Graphical Compiler for High Level LSI Design," *National Computer Conf.*, pp. 289-295 (1978).

Bre72a.
M. A. Breuer, Ed., *Design Automation of Digital Systems, Vol. 1 Theory and Techniques*, Prentice-Hall, Englewood Cliffs, NJ (1972).

Per77a.
G. Persky, D. N. Deutsch, and D. G. Schweikert, "LTX - A Minicomputer-Based System for Automated LSI Layout," *Jnl. of Design Automation and Fault-Tolerant Computing* **1**(3) pp. 217-255 (May 1977).

Shi80a.
H. Shiraishi and F. Hirose, "Efficient Placement Techniques for Master Slice LSI," *Procs. 17th Design Automation Conf.*, pp. 458-464 IEEE ACM, (1980).

Lee61a.
C. Y. Lee, "An Algorithm for Path Connections and Its Applications," *IRE Trans. on Electronic Comps.* **EC-10** pp. 346-365 (Sept. 1961).

Sou80a.
J. Soukup, "Global Router," *Jnl. of Digital Systems* **4**(1) pp. 59-69 (1980).

Hig69a.
D. W. Hightower, "A Solution to Line-Routing Problems on the Continuous Plane," *6th Ann. Design Automation Workshop*, pp. 1-24 (1969).

Wei67a.
A. Weinberger, "Large Scale Integration of MOS Complex Logic: A Layout Method," *IEEE Jnl. of Solid State Circuits* **SC-2**(4) pp. 182-190 (Dec. 1967).

Sou82a.
J. R. Southard, A. Domic, and K. W. Crouch, "LBS - Lincoln Boolean Synthesizer," Technical Report 622, MIT Liconl Laboratory (1982).

Sav83a.
J. E. Savage, "Three VLSI Compilation Techniques: PLA's, Weinberger Arrays, and SLAP, A New Silicon Layout Program," in *Algorithmically-Specialized Computers*, ed. L. Snyder, L. J. Seigel, H. J. Seigel, D. Gannon, Academic Press (1983). to appear

Joh79a.
D. Johannsen, "Bristle Blocks: A Silicon Compiler," *Proc. 16th Design Automation Conf.*, pp. 310-313 (June 1979).

Rup81a.
C. R. Rupp, "Components of a Silicon Compiler System," pp. 227-236 in *VLSI 81: Very Large Scale Integration*, ed. J. P. Gray, Academic Press, London, New York (1981).

Sis82a.
J. M. Siskind, J. R. Southard, and K. W. Crouch, "Generating Custom High Performance VLSI Designs from Succinct Algorithmic Descriptions," *Procs. Conf. on Advance Research in VLSI*, pp. 28-40 MIT, (Jan. 1982).

Flo82a.
R. W. Floyd and J. D. Ullman, "The Compilation of Regular Expressions into Integrated Circuits," *JACM* **29**(3) pp. 606-622 (July 1982).

Rei82a.
S. P. Reiss and J. E. Savage, "SLAP - A Methodology for Silicon Layout," *Procs. of the Int. Conf. on Circuits and Computers*, pp. 281-285 IEEE, (Sept. 28 - Oct. 1, 1982).

Joh83a.
S. C. Johnson, "Code Generation for Silicon," *Procs. 10th Ann. Symp. on Princs. of Programming Languages*, (January 24-26, 1983).

Kan79a.
E. Kant, "A Knowledge-Based Approach to Using Efficiencey Estimation in Program Synthesis," *IJCAI-6*, pp. 457-462 (1979).

The Intersection of VLSI and Software Engineering

for Testing and Verfication

Authors:

Zen Kishimoto
GTE Laboratories
40 Sylvan Road
Waltham, Mass. 02254

Daniel Lubzens
Microelectronics Research Ctr.
Technion
Haifa, Israel

Edward Miller
Software Research Associates
P.O. Box 2432
San Francisco, Calif. 94126

W. Overman
Aerospace Corp.
Los Angels, Ca 90009

Vijay Pitchumani
Syracuse University
Electrical & Computer Engineering
111 Link Hall
Syracuse, NY 13210

R. Ramseyer
Honeywell, Inc.
Systems & Research Cener
2600 Ridgeway Parkway
Minneapolis, MN 55413

Jean-Claude Rault
Agence de l'Informatique
Tour Fiat - Cedex 16
92084 Paris-La Defence
France

1. Introduction

There is a large intersection between VLSI design
and Software Engineering in the areas of Software
Engineering. We first investigate the state of the art of
Software and Hardware (VLSI) testing. Next we look at the
large intersection between the two areas. Finally we look
at formal verification techniques and how they me be used in
the future.

2. Software Testing

In this section, we summarize state-of-the-art
software testing. Since software testing covers a wide
spectrum, we divide it into eleven different areas and
report progress of each area. Among the eleven, we included
a few that are usually not considered in software testing.
These include testability analysis, portability testing and
testing multiple processes. Based on comparisons between
VLSI and software, we feel that these areas should be
further investigated. It is our hope that our covering them
stimulates research.

The following are the eleven areas of interest.

1. Theoretical Foundation

2. Manual Process

3. Static Analysis

4. Dynamic Analysis

5. Performance Analysis

6. Verification

7. Revalidation

8. Testability Analysis

9. Portability Testing

10. Multiple Processes

11. Management Issues

2.1 Theoretical Foundation.

Testing has been an informal process rather than a formal and rigorous process. Most of the techniques and methods successfully used for testing are ad hoc and intuitive. Theoretically sound methods have tended to generate too many tests that have too many restrictions in their applications.

Research has been conducted to make testing more formal and practical. The research has concentrated on: application of graph theory, study of programming languages, application or reliability theory, and derivation of program testing theory.

Graph theory techniques [1] are used to model the control flow and data flow in a program. These two flows are usually modeled as a directed graph. Because of this modeling, some level of automation has become possible for testing. Automatic test generation and data flow analysis are good examples for the automation of testing using a directed graph. These two concepts will be discussed later in this chapter.

Studies of programming languages have resulted in the identification of error-prone constructs for a given programming language and common programming mistakes [2,3]. Such findings provide a foundation for the generation of a set of effective tests.

Reliability theory was developed for hardware and has been successfully used for hardware. The use of reliability theory, however, has been controversial [4-6]. The success of reliability theory largely depends on the theoretical assumptions of the software modeling process. The practical use of this theory is still limited, although it is often used to estimate the remaining errors in a given program and to determine the termination of the testing phase.

Program testing theory focuses its attention on the error detecting capability of tests. Goodnough and Gerhart [7] pioneered a work in this area and stressed the importance of program specification for test generation. Howden [8] considered the effectiveness of path testing, which is a program structure oriented testing technique. Weyuker and Ostrand [9] strengthened the work of Goodnough and Gerhart and derived a test generation method that exploits both program code and specification. Richardson and Clarke [10] applied a technique called symbolic execution [11-15] (which will be discussed later in this

chapter) to the work of Weyuker and Ostrand and made the
procedure in their method more formal. They also expanded
the method to support formal verification of a program.

2.2 Manual Process.

Manual process includes the techniques that do not
involve any automatic means of examining software. They are
formal review [16] inspection [16,17], and peer review
[16,18]. Formal review is a technique that provides
judgement by a panel of specialists about the current
quality of a system. Inspection is a method of thorough
analysis of various parts of a software system. Peer review
is a process by which project personnel study and evaluate
code, documentation, or specifications. These three are
widely discussed but only inspection is widely used.
Inspections are known to be effective when well used. It
has been observed that programmers do not like these methods
as they do not like others disclosing their errors.

2.3 Static Analysis

Static analysis is an automatic means of examining
certain features of computer programs and collecting the
necessary information from them without executing them.
Under static analysis, we can list such tools as code
auditor [16,19], control structure analyzer [16,20], cross-
reference generator [16,19,21], data-flow analyzer [16,22],
and interface checker [16,19,21].

The merits of this technique are: 1) short
analysis time, which means that it is inexpensive to do, 2)
freedom of application to part or all the program and 3)
reusability of the analysis results for other analyses, and
4) ability to detect certain kinds of errors.

Errors in the following areas can be detected by
performing static analysis: control flow (by control
structure analyzers), data flow (by data flow analyzers),
control flow between components, modules or procedures of a
system (interface checker) and notation or programming
standards and practice (code auditor). Since certain kinds
of errors cannot be detected by static analysis, dynamic
analysis is required, which is discussed in the next
subsection.

The information extracted from a program by
performing static analysis includes control flow graph
[22,23], intermediate codes [22], cross reference
[16,19,21]. As the notion of programming environment [24]
is increasingly adopted among software engineers, static

analysis becomes an indispensable tool to set up the
foundation for programming environments.

2.4 Dynamic Analysis

Unlike static analysis, dynamic analysis executes
a program and compares the outputs produced by the program
with the expected outputs. Mismatches between the two
suggests the existence of errors. Dynamic analysis consists
of three steps: test generation, test execution and output
validation.

Test generation can be done using on different
kinds of information as a base: specification, design,
program code, and sensitivity to seeded errors. Test
generation based on specification is exemplified by
techniques called cause/effect graphing [25], condition
table method [7] and test plan generation based on the
finite state machine [26]. These techniques generate tests
based solely on the specification; thus, tests can be
generated before program development.

Design based test generation [27,28] identifies
functions in the design and generates tests to exercise
these functions. There are two groups of test generation
based on program code. The first group is based on pure
code coverage and the other is based on testing the
functions implemented in the program. For the first group,
the programmer does not concern himself with the specific
function computed by the program. His or her only concern
is how much the code has been exercised. Many testing
criteria have been suggested but the coverage measure known
as C1 [29] based on the control flow graph is the most
widely used criterion. C1 measure requires that all the
branches in the control flow graph be exercised at least
once. In practice, establishing 80 to 90% [30] of C1
measure is known to be enough for large-scale programs.
Code coverage has been widely used mainly because it is easy
to see the progress of testing and to show which section of
program code should be exercised to satisfy the coverage
criterion.244 Many tools called "test coverage analyzers"
[23,31] have been developed based on this technique.
Automatic test generation is usually considered for this
technique. A few tools [14,15,32] are equipped with the
automatic test generation capability.

The second approach, which derives the function
information from program code and generates tests with this
function information, includes domain testing [33]. Domain
testing concerns only the errors in the domain of functions.
The approach that derives tests from both specification and

program code is claimed to be more effective than other
approaches [9,10].

Mutation testing [34] is a technique that
generates tests based on sensitivity to the seeded errors.
Among the techniques mentioned in this section, only
cause/effect graphing and coverage based testing are widely
used. Other techniques are still in their infancy.

Drivers [25], stubbing [25] and test languages
[35] are test execution techniques that allow the programmer
to test partially developed programs. These techniques
simulate the undeveloped calling modules and called modules.
A technique known as dynamic assertion that collects
execution profile may be included here but is discussed
under verification.

For the output validation step, it is important to
prepare the expected output so that the produced output can
be validated against them. Program code based testing
suffers from the lack of this information. It is usually
assumed that the test oracle [33] exists that can determine
the correctness of the produced output. A few tools
[35,36], have the capability of validating the produced
output automatically.

2.5 Performance Analysis

Software testing emphasis has been placed on
logical correctness rather than performance correctness. If
logically correct software does not meet the performance
requirements, however, it is of little use, especially in
real-time programming environments.

There are two types of state-of-the-art
performance analysis. The first involves estimating the
execution time while selection of the algorithms is being
considered. The second is to validate the performance
against the required performance by monitoring execution
after the software has been developed. An example of the
first one is the analytic modeling of system designs [16].
In spite of its success in particular systems, there is
little transferable technology available. Execution time
estimator/analyzer [16,37] and software monitor [16] are
examples of the second type. They both monitor the
execution, provide the execution characteristics of a
program, and identify performance bottlenecks. These tools
are commercially available for most systems.

2.6 Verification

Since verification will be covered later in this paper, in this section we place emphasis on the intersection of testing and verification. Two techniques lie in this intersection: assertion and symbolic execution.

Inductive assertions [38] are assertions that are used to prove the correctness of a given program. They are not actually executed, but are usually examined manually by the programmer. Assertions used for testing are called dynamic assertions [23,31] because they are checked during the execution of a program. Dynamic assertions are normally much simpler than inductive assertions. They usually check simple violations, such as assigning out-of-range values to variables and array index boundary violations. The number of violations is reported after the execution. Some tools [31] have the capability of halting execution of the program after a preset number of violations has been detected.

The use of dynamic assertions increases overhead; hence, only simple assertions are used for testing. The use of inductive assertions for dynamic assertions is not practical as it increases overhead too much to be usable. Moreover, the derivation of an inductive assertion is usually difficult. The use of dynamic assertions in place of inductive assertions for proof of correctness is not suitable because dynamic assertions are too simple to be used in this fashion.

Symbolic execution [11-15,39] was developed as a compromise between correctness proof and testing. The use of symbolic execution, however, has been limited to testing rather than verification. It has been used for symbolic testing and generation of test data. With one exception, work on symbolic execution is still at the research stage. Recent literature suggests the use of symbolic execution to prove the correctness of a program. Two approaches have been considered. One approach [40] uses symbolic execution with inductive assertions to prove the correctness of a program. The other [10] uses symbolic execution to derive the function information from both specification and program code. It then matches the two to verify the correctness of a program.

2.7 Revalidation

We deliberately used the term "revalidation" instead of regression testing [16,25,41] because regression testing is only one aspect of revalidation. Regression testing is a common term used to describe the validation of modified computer programs and is applied to an entire program. This testing maintains a basic set of test cases that exercise major functions of the program. After a program is modified, it is regressed on the test cases. A good example of the set of tests prepared for regression testing is a validation suite [42]. A validation suite is a set of small programs used for validating a compiler. The problem with regression testing is its informality. There are seldom rigorous methods of selecting the basic set of tests or update tests when the functional specification changes.

There is little work reported in the area of revalidation [35,36,41,43] aside from regression testing. Most work is still at the research stage. Major issues of program revalidation are: the determination of scope of revalidation, further test generation and reuse of the original set of tests. The determination of scope of revalidation concerns integration level testing for modified programs i.e., which module or group of modules should be revalidated. No particular method is suggested for performing integration testing. However, Miller [44] gives a guideline for integration testing. Modules that need testing are: modules calling the modified module, modules called by the modified module and modules sharing the common data with the modified modules. Further tests may be necessary if the quality of the original tests is poor or if there has been a change in the functional specification. One article [43] adopted partition testing [9, 10] to determine the set of tests necessary for the modified program. It also showed a method to enhance the original set to satisfy the requirement for the modified program. Reuse of the original tests is important to minimize the cost of revalidation. Two articles [41,43] report the selection a subset of previously used tests whose executions exercise modified sections of the program.

2.8   Testability Analysis

Much research has been conducted on testability analysis in hardware. In contrast, testability analysis for software has been neglected. Testability of a given program is defined to be the effort needed to test the program. Because of the high cost of testing (about 50% [25] of software development cost), reduction in testing cost reduces the total cost of software development. Surprisingly then, there is little published work available in this area. There is a particular lack of research where the testability has been quantified. As far as we know, there is only one work [45] reported that actually computes testability based on the control flow of a given program.

In considering testability measure, two points are important: complexity and testing strategy. Intuitively, a complex program is harder to test than a simple program. There is no doubt that complexity plays a major role in testability. It is not clear, however, how complexity and testability are related.

The second point is that testability may vary depending on the testing strategy adopted. Suppose a programmer takes a criterion that requires testing all the statements at least once, then the number of statements in the program can be used as a crude measure for testability. This measure is crude because depending on how we choose tests to satisfy the criterion, the number of tests (effort to test) may be different and the number of statements may not reflect it. When a programmer uses a different testing criterion on the same program, the testability measure may become different. If he requires that all the paths in the control flow graph of a given program must be traversed, the number of static paths (paths solely based on the graph) may be a crude measure for this particular testing strategy. Again such a measure is crude because not all the paths are feasible. In any event, the number of tests (effort to test a given program) for a given program usually differs according to the different testing strategies.

In estimating the number of paths for the second criterion, we can associate complexity measure based on control flow, such as McCabe's [46], with testability. According to his complexity measure, a complex program contains more paths than a simple program. The correlation between complexity and testability, however, seen here exists for a particular complexity measure and a particular testing strategy. More work is needed to develop a general testability measure. In particular, when the characteristics of a program are considered, both control flow and data flow must be examined. Therefore, to derive a good testability measure, information for both flows must be taken into account. At the same time, further investigation should be done into hardware testability as it may provide further insight into tackling the problem of software testability.

2.9 Portability testing.

Portability testing requires asking two questions:

⊕ how we can determine if a given program is portable?

● After a computer program has been transferred from one machine to another, how should this program be tested?

Since programs written in assembly languages usually are not portable, we only consider programs in high level languages, such as FORTRAN.

To assist in determining if a given program is portable, there is an automatic tool [19] which detects the use of non standard features of a language. Non standard features are those not found in the standard language such as machine dependent system utility calls, or features found in the language dialects. Finding information to answer to the second question is more difficult. We could not find any particular work on this subject. However, changes needed to make the program operational on the new machine can be considered as changes done because of environment changes. Swanson et. al [47] classified the changes performed in the maintenance phase into three categories: corrective, perfective, and adaptive. Regression testing is widely used for validating modified programs. Based on the similarity just pointed out, we may adopt the same approach to validate the transferred program. Again the preparation and modification of tests for regression testing are difficult issues. For a particular case, where a compiler is self-compiling, the source code of the compiler itself may be used for regression testing. Since it is necessary to carry a source of the compiler to the new machine, this is a cost-effective approach. How many different features are exercised by doing self-compilation is left unanswered.

2.10 Multiple Processes.

Most of work on software testing has treated a single program (process) on a single computer (processor). There is scant information available for testing multiprocesses running on a single processor (multiprogramming environment); much less multiprocesses running on multiprocessors. Multiprocesses are linked with real programming environments. With the progress of hardware technologies, multiple processing has become more common. The data flow machine [48] is one example.

Two of the main issues in testing multiprocesses are the irreproducibility and time-dependent test results. Brinch Hansen [49] introduced a technique to solve these problems. This area needs further investigation to attain the present sophistication level of VLSI technique.

2.11 Management Issues.

We have discussed many issues relevant to **tes**ting. These issues, however, are meaningless unless the testing effort is well coordinated and well managed. We consider the following four points important as management issues: progress monitoring, cost and time assessing, good testing team, and developed tests archiving.

The ability to monitor testing progress enables a programmer to identify untested sections of a program and generate additional tests to complete testing. Based on this information, the remaining testing effort can be estimated so that time, computing resources and personnel allocated to the current testing effort can be adjusted.

Assessing the cost and time for testing is important so that the proper testing methods can be selected for testing a given program. Different testing techniques and methods establish different levels of program reliability with different time and cost requirements.

A good testing team is necessary for the success of testing. It is known that a programmer tends to overlook his or her own mistakes [25]. Therefore, having an independent testing team is recommended. Two points are particularly important to remember in managing the testing team. The first point concerns the coordination between the development team and the testing team. The second point concerns the testing team itself. Testing often starts while program development is ongoing. Psychological contention between the development and testing teams is predictable and remedies for it should be prepared. Furthermore, the testing team should be given a reasonably high priority in accessing computer resources, as studies [50] report that high turnaround time often means the early termination of the testing phase. The selection of an optimal number of personnel who are appropriate for testing contributes to the success of testing, although no particular methods for the selection are known.

Keeping the developed tests and information about them for the future is often neglected. The high cost of developing a good set of tests encourages programmers to retain their tests for future testing. Such tests can be used for revalidation of a program after it is modified in the future. They, along with their documentation, also can provide the programmer information about what testing and how much testing has been performed on the original program. Without such tests and their information, the entire testing effort may have to be repeated, which is usually not allowed because of tight cost and time requirements in the maintenance phase.

3. Hardware Testing

3.1 Physical Device Testing

The techniques employed in testing digital hardware have not changed much in the last 20 years. The method of doing functional, where functional testing implies testing at speed, and nonfunctional testing, where nonfunctional implies static testing, are the same today as they were in the 60's. The major difference is that today we use computers to automate large portions of the generation and application of the test data. As the complexity of digital systems have grown over the years, it has not only become convenient but rather become necessary to use a high speed computer to generate test data and then to run ·that test data via automatic test equipment on today's complex chips. Nowhere is this more evident than in the Very High Speed Integrated Circuits program currently underway and funded by the Department of Defense.

3.1.1 <u>Testing Large Scale Computer Systems in the Late 1960's</u>

The 1960's were to computer automated design as the 80's are proving to be to computer aided test. Many innovative software tools were developed during the 1960's that facilitated going from logical equations to hardware for the logic designer. Wirewrap lists for boards and backplanes could be generated by computers from simple coding forms by taking information from the logic designers drawings. This eliminated time and expense from the manual conversion techniques used before this. By the early 70's, logic designers were sitting at their desks with terminals designing logic and automatically and interactively generating wire lists and the appropriate text on those wire lists in real time.

Unfortunately, the same progress was not made in the area of test and debug. About half of the "design time" in the life cycle of an advanced development project for large scale digital systems was spent designing the tests for that system. Huge amounts of time and energy were spent with logic designers pouring over sheet after sheet of logic and figuring out the state of that logic, on a clock by clock basis, given an initial set of conditions. A typical scenario for a test might be as follows:

- clear all flip flops

- set flip flop A, C, D and E

- issue one clock

- check that flip flop B has set and A has reset

- clear all flip flops

The above examples appears trivial; however, it illustrates the monotony, tedium and time consuming labor involved in testing the simplest of circuits using this technique. The designers had to scrutinize large amounts of logic and select appropriate initial conditions. Then, they would have to trace through their designs on a clock by clock basis and determine the state of the logic after each clock pulse. All information had to be written down by hand on large sheets of paper for use in the laboratory. A nominal subsystem of the 60's containing 100,000 gates would take many months to test and debug by this procedure.

The above mentioned problems in the area of design for test and test/debug are amplified greatly now that the systems of the 60's are becoming the chips of the 80's. Not only is the complexity there but also problems of control, access and observability are exacerbated by the complexity of the chip and the limited number of pins. Honeywell, a VHSIC contractor, has the situation under control for the VHSIC phase 1 program. Although formal verification techniques are still a bit in the future as will be discussed later, the issues involved in test and debug of the Honeywell VHSIC chips will be discussed below.

3.1.2 Testing VHSIC Chips in 1982

Honeywell has designed and is implementing two integrated circuit chips for its VHSIC program. These chips are intended for electro-optical (EO) signal processing applications. One chip is a controller capable of controlling other specialized processing chips. The second chip is an arithmetic processor with parallel, pipelined processing features.

Honeywell's VHSIC chips have been designed to be easily tested using an external tester. This feature requires a few additional pins on the chips. The design also permits a system composed of many EO chips to perform a thorough self-test. Little additional logic is required beyond that needed for the external testing. The features of the testing approach are outlined below.

3.1.3 Chip Partitioning

For testing purposes, the chips were "divided" into modules. These modules correspond to different functional units on the chip. Two criteria were used to select a section of logic as a module: the complexity of the logic should be small, and the flip-flops included in the section should provide most of the inputs to the combinational logic and should receive most of the outputs from the logic.

3.1.4 Observability

All flip-flops within a module are connected during testing so they can operate as a shift register. These shift registers are individually addressable providing quick access to most inputs and outputs from a module. Dividing the chips into modules also makes it simpler to develop a self-test procedure for the chips.

Honeywell's approach to forming shift register paths is called NFT (non-functional test). Logic is designed using a set of NFT design rules. The main requirements of the NFT design rules for VHSIC are:

- All logic on a chip must be synchronous.

- A single-phase clock is used throughout the design for NFT purposes.

- Edge-triggered histables are used.

- All bistables in the circuit are connected to form the NFT diagnostic shift register (DSR).

- Any input to the circuit must generate a defined output.

By specifying that all bistables (storage elements) be configured into one or more DSRs, the NFT approach provides a means to access the internal nodes in a digital circuit. This is implemented by adding control logic to allow three modes of operation for the circuit under test: normal mode, reset mode, and diagnostic shift mode. In the normal (functional) mode, the bistables perform their normal logic functions. In the diagnostic mode, they can be reset or configured into a DSR, thus allowing data to be shifted into and out of any bistable in the circuit. The normal system clock is inhibited in the meantime. This enables the bistables to act as additional pseudo-input and output access points to the circuit

effectively partitioning the circuit into blocks of
combinational logic called subsections. This concept is
illustrated in Figure 1.

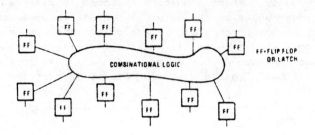

a. Normal Functional Logic

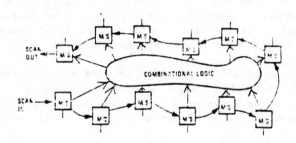

b. Serial Shift Register Logic Added

Fig. 1   Non-Functional Test.

3.1.5 Test Interface

Each chip contains a test interface section. The
test interface has a serial data in, a serial data out, and
three or four control lines that connect to the external
tester through pins. The interface also contains a control
register that can be loaded serially with information for
selecting the module to be accessed, for controlling the
clock, and for specifying the testing operation to be
performed.

The control inputs to the interface specify a
particular operation to be performed during each period.
Some operations that can be specified are:

- Load (serially) the control register

- Load a buffer register with the clock control bits

- No operation

- Issue a clock pulse (to the addressed module)

- Self-test operations

The test interface is designed so that individual
chips can be controlled and tested by an external tester, or
a complete system of chips can be tested. With a system of
chips, the test interface lines from the external tester are
connected to the controller chip and are also routed in
parallel to all arithmetic chips.

24

The test interface in the controller chip is also designed so that interface signals can be generated and received by the sequencer portion of the chip. Hence, the chip can be operated in a self-test mode whereby the non-sequencer portion of the controller chip and any connected arithmetic chips can be tested by the sequencer.

3.1.6 Test Vector Generation

The NFT vectors are a series of predefined bit patterns that are executed as test steps. They are applied to the digital circuit to provide hardware logic test without regard to the functionality of the hardware. These

NFT test vectors are generated from the Honeywell ORION Test Generation (OTG) system developed at the Large Information System Division (LISD) in Phoenix.

The OTG system is a software package that provides automatic test-pattern generation for digital circuits using the NFT design-for-test methodology. The system, developed and modified by Honeywell for 15 years, is part of LISD's complete design automation system package.

Test vector generation is based on stuck at 1 or 0 fault assigned at the gate level. The system can also handle short faults and input-diode short fault modes. Circuit design input to OTG must follow the NFT design rules.

When generating the test vectors, the OTG system performs three major functions:

1. Preprocessing of the input circuit description.

2. Test vector generation.

3. Post-processing of the test-generation output.

Preprocessing entails unloading the input-circuit description and from it creating a gate-level circuit image that can be simulated. Functional models of the gates are then inserted to create the final circuit image. Generation of the target models is also done in preprocessing. A target is a bounded set of combinational logic that is driven by and drives into NFT shift-register bistables. The target is defined by the target-model generator program. The target-model generator then searches for all the combinational logic between the set of bistables and other sets that can be used to bound the logic and allow input to the target.

Two user input data files are required by OTG: a structural file of the macrocell and a library file of compound gates. When the circuit-image input is completed, OTG generates a set of test vectors by iterating the following procedure:

1. A gate in the circuit is selected and assigned a stuck at 1 or 0 fault.

2. A path is sensitized back to the circuit primary inputs to determine an input vector that will exercise the faulted gate. A path is also sensitized to the circuit outputs to confirm that the fault is visible.

3. Having selected this input vector, a fault-free output response is obtained using a gate-level simulation of the circuit. This will be used as a compare vector for the first input vector.

4. A stuck at 1 or 0 is selected, and simulation is performed to determine if the output pattern changes when compared to the no-fault case. If it does not change, another stuck at 1 or 0 fault is tried. If it does change, the resulting output pattern is saved in a "fault table", and the next stuck at fault is tried.

5. Step 4 is repeated until all the stuck at 1 and 0 faults have been tried for this first input test pattern.

6. Steps 1 through 5 are repeated to select and test for a new input test vector. For this second test pattern, any fault detectable by the first pattern will not be simulated again.

This procedure is continued until the desired percentage of the possible stuck at faults have been detected. The results of the procedure are a set of test vectors that can be used to test the physical implementation of the circuit.

Post-processing reformats the test-generator output data into the appropriate readable forms. Test vectors are set up for application on the test system, and test generation statistics generated.

3.1.7 NFT Test Procedure

A shift-path test is first executed to ensure that the DSRs are connected and operating correctly. One way to do tis is to reset or master clear all the bistables to a 0000 ... pattern and then shift the data out. As part of the design, the bistables are connected so that data bits are always inverted between bistables. Thus, a 1010 .... pattern is expected for the data shifting out. If this pattern is not read out, there is a fault in the shift mechanism. The fault should be at the bistable corresponding to the bit position in the bit-serial data stream that came out incorrectly.

Once it is determined that the shift operation works incorrectly, the test vectors can be loaded into the flip-flops as bit serial strings. The system is clocked functionally and the results are shifted out and compared to what they should be. The same process is then repeated for the next test vector. When a fault is detected by NFT, the bistable containing the error are identified. They may then be used to trace the error condition to the faulted gates. The practical results of using the NFT approach have shown that most bridging faults are also detected.

The NFT test system currently does not automatically generate the location of the faults for several reasons. Because of the number of gates on a VHSIC chip, a large memory is required to store the fault signatures in the fault table and a large amount processing to generate the fault dictionary. The presence of multiple faults will also make the use of fault signatures more difficult if not impossible. New deductive methods are being developed to reduce the problem of fault isolation and to make it more manageable (such as to fault isolate down to a number of gates instead of a single gate).

3.1.8 Self-Test

The importance of the self-test capability is well recognized, especially for field operation where special equipment is not readily available for testing. The VHSIC chips are capable of self-testing at high speed under control of the test hardware and firmware built into the controller chip.

The test interface logic of the controller chip has been designed so that a "hardcore" section of the controller chip can perform a self-test of the rest of the controller chip and arithmetic chips connected to it. This hardcore section consists of the microprogram sequencer, control ROM, pipeline register, and the test-interface logic. When no external tester is connected to the controller chip, an "external test enable" signal switches the source of the test signals from external lines to a set generated by the microprogram sequencer in the controller chip. The microprogram sequencer will control the test interface via microcode. The microprogram sequencer and associated hardcore sections will remain in functional mode for test control independent of commands sent to the test interface while the rest of the controller chip and the arithmetic chips are controlled by the test interface. Therefore, the microprogram sequencer can send test vectors and receive response vectors from any logic section just as an external tester would.

Since it is not feasible to store all test vectors and response vectors required for full NFT in the controller's ROM, the controller contains an on-chip test vector generator (TSTV) and a signature analysis register

(SAR). Selftesting for a chip is carried out by first generating pseudo-random test vectors to be applied to the subsection inputs and sending the corresponding output to the SAR. After applying a predetermined number of test vectors to the circuit under test, the content of the SAR is then compared with a known correct signature. This self-test approach is meant to serve as a go/no-go test that can detect faults occurring on the chips. No fault location below chip level is intended. Successful completion of the self-test would indicate a high degree of confidence that the chips are operating properly.

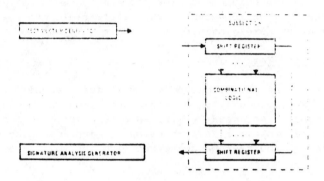

Fig. 2   Signature Analysis Testing.

Figure 2 shows a block diagram of the self-test implementation. The subsection registers can be loaded serially from the TSTV as well as from the NFT serial input. Also, the contents of the subsection registers can be serially shifted into the SAR. The same shift-paths used for the NFT are used for the signature analysis during self-test. The sequence of operations required to generate a signature is as follows:

1.   Load initial test vector into TSTV.

2.   Shift contents of TSTV into subsection input registers, and generate a new test vector. .

3.   Clock the subsection registers in functional mode so that the combinational logic output is loaded into the subsection output registers.

4.   Shift the contents of the subsection output registers into the SAR.

5.   Repeat steps 2 through 6 for each test vector to be applied.

FIGURE 3.

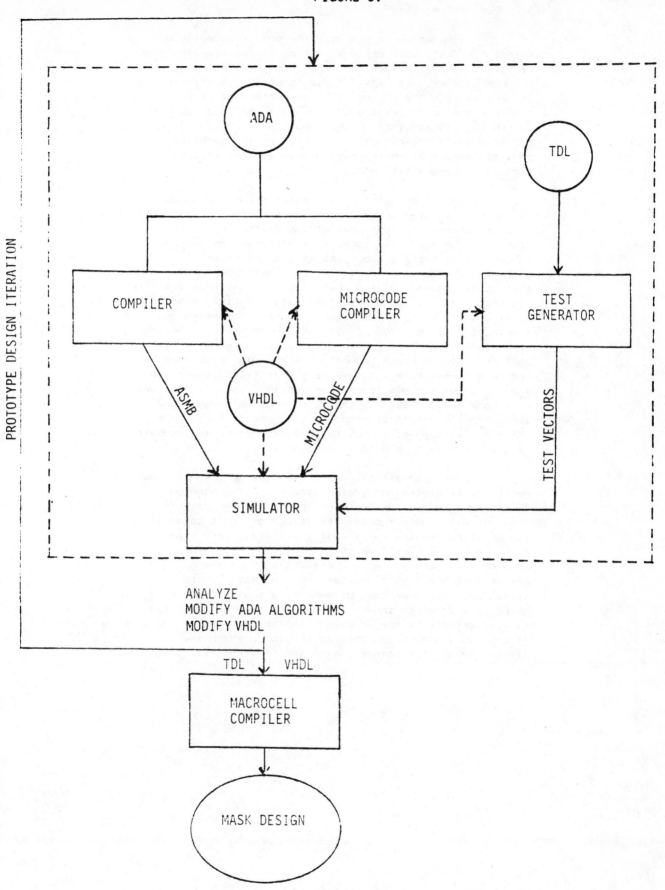

Figure 3 shows such a grand scheme currently coming into focus at Honeywell's Systems and Research Center.

3.2 Device Simulation

Simulation is probably the most frequently used
method for VLSI verification. The most accurate simulation
method is circuit simulation.[1] In this method a computer
program simulates as close as possible all the physical
properties of a given circuit. It enables the user to
simulate the response of such circuit to any desirable input
waveforms. In addition to the input waveforms the user
should specify the circuit net-list, and the detailed
physical models of the circuit's devices (transistors,
registers, capacitors, etc.).

The accuracy of a simulation program depends
strongly on the device model, that describes the relations
between currents and voltages at the device terminals.
Since most devices have capacitive effects, the current-
voltage relations are expressed as a first order
differential equation in time. The models are derived from
theoretical considerations when possible, and from empirical
equation that are found experimentally, in other cases. The
equations are usually non linear, to handle them in the
simulation the equation are linearized in parts. The models
are usually a part of a given simulation program, however in
some cases the user can specify a particular model from a
choice of a few possibilities (e.g., in SPICE2 there are
three choices for MOS transistor model).[2] Usually the models
have some free parameters that should be entered by the
user, these parameters depend on the process (e.g., the
threshold voltage of an MOS transistor), or on the geometry
(e.g., the area of a diffusion capacitor).

The process parameters are usually given by the
manufacturer of the integrated circuits. They can be
extracted from devices that are specially fabricated on a
test circuit. Only approximate values of these parameters
can be found, as the details of the process vary from batch
to batch, as well as from chip to chip on one wafer.
However it is usually a good assumption that the process
parameters, are almost constant on one chip. These
variations in the process parameters are usually given as
large tolerances on the parameters, or as a set of three
values for each parameter: Typical, low, and high. The user
of a circuit simulation program should cover in the
simulation all the points inside the n-dimensional volume

that encloses all the possible allowed combinations of
parameters values in the parameters space. A full coverage
is impractical, the common practice is to use the typical
values and a few extreme points. In addition it is
necessary to simulate the circuit on a range of temperatures
(as most models use also the temperature as a parameters),
again simulation at extreme ranges of temperatures is
usually sufficient.

The net list is the input that includes all the
data that can be extracted from the topology and the
geometry of the layout. The topology includes information
on the connectivity graph of the circuit, and the geometry
includes information on device parameters such as length and
width of transistors. This data is extracted automatically
from the layout of the verified VLSI circuit.

The input waveform voltages are given by the user
at discrete time points. The output waveforms are
calculated at the same time points. The input waveforms
typically represent the digital data at the input ports of
the circuit. The user at simulation program, should
generate a test that will cover enough cases to quaranty a
proper operation of the circuit. The problem of generation
a test with large enough coverage is similar to the same
problem in logic simulation, however as circuit simulation
is used usually for smaller circuits this problem is less
severe. In addition, it is possible to vary, in the input
waveforms, the voltages of the logical levels, as well as
the rise time and the fall time. The last changes are of
analog nature, usually it is enough to simulate the extreme
cases.

The algorithm used by the circuit simulator
involves the transformation of the differential equations of
the electronic circuit into algebraic difference equations,
this is done by implicit integration. Then the algebraic
equations are solved by iteration. The time needed to
perform the mentioned algorithm increases approximately
linearly with the number of nodes. However two mechanisms
increase the calculation time: First, it is necessary to
decrease the integration time-step to keep the truncation
errors constant. Second, the number of iterations in each
step increases with the number of nodes, and with the
complexity of the circuit. The result of these effects is
that the simulation time is proportional to $ n sup alpha $
$ (1 < alpha < 2) $. Experimental results show that for
typical circuits $ alpha = 1.5 sup 3 $. Logical simulator
are much faster than circuit simulator, because the
calculation time is proportional to the number of nodes, and
in addition each time iteration is faster because of simpler

equations.

It is not practical to simulate large circuits with circuit simulators a typical run time is 30 minutes for a circuit with 100 transistors, over 1000 time points, using SPICE2 on IBM 378-158. With this number one gets that simulation of a VLSI circuit with 100,000 transistors will take 20 days. Since each simulation should be tested with a few possibilities of parameter sets another factor of 10 should multiply the above run times, thus even the usage of faster computers will not help much. The practical solution is to circuit-simulate only small portions of the VLSI, then the full circuit is simulated with less accurate simulators such as timing or logic simulators. In the last method the verification is less complete than in full circuit simulation, and its validity depends much on the experience of the user. Mixed mode simulators (such as SPLICE) that include circuit, timing, and logic simulators in one package, can help the user, but is still the user responsibility to decide how to divide the circuit and which simulator to apply to each part.

Usually it is impossible to use the hierarchy of the circuit in circuit simulators because each instance of circuit macro (a cell) receives different inputs with varied levels and timing. However in a structured design methodology it is possible to by-pass some of the problems. For example in two phase clocking methodology[4,5] the VLSI circuit can be built of small parts with inputs active on one phase and output enabled in the second phase. In this design timing problems are negligible, providing that each part of the circuit was circuit-simulated carefully to assure that the delay, in each part, is shorter than the clock period.

Circuit simulation is a powerful verification tool, its two main disadvantages are long execution time, and the necessity to use parameters that are of analog nature. A silicon compiler that will take care of the physical design of a circuit will probably relief the user from the burden of circuit simulation.

4. Intersection

In a recent paper co-authored by E. H. Frank and R. F. Sproull and entitled: "Testing and debugging custom integrated circuits" one can read:

"Although designing a custom integrated circuit does not seem to be more difficult than designing software

of comparable complexity, testing and debugging a chip is
much more cumbersome than testing and debugging software....
The problem, therefore, is how to make testing and debugging
custom integrated circuits as easy as testing and debugging
problems."

Proffered among the software engineering
community, such a statement can only be met with smiles.

On the other hand, one can hear from members of
the software engineering community similar statements put in
the other way around. For instance, during a panel session
in a recent meeting on software engineering, I have been
amused to listen to a compiler designer envying VLSI
designers for their luck in being able to test thoroughly
the products they design.

While comparing respective complexity of design
and easiness of testing in VLSI engineering and software
engineering seems to me a moot question, I am feeling that
mutual carry-overs between the two areas are worth
investigating.

In the following, we will review several general
techniques and approaches are used in both software
engineering and electronic systems engineering.

4.1 Levels of Design Verification

Schematically, design verification occurs at three
levels:

1. at the specification stage

2. during implementation

3. after implementation

4.2 Approaches

Three main approaches to performing verification
are common:

1. analyze the specifications for assuring their
    consistency and completeness (level 1)

2. derive from implemented parts assertions and/or
    specifications, and check them against the initial
    specifications (levels 2 and 3).

3. analyze implementation for consistency, absence of faults (levels 2 and 3).

4. test implementation (level 2 and 3).

4.2.1 Specification Analysis

For the first approach, software engineering and VLSI engineering are on a par; even the two disciplines may call on common tools and techniques. A main quality of a specification technique is to be independent from the technologies involved in implementation.

I feel that much should be shared among the two disciplines and this the higher as the level of abstraction.

4.2.2 Extraction of Higher Level Descriptions From Lower Level Descriptions

Availability of such a capability requires use of some procedure that allows one to keep record of successive transformations from higher level descriptions to low level descriptions and to easily backtrack bottom up.

IC designers have felt the need for extractors for quite a while; those extractors correspond to those analyzers used for retrieving logic or electrical schematics from mask geometric descriptions; several such extractors are in use. However, their implementation is cumbersome and their operation uneconomical; this is because current IC CAD systems are not integrated enough.

4.2.3 Implementation Analyses

In this category fall all kinds of tools that have as input data implementation descriptions (code, logic or electrical schematics, mask layout...).

VLSI

electric simulators
logic simulators
delay analyzers
thermal simulators
parasitics analyzers
design rule checkers
EMC analyzers
quantization effect analyzers
testability analyzers
fault analyzers
performance analyzers

sneak circuit analyzers

SOFTWARE

language standard enforcers
coding standard enforcers
complexity analyzers
fault pattern sniffers
numerical precision effect analyzers
test coverage analyzers
static and dynamic analyzers
maintainability analyzers
modularity analyzers
performance analyzers

4.2.4 Test Data Preparation and Generation

Preparation of test data for digital systems or computer software involves one or two basic approaches:

1. A deterministic approach in which through direct synthesis or fault analysis input data detecting a given set of faults or executing a given set of entities are analytically determined.

2. A probabilistic approach in which input data are randomly drawn either on-line or off-line.

In both approaches, the main problem is assessing the thoroughness of the test data so obtained with respect to both the input domain and the possible faults.

Instances of application of both approaches are known for both program testing and circuit testing.

4.2.4.1 Deterministic Approach

4.2.4.1.1 Fault Simulation

This technique is in much use for preparing test programs for digital circuits. Today scores of logic simulators with fault simulation capabilities are available. Quality of testing sequences is then measured by means of the fault coverage they provide, i.e., the percentage of potential faults they are able to detect. Here potential faults means those that can be modeled economically; consequently, the list of potential faults taken into account is far from being exhaustive.

The software counterpart of hardware fault simulation is mutation analysis that has been investigated only by a few research groups.

One will notice that hardware fault analysis and mutation analysis are based on the same assumptions:

a)   The "almost correct" assumption:

   ● Software "good" programmers do not provide grossly incorrect programs but programs that are "almost" correct.

   ● Hardware faulty circuits are affected by only a limited number of faults; this is the conventional single fault assumption.

b)   The "coupling effect" assumption.

The occurrence of complex faults is coupled to simple and easy to detect faults. For hardware, this assumption corresponds to the classical stuck-at faults assumption.

For software, one remarks that test data that distinguish all programs differing from a correct one by only simple errors are so sensitive that they also implicitly distinguish more complex errors.

4.2.4.2 Test Data Synthesis

Here the problem is determining directly test data able to detect a given fault; the problem data are a description of the circuit or the program under consideration, a description of the faults (nature and site) for which detection test data are sought.

For hardware, numerous techniques have been proposed during the past 20 years. They may be put into several general categories:

   ● Algebraic versus heuristic techniques.

   ● Structural versus functional techniques.

Probably the most popular technique is path-sensitizing well represented by the well-know D-algorithm.

As far as software is concerned, test data synthesis seems to be neglected. However, one can mention a few attempts that are directly inspired by hardware practice:

36

a)   The technique of cause-effects graphs in which
     program functions are described by decision tables
     that parallel logic circuits; the equivalent logic
     circuit can then be handled by algorithms similar to
     the D-algorithm.

b)   The technique of finite-state machines in which
     software behavior is modeled by finite-state
     machines. Here the mathematical arsenal of finite-
     state machine theory can be called into play.

We have the feeling that this approach could be
exploited to a wider extent in particular in conjunction
with software specification techniques.

4.2.5   Probabilistic Approach

This category of approach gather those techniques
that involve sampling.

4.2.5.1   Random Test Data Generation

A technique, common for digital systems, consists
in analyzing the fault coverage of input data drawn
randomly, or best according to given laws of occurrence.
Here the basic tool is a fault simulator; most logic fault
simulators provide facilities for implementing such a
procedure.

We do not know of any direct application of this
approach to software. However, one should mention its use
in quantitative assessment of software reliability. For
instance, E. J. Nelson proposes procedure wherein input data
sets are selected randomly according to an operational
utilization profile and software reliability is defined as
the probability of using input data that lead to correct
results.

4.2.5.2   Comparison Testing

In this technique, the device to be tested is
exercised in parallel with a reference device by random
input data. The question is determining the number of
random input data to be used to reach a given level of
confidence. This technique is implemented by commercial
automatic test equipment.

This technique can be transferred to software in
the case where two versions of a same software are
available. One version can be the program actually
implemented, the reference version a prototype or an

executable specification.

5. Formal Verification

In practice, verification of software and hardware
is most commonly done by running test cases, either directly
on the software or hardware to be verified, or on a piece
that simulates it. Short of exhaustive test case runs,
which is impractical for most designs, such verification is
incomplete. Formal verification offers the potential for
complete verification.

Formal verification involves proving
mathematically the equivalence between two descriptions. It
is not test case oriented. Usually one description is the
specification of the expected behavior, and the other an
implementation.

The specification may be assertions about the
machine state at various control points. These assertions
specify, usually in the language of first order predicate
calculus [59,62], the expected relationships among the
machine variables. For instance, for a sequential hardware
that multiplies two numbers by repeated shift and add, an
informal assertion at some point in the multiplication loop
would be: "The result obtained thus far is the product of
the multiplicand and the rightmost m bits of the
multiplier." m itself will be a loop variable and will
change in every pass. The bits constituting "the result
obtained thus far" will have to be specifically identified.
The length of this partial result will be a function of the
loop variable m. Of course, the above assertion will have
to be stated formally and precisely to make mechanical
verification possible.

Floyd's inductive assertion method [60,62]
requires enough assertions to break each loop in the control
flowchart. This will create a finite number of paths in the
flowchart. Each path will have assertions at its head and
tail but none in between. For each path, if control starts
from a state satisfying its head assertion and follows the
path, then it must lead to a state satisfying its tail
assertion. For instance, suppose a path consists of the
statement "A <- A+1," and its head and tail assertions are P
and Q respectively. Each free occurrence of A in Q refers
to the "new" value of A, and each free occurrence of A in P
refers to the "old" value of A. Since new A = old A + 1,
substituting (old) A+1 for (new) A in Q should give the
required precondition for the path. The head assertion must
imply this required precondition, for correctness of this

path. In other words, "P implies $Q sub A+1 sup A$" must be valid for the path to be correct, where $ Q sub A+1 sup A $ denotes Q with each free occurrence of A replaced by A+1. This condition for path correctness is called "verification condition" (VC).

In general, a mechanical verifier for inductive assertion-based verification will have (i) a "verification condition generator" or VCG, to generate the VCs for all the paths, based on the semantics of the language, and (ii) a theorem prover to prove all the VCs valid, based on the axioms about the functions and predicates appearing in the VCs. If all the VCs are proved valid, the design is correct with respect to the assertions.

Some work has been reported on formal verification of hardware. Wagner [70] describes a formal method for proving the equivalence between two descriptions. An example shows how a particular gate level implementation is equivalent to the behavioral specification of a latch. Smith et al [69] describe "Static Analysis System" (SAS), which proves the equivalence between two combinational logic units. Such a system would be useful for comparing a gate level implementation mechanically synthesized from a register transfer level description, and one manually synthesized from the same description. The mechanical synthesizer need not be smart. Its output could be technology independent, and need not be optimized in any way. A one-to-one correspondence between latches, primary inputs and primary outputs of the two designs is required for the above comparison. Proof of equivalence between two combinational logic units is exponentially complex in general. SAS employs heuristics that usually work well. Pitchumani [65,66,67] describes an inductive assertion method for register transfer level verification of synchronous designs. The language semantics specifies how a variable t representing current time, measured in elapsed clock cycles, changes for each construct in the language. This variable t may appear in assertions but not in the hardware description itself. Assertions are useful for proving the realtime characteristics of hardware designs. Umrigar [71] describes the formal verification of a UART (Universal Asynchronous Receiver Transmitter) based on the above method.

A hardware description may be a behavior description (as most register transfer level descriptions are), or a structure description (as most gate level descriptions are). Formal verification of a design from its structure description is in general more difficult, since such a description is usually at a lower level than a behavior description. To use the inductive assertion method on the structure description of a synchronous design, the designer can gives one big assertion that is valid for each clock cycle of machine operation. The verification condition can then be derived based on the requirement that starting from this assertion and executing one clock cycle of activity must lead the machine back to the same assertion.

"Symbolic execution" [57,58] is a more general form of simulation. The inputs and initial values of storage elements may be symbolically specified. Every assignment executed during simulation will cause a symbolic expression, rather than a specific value, to be computed and assigned to the destination variable. Since the exact values of variables may not be known, it may not be possible to resolve branch conditions unambiguously. In such cases, symbolic simulation will follow both branches, thus creating a symbolic execution tree. Each node in the tree has a "path condition" or pc, and the current values of the variables. Both of these are in terms of the symbolic inputs and the symbolic initial values of the storage elements. The pc associated with a node specifies the condition that must be true for execution to reach that node from the root of the tree. The pc for the root of the tree is the predicate obtained by substituting the symbolic initial values of variables in the initial assertion. At each branch point, the pc for each outgoing branch is obtained by ANDing and pc of the incoming branch with the branch condition of the outgoing branch.

In general the symbolic execution tree may not be finite. If assertions are given for some control points in the hardware description program, then their validity may be verified (manually or by a theorem prover) at all instances of these control points in the symbolic execution tree. This verification is done by substituting in each assertion the symbolic expressions for the variables at this node, and determining if the path condition pc for the node implies the resulting predicate. For an infinite tree, the tree may be truncated to a finite depth, and verification obtained for this finite tree. Because of the pruning, such verification is not complete. If all the loops are cut by assertions, then complete verification is possible by using symbolic execution to establish the correctness of paths from assertions to assertions, as required by the inductive assertion method. For each path, symbolic values are assigned, at the head of the path, to the variables. The pc for the head is set to the head assertion with the symbolic values substituted. By symbolic execution, the pc and the symbolic expressions for the variables are computed for the tail of the path. The verification condition is then the predicate that the tail pc implies the tail assertion with the symbolic expressions for the tail substituted for the variables.

Formal verification requires a mechanical theorem prover to prove the verification conditions. The current state of the art permits formal verification of programs of "modest" size, with some user guidance. Theorem proving required for hardware verification is not different, hardware designs of "modest" size can be formally verified too. An example of software verification possible today is that of SIFT [64], a fault-tolerant flight control system, based on redundancy and software-implemented majority voting. The proof has been performed using STP [68], a specification and verification system. The required reliability of the SIFT computer system is so high that even a large number of test case runs can not offer the level of confidence desired. Validation of SIFT involved proving that the predicate "system safe," defined informally as "the replication of each of the tasks is sufficient so that the voting can mask the effects of the faults present in the system," is true. Ref. [64] describes how this was verified using a hierarchy of specifications. Each level in the hierarchy specifies an abstract view of the system as a set of primitive predicates Pi and functions Fi. Each level is related to its next lower level by describing the functions and predicates of the former in terms of those of the latter. With this mapping, one must prove that each property derivable from a higher level specification is derivable from its next lower level specification. by induction, properties derivable from the highest level are also derivable from the lowest level.

There are some practical problems in formal verification. First order predicate calculus is undecidable [62]. i.e., If a first order formula is valid, then a mechanical theorem prover is guaranteed to find a proof. However if it is not valid, the theorem prover may not terminate. Such a case may arise if the design or the assertion is incorrect, or if an axiom needed for the proof of a verification condition is not supplied. It is common for some property (e.g., commutativity) of a commonly used function to be left out, when it is needed for the proof. Since theorem proving is an exhaustive search for a proof or counterexample, heuristics speed up the proof process [56]. Ref. [59] briefly describes some search strategies. Many current theorem provers require the user to have at least a partial knowledge of theorem proving concepts to efficiently guide the theorem prover. Most hardware designers will need some training both on inventing assertions and on theorem

proving concepts for formal hardware verification to become
practical. The space and time problems experienced by the
theorem provers will ease with advances in computer
technology. However the number and size of the theorems to
be proved will also increase as designs get larger. For the
foreseeable future, user guidance in some form will be
required for theorem proving. The process of inventing
assertions forces a designer to understand his design
better. This itself may reveal some errors even if no
proof, mechanical or manual, is attempted.

The formal specification of the design must
correctly and completely capture the intended behavior. In
the end, this must be determined by manual inspection. For
a sequential multiplier, the final assertion "The product
register contains the product of the two argument registers"
may not be enough. A design that clears all three registers
to zero and does no multiplication at all will trivially
satisfy the specification. The formal specification must be
complete enough to exclude such designs.

For hardware, timing verification is usually a
separate step from logic verification. The timing
verification verifies that signal paths are not so long that
signals do not reach their destination in time ("setup"
requirement), nor so short that a new signal launched by a
clock pulse from a source reaches a latch while it is still
responding to the same clock pulse ("hold" requirement).
Ideally one would like to separate logic verification from
timing verification. The logic verification can be done by
teating the latches as primitives and simulating the gates
in rank order with zero delay assumption. The timing
verification can be done by ignoring the actual functions
performed by logic gates and only noting their inverting or
non-inverting behavior, to account for different rising and
falling propagation delays [61]. Such a separation has the
advantage that even if the logic is verified incompletely,
timing can be verified without relying on test cases. There
are some factors that make this ideal approach not always
possible. First, complete timing verification usually
assumes that a signal from a latch fed by clock Ci must
reach a latch fed by clock Cj in the time from a Ci pulse to
the next Cj pulse. In a particular design, it is possible
that such a path never gets sensitized, or does get
sensitized but only one or more cycles after the next Cj
pulse. Whether this is the case can only be determined by
taking the logic of the gates into account [63]. Secondly
logic gates are analog circuits. Manufacturing tolerances
make gate propagation delay a random variable with a
significant standard deviation. In addition, rise and fall
times are finite and non-zero. These make a meaningful

digital timing model for a logic gate difficult to obtain.
A worst case model will be dismissed as being too
conservative by designers who are always pushing the
technology to its limits. The effect of a slow gate on a
path may be offset to some extent by a fast gate on the same
path. One solution currently practiced is to identify some
critical paths, and do a detailed circuit level simulation
of these paths to verify timing. Such simulation is time
consuming and can not be applied to all paths. The
completeness of such verification depends on all the
critical paths being identified. It appears that designers
will have to become more conservative in order for complete
separation of logic and timing verifications to occur.

This section has examined verification. Formal
verification is not fully practical yet. Advances in
computer technology may make them more practical. For the
foreseeable future, user guidance of some sort will be
required to direct the theorem provers. Designers will need
some training in inventing assertions and in theorem proving
concepts for formal verification to become more practical.

6. Conclusions

There is a large intersection between software
testing and verfication and VLSI testing and verification.
In both areas we look to formal verification to provide
techniques to provide functional correctness assurance.

References

[1] M. Paige, "Program Graphs, an Algebra, and Their
     Implication for Programming," IEEE Trans. on Software
     Engineering, September 1975.

[2] S. Gerhart and L. Yelowits, "Observations of
     Fallibility in Applications of Modern Programming
     Methodologies," Trans. on Software Engineering,
     September 1976.

[3] T. Ostrand and E. Weyuker, "Software Error Data
     Collection and Analysis," IEEE Phoenix Conference on
     Computers and Communications, May 1982, pp. 209-213.

[4] P. Moranda, "Software Reliability Revisited," IEEE
     Computer, Vol. 11, No. 4, April 1978, pp. 92-94.

[5] G. Myers, "Software Reliability is Not an Equation,"
     IEEE Computer, Vol. 11, No. 6, June 1978, pp. 82-83.

[6] P. Moranda, "Software is Not a Warm Blanket," IEEE
     Computer, Vol. 11, No. 7, July 1978, pp. 131-132.

[7] J. Goodnough and S. Gerhart, "Toward a Theory of Test
     Data Selection," IEEE Trans. on Software Engineering,
     Vol. SE-1, No. 2, June 1975, pp.156-173.

[8] W. Howden, "Reliability of the Path Analysis Testing
     Strategy," IEEE Trans. on Software Engineering,
     September 1976.

[9] E. Weyuker and T. Ostrand, "Theories of Program
     Testing and the Application of Revealing Subdomains,"
     IEEE Trans. on Software Engineering, Vol. SE-6, No. 3,
     May 1980, pp. 236-246.

[10] D. Richardson and L. Clarke, "A Partition Analysis
     Method to Increase Program Reliability," Proc. 5th
     Int't Conf. on Software Engineering, March 1981, pp.
     244-253.

[11] W. Howden, "DISSECT: A symbolic Evaluation and Program
     Testing System," IEEE Trans. on Software Engineering,
     Vol. SE-4, No. 1, January 1978, pp. 70-73.

[12] J. King, "Symbolic Execution and Program Testing,"
     Comm. ACM, Vol. 19, No. 7, July 1976, pp. 385-394.

[13] R. Boyers, B. Elpas, and K. Levitt, "SELECT: A Formal System for Testing and Debugging Programs by Symbolic Execution," Proc. int'l·conf. on Reliable Software, 1975.

[14] L. Clarke, "A System to Generate Test Data and Symbolically Execute Programs," IEEE Trans. on Software Engineering, Vol. SE-2, No. 3, September 1976, pp. 215-222.

[15] C. V. Ramamoorthy, S. F. Ho, and W. T. Chen, "On the Automated Generation of Program Test Data," IEEE Trans. on Software Engineering, Vol. SE-2, No. 4, December 1976, pp. 293-300.

[16] Software Validation, Verification, and Testing Technique and Tool Reference Guide, NBS Special Publication 500-93, 1982.

[17] M. E. Fagan, "Design and Code Inspections to Reduce Errors in Program Development," IBM Systems Journal, No. 3, 1976.

[18] E. Daly, "Management of Software Development," IEEE Trans on Software Engineering, May 1977.

[19] B. G. Ryder and A. D. Hall, "The PFORT Verifier," Computer Science Technical Report, No. 12, Bell Labs, March 1975.

[20] R. Fairley, "Tutorial: Static Analysis and Dynamic Testing of Computer Software," IEEE Computer, Vol. 11, No. 4, April 1978, pp. 14-23.

[21] C. V. Ramamoorthy and S. F. Ho, "Testing Large Software with Automated Software Evaluation Systems," Proc. Int'l Conf. on Reliable Software, 1975.

[22] L. Osterweil and L. Fosdick, "DAVE - A Validation, Error Detection, and Documentation System for FORTRAN Programs," Software - Practice and Experience, September 1976, pp. 473-486.

[23] C. Gannon, "JAVS: A JOVIAL Automated Verification System," Proc. CompSac '78, November 1978, pp. 539-544.

[24] L. Osterweil, "Software Environment Research: Directions for the Next Five Years," IEEE Computer, Vol. 14, No. 4, April 1981, pp. 35-44.

[25] G. Myers, _Software Reliability: Principles and Practices_, John Wiley and Sons, Inc., 1976.,

[26] A. Davis, "The Design of a Family of Applications-Oriented Requirements Languages," _IEEE Computer_, _15_, _5_, May _1982_, pp. _21-28_.

[27] T. S. Chow, "Testing Software Design Modeled by Finite-State Machines," _Trans. on Software Engineering_, Vol. SE-4, No. 3, May 1978, pp. 178-187.

[28] W. Howden, "Functional Program Testing," _IEEE Trans. on Software Engineering_, Vol. SE-6, No. 2, March 1980, pp. 162-169.

[29] _Summary of Software Testing Measures_, Software Research Associates Technical Note, TN-843A/3, May 1982.

[30] E. Miller, "Some Statistics from Software Testing Service," _ACM SIGSOFT Software Engineering Notes_, Vol. 4, No. 1, January 1979, pp. 8-11.

[31] L. Stucki, "Automatic Generation of Self-Metric Software," _Proc. 1973 IEEE Symp. on Computer Software Reliability_, 1973.

[32] E. Miller and R. Melton, "Automated Generation of Test Case Datasets," _Proc. Int'l Conf. on Reliable Software_, April 1975.

[33] L. White, "A Domain Strategy for Computer Program Testing," _IEEE Trans. on Software Engineering_, _Vol. SE-6_, No. 3, May 1980, pp. 247-257.

[34] R. Lipton and F. Sayward, "The Status of Research on Program Mutation," _Digest of the Workshop on Software Testing and Test Documentation_, 1978, pp. 355-373.

[35] D. Panzl, "Automatic Revision of Formal Test Procedure," _Proc. Third Int'l Conf. on Software Engineering_, May 1978, pp. 320-326.

[36] R. Hamlet, "Testing Programs with the Aid of a Compiler," _IEEE Trans. on Software Engineering_, July 1977, pp. 297-290.

[37] C. V. Ramamoorthy and K. H. Kim, "Software Monitors Aiding Systematic Testing and their Optional Placement," _Proc. the First National Conf. on Software Engineering_, September 1975.

[38] Z. Manna, <u>Mathematical Theory of Computation</u>, MacGraw Hall, 1974.

[39] C. V. Ramamoorthy, Y. Mok, F. Bastani, G. Chin and K. Suzuki, "Application of a Methodology for the Development and Validation of Reliable Process Control Software," <u>IEEE Trans. on Software Engineering</u>, Vol. SE-7, No. 6, November 1981, pp. 537-555.

[40] S. Hantler and J. King, "An Introduction to Proving the Correctness of Programs," <u>ACM Computing Surveys</u>, Vol. 8, No. 3, September 1976, pp. 331-353.

[41] K. Fisher, "Test Case Selection Method for the Validation of Software Maintenance," <u>Proc. CompSac '77</u>, November 1977, pp. 421-426.

[42] J. Goodnough, "The ADA Compiler Validation Capability," <u>IEEE Computer</u>, Vol. 14, No. 6, June 1981, pp. 57-64.

[43] S. S. Yau and Z. Kishimoto, "A Method for Revalidating Programs in the Maintenance Phase," <u>submitted to Journal of System and Software</u>, North-Holland Pub. Co.

[44] E. Miller, <u>Methodology for Comprehensive Software Testing</u>, RADC, RADC-TR-75-161, June 1975.

[45] S. Mohanty, "Models and Measurements for Quality Assessment of Software," <u>ACM Computing Surveys</u>, Vol. 11, No. 3, September 1979, pp. 251-275.

[46] T. McCabe, "A Complexity Measure," <u>Trans. on Software Engineering</u>, December 1976.

[47] E. Swanson, "The Dimensions of Maintenance," <u>proc. Second Int'l Conf. on Software Engineering</u>, October 1976.

[48] Special issue of <u>IEEE Computer</u>, February 1982.

[49] B. Hansen, "Testing a Multiprogramming System," <u>Software Practice and Experience</u>, April-June 1973.

[50] E. Miller and W. Howden, <u>Tutorial: Software Testing & Validation Techniques</u>, IEEE Computer Society Press, 1981.

[51] A. L. Sangiovanni-Vincentelli, "Circuit Simulation," in "Computer Design Aids for VLSI Circuits," edited by P. Antognetti, D. D. Pederson, and H. De Man, Sijthoff

& Noordhoff (1981).

[52]   A Valdimirescu and S. Liu, "The Simulation of MDS
        Integrated Circuits Using SPICE2," Memorandum no
        UCB/ERL MB0/7, Electronics Research Laboratory,
        University of California, Berkeley (1980).

[53]   H. De Man, G. Arnout, P. Reynaert, "Mixed-Mode Circuit
        Simulation Techniques and Their Implementation in
        Diana," in "Computer Design Aids for VLSI Circuits,"
        edited by P. Antognetti, D. O. Pederson and H. De Man,
        Sijthoff & Noordhoff (1981).

[54]   C. A. Mead, L. Conway, "Introduction to VLSI Systems,"
        Addison Wesley (1980).

[55]   D. Noice, R. Mathews, J. Newkirk, "A Clocking
        Discipline for Two-Phase Digital Systems," in
        proceedings of IEEE international conference on
        Circuits and Computers, 1982.

[56]   R. S. Boyer and J. S. Moore, A Computational Logic,
        ACM Monograph Series, Academic Press, New York, 1979.

[57]   J. A. Darringer, "The Application of Program
        Verification Techniques to Hardware Verification,"
        16th Design Automation Conference Proceedings, San
        Diego, CA, pp. 375-381, June 1979.

[58]   J. A. Darringer and J. C. King, "Applications of
        symbolic Simulation to Program Testing," Computer, pp.
        51-60, April 1978.

[59]   B. Elspas, K. N. Levitt, R. J. Waldinger, and A.
        Waksman, "An Assessment of Techniques for Proving
        Program Correctness," Computing Surveys, Vol. 4, No.
        2, pp. 96-147, June 1972.

[60]   R. W. Floyd, "Assigning Meanings to Programs,"
        Proceedings of Symposium on Applied Mathematics,
        Mathematical Aspects of Computer Science, Vol. 19, J.
        T. Schwartz, Editor, American Mathematical Society,
        Providence, pp. 19-32, 1967.

[61]   R. B. Hitchcock Sr., "Timing Verification and the
        Timing Analysis Program," ACM IEEE 19th Design
        Automation Conference, Las Vegas, pp. 594-604, June
        1982.

[62]   Z. Manna, Mathematical Theory of Computation, McGraw-
        Hill, 1974.

[63]   T. M. McWilliams, "Verification of Timing Constraints
       on Large Digital Systems," 17th Design Automation
       Conference, Minneapolis, pp. 139-147, 1980.

[64]   P. M. Melliar-Smith and R. L. Schwartz, "Formal
       Specification and Mechanical Verification of SIFT: A
       Fault-Tolerant Flight Control System," IEEE Trans. on
       Computers, Vol. C-31, No. 7, pp. 616-630, July 1982.

[65]   V. Pitchumani, Methods of Verification of Digital
       Logic, Ph.D. Dissertation, Syracuse University, 1981.

[66]   V. Pitchumani and E. P. Stabler, "A Formal Method for
       Computer Design Verification," ACM IEEE 19th Design
       Automation Conference, Las Vegas, pp. 809-814, June
       1982.

[67]   V. Pitchumani and E. P. Stabler, "An Inductive
       Assertion Method for Register Transfer Level Design
       Verification," accepted for publication in IEEE
       Transactions on Computers, to appear soon.

[68]   R. Shostak, R. Schwartz, and P. M. Melliar-Smith,
       "STP: A Mechanized Logic for Specification and
       Verification," SRI International, December 1981.

[69]   G. L. Smith, R. J. Bahnsen and H. Halliwell, "Boolean
       Comparison of Hardware and Flowcharts," IBM Journal of
       Research and Development, Vol. 26, No. 1, January
       1982.

[70]   T. J. Wagner, "Hardware Verification," Ph.D.
       Dissertation, Stanford University, 1977.

[71]   Z. D. Umrigar and V. Pitchumani, "Formal Verification
       of a Realtime Hardware Design," Syracuse University,
       1982.

DEVELOPMENT ENVIRONMENTS

FOR VLSI AND SOFTWARE ENGINEERING

Randy Katz, Walt Scacchi, and P. Subrahmanyam
[1]

Abstract

We describe environments for VLSI and software
development. Many similarities exist because of the
common difficulties of building complex systems in
either software or hardware. We indicate what these
similarities are, such as support for the complete
system life cycle, as well as the differences, for
example, the overwhelming need for simulation aids in
the VLSI design domain. Development environments of
the future will have to be able to support both
disciplines, because distinctions between the two
continue to disappear, and because large systems need
to incorporate both hardware and software components
in their designs.

OVERVIEW

This report elaborates on the discussions of the
Design Environments Working Group that took place at
the Workshop on VLSI and Software Engineering, in Rye,
N. Y., in October, 1982. Our purpose is to address how
environments for hardware/VLSI design and program
development are similar and different, survey the
available development environments, and speculate on
what will be available in the near and long term
futures. While our working group was not able to come
to a consensus on what constitutes the ultimate
development environment of the future, we were able to
identify many of the most desirable features. We
believe that these can be attained with extrapolations
of available technology. Our most significant
observation is that future environments for system
development must encompass both the hardware and
software design. This is because the two design
approaches share much in common, and because future
systems will require elements of hardware and software
design, as distinctions between the disciplines
continue to blur.

----

[1]R. Katz, Computer Sciences Department, University
of Wisconsin-Madison, Madison, WI 53706; W. Scacchi,
Computer Science Department, University of Southern
California, Los Angeles, CA 90089; P. Subrahmanyam,
Computer Science Department, University of Utah, Salt
Lake City, UT 84112

The report is organized as follows. In the next
section, we describe the guiding principles behind
environments for hardware and software developement.
Since engineering support for the complete system life
cycle is a crucial aspect of development environments,
section 3 defines the life cycles for both hardware
and software development. Section 4 describes the
basic functions of a development environment. In
section 5, we discuss what is similar and what is
different in the current environments for VLSI and
software. Finally, in section 6, we describe the
state-of-the-art in design systems for VLSI and
software development, and look to what should be
available in the near term future. We also speculate
on what could be available in the more distant future,
tempering the view with some of the difficulties
likely to be encountered in developing future design
systems. Section 7 contains our summary and
conclusions.

2. GENERAL PRINCIPLES

The following "list of principles" represent our view
of the most important features of a development
environment for either hardware or software design.
Any future design system must give careful attention
to the provision of these features.

- Easy-to-Use User Interface: The users of a
  design system are designers, not design
  system implementors, and should not have to
  learn the intricacies of a complex system to
  get their design tasks completed. The
  interface should use menus extensively,
  helping to lead designers through the system
  with little effort. It should be able to
  operate in both expert and novice user mode,
  so as not to hinder the experienced user.
  Finally, graphical display of information,
  especially design data, presents it in a
  more meaningful way, and should be used.

- Integrated Support for the Entire System
  Life Cycle: The environment should support a
  system development project through its
  entire life cycle, from inception through
  completion. Most development systems only
  provide help for a piece of the overall
  problem. Support should be included for
  project management (eg., budgeting and
  scheduling), as well as design,
  implementation, maintenance, and validation
  of a system being constructed.

- Layered, Portable, Evolvable Development
  Environment: No single development system
  will be suitable for all computing
  environments, application domains, and
  application team organizations. Therefore,
  it will be important that the environment be
  structured to facilitate the incorporation
  of alternative implementations of components
  of the development environment. For
  example, a simpler user interface package
  would be used with dumb terminals than if
  sophisticated engineering workstations were
  available. It should be possible to
  personalize the environment to a given

application domain. Configurable language-directed text editors are examples of tools that provide such a capability. In addition, the development environment itself will evolve over time through incorporation of new facilitates and components, and provision must be made to make this evolution as effortless as possible. Clean interfaces between components will be critical.

- Environment Does Not Restrict Methodology: Development environments should aid the design process without constraining it. Several methodologies should be supported by the environment, since different methodologies may be appropriate for different components of the overall system. The design system must provide adequate performance, so as not to restrict designers from rapidly iterating between the stages of the life cycle.

3. ENGINEERING THE SYSTEM LIFE CYCLE

The "life cycle" of a system development project denotes the set of formal activities that occur in producing a system. These activities span from the conception of a system through its routine use and evolution. Ideally, we would like to support these activities with automated tools and a system engineering methodology for their use [BOSC82]. While comprehensive life cycle support is the goal, we do not yet understand what is required to provide this to project managers and system engineers alike. Nonetheless, we can describe what our current understanding is and where there is need for further investigation.

The development and evolution of a VLSI or software system follow a similar, but distinct course. These activities (or "stages") of the life cycle for VLSI or software system include:

- Initiation and Acquisition: making a commitment to acquire or develop a new computing system

- Requirements Analysis: determining why the system is needed and what resources must be available to support its development and use

- Selection and Partition: determining whether the system components are available and choosing between alternative divisions of hardware and software components to be built

- System Specification: describing what computational functions the desired system is to perform

- Architectural Design: organizing and dividing system functions across computational modules and people who will build them

- Detailed Design: designing algorithms and procedural units that realize the computational modules

- Implementation: coding and integrating designed components in preparation for installation in another environment

- Testing: verifying that the implemented system fulfills system specifications while validating its performance

- Documentation: providing a written record of what the system does and how to use it

- Use: operating the developed system under a variety of idiosyncratic circumstances according to the discretion of its users together with the mistakes they make in using it

- Evaluation: evaluating the operation, performance, and applicability of the system in light of changing circumstances

- Evolution: enhancing, tuning, repairing, and converting the installed system to maintain its useful operation

However, the apparent sequential order of these activities does not reflect the order we have actually observed [KLIN80, SCAC81, SCAC82].

The real work of system development entails articulating a variety of system descriptions, transforming these into an operational system, and evaluating them and the developed system to establish a basis for its improvement. This work is by necessity incremental, iterative and ongoing. However, we are not yet at a point where system engineering environments are available to thoroughly support this work. Thus, much of this work must either be done manually or else shoe-horned into some existing tool assembly during system development.

Although these system life cycle activities are familiar to most system engineers and project managers, the organizational arrangements that affect the ease by which these activities can be completed are less familiar. It is not that system developers are not aware of these conditions; instead, it is more a matter of the extent to which these social conditions are explicitly accounted for when organizing and performing hardware or software system development [KLIN82, SCAC82]. Nonetheless, the grouping of system life cycle activities listed above does provide a simple conceptualization of the history, organization, and performance of a system development effort that we can further examine.

3.1 Initiation and Acquisition

A software or VLSI system is initiated when participants propose it make the decision to acquire it. Acquisition denotes a binding commitment of organizational resources needed to perform system development. The proposed system somehow meets local "needs" that existing systems do not. The needs substantiate the decision to acquire the system. However, on closer examination, the possible range of conflicts within identified needs is large. For example, the need to acquire a new computer-aided design system for VLSI development may depend upon (a) overcoming organizational contingencies such as frequent failures or delays with the existing circuit design facilities, (b) the perceived ease with which design activities (or designers) can be better controlled, (c) the apparent technical benefits arising from standardized circuit patterns generated by the new system, (d) whether users are convinced that the new system will make their work more satisfying or entertaining, (e) possessing a "state of the art" VLSI design workstations that will help attract or retain talented engineering staff, and (f) reducing the lead time necessary for complex circuit development. The point here is not whether all of these needs can be met; instead, whose agenda are they on, how are they prioritized, who determines the priorities, and whose interests are met when some need is fulfilled. In any case, this organizational phase of a system's life cycle puts the development effort into motion and shapes its direction.

3.2 Requirements Analysis

Participants are concerned with two kinds of system requirements, non-operational and operational. Non-operational requirements indicate the **package** of computing resources that the new system assumes must be in place to ensure its proper operation.[2] These requirements may indicate that certain development tasks or production processes be structured to be compatible (i.e., made efficient) with the new system. On the other hand, operational requirements for a system are expressed in terms of its performance characteristics (e.g., response time), standard interfaces, engineering quality practices, testability, reusability, user-orientation, and so forth. Finally, requirements for the system to be cost effective, produced within resource constraints, delivered on schedule, and easy to use and manage have both operational and non-operational implications. Taken together, none of these requirements specify what the system's operations are. Instead, they outline preferences of participants to achieve a certain kind of engineering discipline through the life cycle of the system under development. Subsequently, these requirements form the criteria for evaluating the success of the system development

---

[2] A computing package consists of not only hardware and software systems, but also organizational facilities to operate and maintain these systems, organizational units to prepare data and analysis, skilled staff, money, time, management attention, application-specific know-how, staff commitment to modern engineering practices, and policies and procedures for ensuring the orderly production of additional applications [KLIN79, SCAC82].

effort. As such, what we need is some sort of "system requirements planning" facility that can take these preferences and system requirements as input. Managers, users, and engineers could then use the facility to produce plans coordinating their system development activities. Further, such an automated tool must operate with incremental updates to its inputs as well as be interfaced to system development databases. However, such a tool is not yet available.

3.3 Selection and Partition

Once a binding decision is made to acquire a new system, which system will do the job? Should the system be developed with in-house staff or should it be purchased elsewhere? Going with in-house staff facilitates the cultivation of local product and production knowledge useful in system maintenance. But if the system to be developed represents an unfamiliar or unproven technology, uncertainty over project completion within resource constraints may point to a lack of incentives for an in-house effort. Going with off-the-shelf components, on the other hand, requires figuring out whether they will do the job in the target system. Subsequently, what criteria can be used to filter information for readily available components: (1) developer reputation, (2) prior experience of similar users, (3) performance characteristics, (4) quality of available documentation, or (5) ease of fit into local computing arrangements? In any case, uncertainty over what to consider in selecting system components is present. Thus, it is very likely that the system selection will be influenced either by the mobilization of participants favoring one component set, or by the participants whose input is trusted by those making the decision.

How to partition a system into hardware and software components is a related problem. Partitioning a system is more art than science. The final result depends on the order in which partitioning decisions are made. When no ordering prevails, the resulting partitioning tends to be ad hoc and circumstantial. Alternatives to this can be found through experimentation via system simulation, sub-system prototyping, or through the prior experience of system developers on similar projects. However, experimentation to evaluate partitioning trade-offs can be very costly. In short, we lack a notation and calculus for expressing the trade-offs between hardware and software system components as well as the automated tools that support such analyses.

3.4 System Specification

What is the system to do? What are the objects of computation and what operations are applied to them? How can these specifications be represented so that either their internal or external consistency, completeness, and correctness can be checked? Clearly, use of system specification languages and analysis tools helps. If the application domain for the system being specified is bounded and well-understood, then a system generator may be available that produces a working implementation of a system from its specification. Examples in software include the so-called "application generators" popular in business settings, whereas in VLSI we have aids such as PLA generators. However, system generators that transform more general system descriptions into modular implementations are still subjects of advanced research. Subsequently, evaluating or transforming the specifications of either VLSI or software systems is an error-prone, manual activity. But it is not clear that more automation will eliminate difficulties in system specification.

Problems found in specifications may be due to oversights in their preparation or conflicts between participants over how they believe the system should function. Although a system specification language or methodology may serve as a medium of communication among participants, these aids do not resolve conflicts that might exist between participants; instead, they may make them more apparent. Therefore, who decides how to resolve a specification conflict? Who has a visible stake in achieving a particular outcome? How will specification responsibilities be divided among participants? Each of these questions point to tacit or explicit negotiations between project participants that occur in the course of developing system specifications. Further, the outcome of these negotiations will shape how stable the specifications will be and how frequently they must be reiterated.

3.5 Design

Designing a system entails deriving its configuration and detailing the computational procedures and objects from the available specifications. Developing the system's architectural design means articulating an arrangement of system modules (e.g., a "floor plan") that progressively transform the objects of computation into the desired results through local computational units. This articulation includes (1) choosing a system design technique, (2) developing and rationalizing alternative configurations, (3) employing a standardized notation for describing system architecture and module interfaces, (4) determining the order of module development (i.e., top-down, bottom-up, hardest-first, easiest to test, user interfaces first, etc.), (5) mapping system configuration onto staff to divide the labor, (6) performing system design, and (7) renegotiating any of these if local circumstances do them in.

On the other hand, developing a system's detailed design means articulating a symbolic description of the computational procedures organized in the architectural design. This stage of design requires interactive access to user knowledge of the procedures being codified into the system. This knowledge is usually dispersed across many participants with varying degrees of familiarity and commitment to the precision of articulation required for computational codification. Since this knowledge is difficult to access, gather, evaluate, codify and stabilize, system designs will be plagued with errors of omission or misarticulation. As these problems emerge, system designs and possibly the software development

artifacts preceding them will be redefined and reiterated.

3.6 Implementation

System implementation involves coding the design into an operational form. Choice of programming language for software, or layout format for VLSI comes into play here. Techniques for verifying that the implementation systematically realizes the system's design, specifications, and requirements must be considered. Additionally, the choice may be constrained by the kinds of automated optimizations and performance validations sought. However, implementation also includes introducing early versions of the system to users for hands-on evaluation.

Much hand-holding between system engineers and users can take place to smooth the introduction. If users believe that the system is being imposed on them without their earlier participation, then a variety of counter-implementation actions may appear marking their resistance to the system's introduction. Therefore, to ensure the system's integration into an existing computing environment, participants will engage in a series of negotiations to (1) establish sustained service for the new system, (2) get enhancements to the delivered system to improve its fit, (3) eliminate major system bugs, and (4) train new users. But participation of users with the system's developers earlier in the life cycle may obviate the need for these negotiations.

3.7 Testing

In testing a software or VLSI system, we seek to verify that the implementation is a consistent, complete, and correct realization of the system's designs, specifications, and requirements. Formal testing of systems is still very costly and not widely practiced. Ideally, this verification could be controlled through selectively generating test data that allows system developers to evaluate the system's static (control-flow), symbolic, and dynamic (data-flow) behavior. However, most system testing is heuristic and generally performed through system simulation or hands-on operation.

The division of labor in testing a system usually leads system developers to perform isolated tests on system components and users to discover additional problems as the delivered system supports more routine usage. Then, when difficulties ("bugs") appear, a collective effort begins to try to locate the source of the problem. This effort usually entails a partial reconstruction of what transpired and how to make it appear again for further study and correction. Well-organized system development documentation helps, but if it's not available, people who might know about how the system works in its current form must be found and engaged. This situation grows worse if the attribution of responsibility for the bug or its adverse effects is unclear. Thus, if the reconstruction is marked by uncertainty and frequent negotiations, participants may subsequently choose to work around the system anomaly leaving it for other staff to rediscover, reconstruct (again), and attempt to rectify.

3.8 Documentation

Documentation represents the most tangible product of system development activities. However, its utility has a very short cycle unless effort is directed to continually update it. We usually hear more about (and experience) the inadequacy of available system documentation than of it's superlative comprehensiveness.

Standards and incentives for good documentation are few. Users need one kind, developers another, and maintainers possibly a third. If the system development process has been volatile or behind schedule, then documentation may be put off.

Documentation work is labor intensive and revealing of personal communication skills. System evolution continually makes obsolete available documentation unless countervailing support is provided. Further, uncorrected system aberrations may not be documented since they may be used as evidence indicating either a lack of interest or lack of technical competency by certain participants. In short, in order to assure high--quality of the most visible -- and in the long term, the most important products of system life cycling -- development and use of system documentation must be planned, organized, staffed, controlled, coordinated and scheduled in much the same way as the system must be. This suggests that life cycle engineering tools must also support the development and evolution of system documentation in a manner similar to the development of the system itself.

3.9 Use

How systems get used is not well understood from an engineering viewpoint. We do not know the extent to which well-engineered systems are easier to use. But we do know that system use is shaped by (1) the discretion a participant has over when and for what he/she can use the system, (2) how easy it is to learn how to use an unfamiliar system, (3) what kinds of mistakes or error are likely to be encountered in using the system, and (4) how easy it is to integrate the system into the existing computing environment and established work routines [KLIN79, KLIN80, KLIN82]. Each of these arrangements is articulated only after a period of hands-on use of the system. These conditions cannot be thoroughly predicted during initial system development. However, as new systems are cycled through various user groups, the demands placed on the system (ie., its requirements) change and subsequently so must the system. The system also changes because of staff turnover, thereby requiring new staff to (re)negotiate the arrangements which shape their use of the system. Thus, circumstantial conditions in the work setting play a large role in determining the pace at which a system is consumed and evolved.

3.10 Evaluation and Evolution

Local participants regularly evaluate how well delivered systems work and how useful they are. As their experience with a system grows, so will a system's apparent inadequacy. System developers or users will seek enhancements, adaptations, repairs, or conversions as this occurs. System maintenance is really just ongoing, incremental system, development. It is done to improve system performance, to keep the system usable, or to reduce the cost of its use. It can also be supported with the same automated tools used during initial system development. However, systems developed without contemporary engineering aids will be more difficult (and costly) to maintain.

The care and attention to detail by which maintenance work gets done shapes long-term system usability. However, many conditions counter an ideal practice of system maintenance: (1) system users often have more requests for enhancements than can be realized within the local computing environment, (2) poor quality of development documentation complicates the ease of figuring out where to make system alterations, (3) maintenance work often competes with new system development for staff attention, (4) multiple system versions appear when maintenance activities are not coordinated or when unwanted alterations are resisted by users, (5) turnover of system development staff fragments local system know-how, and (6) bureaucratic mechanisms such as "change control boards" create a new source of resistance that must be engaged (or bypassed) in order to keep the system well-integrated as a computing package. As maintenance activities lag, users may begin to take on maintenance work in order to keep the system usable. Otherwise, they work around the system through ad hoc extensions. Subsequently, as this arrangement becomes too demanding for users or as new technological alternatives appear, participants may let the system sink in order to establish the "need" to acquire a new system. This of course marks the termination of one system life cycle and the initiation of another.

3.11 Summary

Overall, there is a high degree of concurrency across the activities occurring during a VLSI or software system's life cycle. Each life cycle activity requires a different kind of description of the system being developed. A complete and consistent description is the desired product of each activity, although these descriptions will often be incrementally constructed and revised. Developing these descriptions using a machine-processable language or formal notation appears to be a key to providing automated life cycle support tools. However, three higher-order problems remain:

- articulating the various system descriptions,

- establishing a mapping or set of transformations between successive system descriptions, and

- evaluating the completeness, consistency, and correctness of the system descriptions vis-a-vis one another.

These activities are by necessity incremental, iterative, and ongoing reflecting many system sub-life cycles. But as we improve our ability to engineer this cycling, a growing array of resources must be provided, new tools will be necessary, new forms or subdivisions of work will emerge, and a more complex web of organizational and technological arrangements will appear which must be managed [KLIN82, SCAC81, SCAC82].

4. COMPONENTS OF A DEVELOPMENT ENVIRONMENT

A development environment for software-hardware systems should ideally consist of a well integrated set of tools that support all the activities occurring during the system life cycle. We delineate here some of the more important components of such a development environment, focusing only on those parts of the overall life cycle that are subsequent to the decision to (re)develop a system. Thus, we do not discuss any managerial tools that might be used in reaching such decisions: these might include, for example, tools that support project scheduling, resource accounting, etc.

In essence, the development of an integrated software-hardware system involves:

- the acquisition of a specification of the problem from the end user(s) of the system,

- the actual design and implementation of the system, and

- the subsequent evolution of the design and implementation as a result of changes in the requirements and/or specifications (until a decision to supplant the system by an entirely new one is eventually made).

The system development process typically involves reasoning at several different levels of abstraction. For instance, these include:

- representation independent or "abstract" problem specifications (wherein the only objects and operations present are those of direct interest in the problem domain),
- high level model dependent "programs" that embody a recipe for the solution of the problem, and
- any other levels of abstraction that facilitate the subsequent implementation in terms of some combination of (1) software executing on one or more general purpose host computers, and (2) special purpose hardware. Two examples of such levels of abstraction are (i) architectural descriptions of systems, and (ii) electrical descriptions of circuits.

It is desirable to have design paradigms wherein the choice of a final implementation medium (hardware or software) is not fixed a priori. This mandates that a uniform perspective be adopted both in the specification of the problem to be solved and, in as far as is possible, in the development of an implementation. Ideally, a problem specification must be representation independent, and as close to the user's conceptualization of the problem as possible. However, there is sometimes a trade-off involved between the use of completely representation independent (axiomatic) specifications (e.g., [GUTT78], [DIJK76], [PNUE79]), and the use of conventional high level languages as "specification" languages that yield specifications that are more or less representation dependent. While there are promising axiomatic specification techniques being investigated, the average (current day) system designer is not yet adept at writing formal specifications; in fact, most tend to be put off by the mere presence of formalism, although there are notable exceptions. A second, and more technical, issue is that it is sometimes not easy to specify a desired behavior axiomatically because of inadequate understanding about the problem domain. In such cases, it may not always be feasible to invest the extra effort required to acquire such an understanding due to project deadlines. Consequently, an alternative specification technique that is viable in such circumstances is useful as a practical alternative: this can generally take the form of an understandable "specification" in a high level language.

4.1 Design Paradigms and Support Tools

Given that a problem specification is available, it is necessary to follow some design paradigm to obtain an implementation that is consistent with this specification. The tools needed to support this design process will in general depend on the particular design methodology adopted. We will here attempt to convey a flavor of some of the concepts involved by considering the tools that are needed in the context of a design paradigm discussed in [SUBR82a, SUBR82b].

Both software and hardware design may be viewed as the process of representing the abstractions of objects and operations relevant to a given problem domain using primitives that are already available [PNUE79].

- When synthesizing programs, the primitives used are those provided by the lower-level abstractions: these may either be chosen from an available library, or be explicitly supplied.

- When synthesizing hardware implementations, the "primitives" available during conventional (i.e., printed circuit board) logic design are in the form of off-the-shelf chips: this is quite analogous to synthesizing programs. On the other hand, considerable flexibility in the number and nature of the primitives is available when doing special purpose VLSI design: this potentially enables the structure of the problem to be more directly mirrored in silicon.[3]

In the event that a truly abstract specification of a system is not viable for some reason, a high-level language program may be viewed as comprising a "specification" of the system, e.g., GIST [GOLD80a], Ada [DOD 80].

Depending upon the availability of axiomatic or high-level problem statements, there are two approaches to system design that one may adopt:

One can attempt to synthesize special purpose (software/VLSI) systems proceeding from abstract, representation independent specifications of problems. This paradigm can potentially mirror the structure intrinsic to a problem directly in an implementation structure in silicon, and thus provide a way of tailoring machine architectures to specific problems. As a consequence of the modularization inherent in such specifications at different levels, parts of the system may either be in software or hardware.

Alternatively, a (more or less representation dependent) specification of the problem in the form of a program can be transformed into a hardware implementation and/or more efficient software implementation.

We now outline some of the prototypical components that need to be present in a development environment to support the design paradigm alluded to above. Briefly, these include tools that help interface with the end user(s), tools that aid in the development and evaluation of a system, and tools that support the evolution of a system after its initial design. We believe that in the long run it is important to base such tools on a reasonably cohesive theory of the various aspects of the design process, rather than to merely have an ad hoc collection of tools. Research therefore needs to be directed into gaining fundamental insights in such areas, rather then emphasize attempts to build fancy "front-ends" for otherwise ill-designed development environments [MCCA79].

4.2 Interacting with the User

To facilitate user interaction at the different levels

_____

[3]In the solution of a specific problem using specific technology, however, the number of primitives is usually quite small -- e.g., pass transistors, boolean logic gates, flip-flops, multiplexors. This is partly necessary to reduce the complexity of the design process at this stage: such primitives are at a very low level; their correct implementation depends critically upon the technological "design rules" and usually require substantial effort to be "debugged". It is somewhat fortuitous that a small number of carefully chosen primitives suffices for a large class of problems.

of abstraction involved in the design process, it is convenient to use different forms of syntactic sugaring (even multiple external representations): e.g., both formal and informal textual forms for high-level specifications, graph representations for networks, and more detailed (color) graphic layouts for viewing lower level circuit structures.

It is possible to build knowledge based "expert" systems that have "natural-language" interactions with a user and aid in the acquisition of the initial problem specifications. Since the problem domain typically determines the most convenient way(s) of interfacing with a user, such user "front ends" should be designed so as to be extensible. We envision the sophistication of such front ends to improve with progress in related areas such as artificial intelligence, and to eventually include more-or-less natural language dialogue, speech recognition, and visual sensors.

4.2.1 Back-End Interfacing: Rapid Prototyping

In order to facilitate interfacing with the other design development tools that form the "core" of an environment, it is useful to minimize the number of different forms that the input to this back-end can assume. We believe that such an interface should allow for both axiomatic specifications and high level language programs.

To facilitate rapid prototyping, it is desirable that the initial specifications be "interpretable" or "executable" to some degree. In particular, in order to ensure that the specifications do in fact embody the user's requirements, it is important to provide for some dialogue with the user that enables a clarification of the system's understanding of the problem. A tool that is able to accept various forms of user queries and answer them, e.g., using formal manipulation systems, a simple database retrieval mechanism, etc., is therefore useful in this context.

In general, it is convenient to have means of prototyping systems at various levels of abstraction, so as to be able to exploit the design details as they are fleshed out. For example, one potential advantage of prototyping at lower level is that more accurate information about various performance metrics can be obtained.

4.3 Design Development Tools

The paradigm of development followed can be viewed, to a greater or lesser extent, as a transformation of the problem statement expressed at a higher level of abstraction into a form that elaborates at a lower level of abstraction the representation of some of the constructs used.

4.3.1 Linguistic Primitives

In order to support specification and reasoning at different levels in the design spectrum, it is important to have appropriate linguistic primitives, and languages that embody these. Examples of the kinds of primitives that are useful include: primitives that enable axiomatic specifications; primitives for parameterization of the design (yielding what are sometimes known as "macro languages"); primitives for describing the composition of design components ("interconnection primitives"); primitives to describe component interfaces, etc. It is important to be able to specify environmental characteristics of systems and performance characteristics [SUBR82c]. These primitives may either be embodied in a "broad spectrum" language, or be viewed as a set of distinct languages.

Several common processes such as editing, pattern matching and replacement, and parsing are used at almost all levels in the design hierarchy and can benefit from language tailored tools such as editors, pattern matchers etc. [SUBR82b, WILE80]. Further, tools that aid in symbol manipulation are useful in computing complexity measures of designs at various stages of development [SUBR82d]. A machine readable documentation of the history of a development, that incorporates the reasons for adopting strategic decisions will aid in the incremental redesign of the systems in responses to evolving specifications.

It has been observed that the global strategy that guides a design depends to a large extent on (1) the performance requirements desired of an acceptable implementation and (2) the characteristics of the global environment that the resulting system is to intended to function in. The tools needed to support the acquisition of information needed for the transformations, and to support the mechanisms of the transformation process itself are therefore important ingredients of a development environment.

4.3.2 Evaluation/Verification

Once a system has been designed, it is usually desired to evaluate its performance along one or more dimensions. Examples of relevant characteristics include, for instance,

- memory and time utilization (in software implementations);

- paging frequency (for virtual memory systems);

- communication traffic density (in distributed systems); etc.

- chip area, response time, throughput, reliability (for silicon implementations);

Tools to measure performance along these and other dimensions, and to support the validation of designs are an important part of an overall development environment.

4.3.3 Simulation and Testing

It is useful to be able to ensure at some intermediate stages in the development of a system, that a design is consistent with the specification and has approximately the right performance characteristics. Although there are a few isolated instances where formal verification is being used in practice, the prevalent modes of improving the probability of a design being correct are still testing and simulation.

In particular, "simulation" is fast becoming a very important tool in the existing VLSI design cycle, whereas it is not as widely used nor as applicable in the milieu of software systems. On the other hand, "software testing" can be thought of as the (software) counterpart of (hardware) simulation. Just as in the case of software it is well known that testing can only help in the detection of bugs and can never demonstrate their absence, simulation of a hardware circuit usually helps in reducing the number of logical and electrical errors in a design, and cannot guarantee their absence.

In software, simulation is typically used only for systems that have characteristics that cannot be deterministically modeled very well, e.g., operating systems. In addition, it is used for software modeling of systems wherein the various interactions in the problem domains are not well understood, e.g., war games.

A circuit may malfunction because of errors in its logical design, or due to unforeseen electrical characteristics of the circuit elements used, or due to fabrication faults during reproduction. "Simulation" in the sense it is used in the hardware domain is used to reduce the probability of the first two happening, whereas "hardware testing" is used to detect erroneous circuit function after fabrication. Simulators in the hardware domain need to model both the electrical characteristics of circuits as well as their logical behavior. It is recognized by now that it is not practical to simulate large circuits at the device level using a simulator like, say, SPICE, because of the computational explosion that occurs. It is therefore important to have hybrid or multi-level (hierarchical) simulators in the development environment that allow simulation at the functional, logical, switch and electrical levels, and that allow for a smooth transition between the various levels.

4.   Test/Simulation Data Generation: Testing Environments

Testing plays an important role both in the software system development life cycle and in the development of hardware systems. However, as pointed out above, there is substantially differing set of requirements in software and hardware testing, mainly because of different interpretations of the terms. In the case of software, duplication is almost error free, and testing relates primarily to testing the design of the logic of programs and their robustness. In hardware design, duplication (i.e., fabrication) is far from error free, and therefore testing plays a major role in both the logical design of the system, and in testing for the correct fabrication of ostensibly correctly designed components.

A set of support tools for test data generation, both for software and hardware and modules, is needed. In addition, it is important to have test beds or "drivers" that allow a software or hardware module to be "plugged in" and tested. In particular, apparatus for physically testing the functionality of fabricated chips is needed, as well as the ability to embed a chip in a software/hardware environment that simulates the actual environment in which the module is intended to function.

4.5 Configuration and Version Control

As any non-trivial system evolves, it typically goes through a cycle of design, implementation, and redesign. Besides being intrinsically quite complex, such a system consists of non-trivial subcomponents that are developed by several people and updated by several others. Further, there are usually multiple versions of a system in existence at any one time, both in the hands of different end users and in use by the designers themselves during the development phase. The utility of tools (even very primitive ones) that aid in keeping track of different versions and configurations of software systems, e.g., various releases to different end users, has been established beyond doubt. We believe that it is important that a richer set of support facilities than those existing in current version control systems like SCCS is needed. Some examples of such systems are the personal information environment developed by Bobrow and Goldstein [GOLD80b] that support a layered network model of software systems (including various perspectives of a program), and systems like SOLID (an evolution of the programmers workbench at Bell Laboratories that facilitates in installing different versions of large systems). The initial experiments with such environments to support evolution of designs has been that a methodology for using the underlying tool is needed for efficient usage (e.g., if a layered network model is to be prevented from becoming a very expensive file system). Of course, it is desirable that such a set of facilities be reasonably well integrated into the remainder of the development environment.

4.6 File and Operating System Services

The development of a sophisticated system environment is critically dependent upon the underlying file and operating system capabilities available. In this sense, such capabilities are so basic that a certain minimal standard is indispensable to enable the development of good environments. On the other hand, once such capabilities are provided, they can be (and are) taken for granted for the most part.

In order to ensure that a system scales smoothly as its functions grow or as the size of the problems it can be applied to grows, it important to have a large enough address space (at least 24 bits, and preferably 32 bits of addressable code space). It has been experienced that space, rather than time is the limiting factor in expanding existing systems, in the sense that once the available space limits have been reached, a radical redesign is needed. Of course, faster machines lead to improved response times and in turn to improved programmer productivity.

File support facilities are also important, particularly the ability to have segmented files and some form of direct accessing mechanism. Here, the addressing capabilities needed are typically larger: 32-bits may be enough for all of the code in a system but not for its data, e.g., dictionaries, medical and legal data bases can contain several billion characters very easily. Robustness of the underlying file system and storage mechanisms then becomes quite important.

Various support features of a similar nature, whose main objective is to free the system designer from low level considerations while providing him a reasonably powerful set of primitives include: good process and memory management, swapping facilities, object management support utilities (e.g., garbage collection, reference counting), interrupt facilities, exception handling, software and hardware dynamic monitoring functions for various performance measurements, etc. In addition, it is important that any software support routines already existing (or that are written in different languages) be easily integratable; in order to facilitate this, mechanisms to enable inter-language communication must be provided. Microprogrammability, and the ability to speed up some of the basic support tools by casting them in hardware must also be feasible to some reasonable degree.

4.7 Database/Library Services

Several of the design functions may be viewed as appropriate manipulations being performed on relevant sets of objects. The integration of various tools therefore involves sharing some of these sets of objects. While it possible to view some of these functions as being provided by a database management system (e.g., [KATZ82]), whether or not they are explicitly labeled as such is largely a matter of taste and/or historical precedence. Examples of the objects manipulated by a system would include libraries of programs (indexed by relevant attributes of the implementations), available implementations of standard (or widely used) hardware modules, cell sets implementing primitive functions and tailored to various technologies, etc. The database facilities should provide for accessing the various library entries when indexed by the relevant attributes. This system should support the evolution of the entries themselves and the existence of several versions of objects that perform similar functions. It is obvious that it include many of the features of version control systems and other environments like PIE [GOLD80b].

4.8 Implementation Services

When the initial start up cost for some component of a development environment is capital intensive, a centralized set of services may be made available to a reasonably circumscribed community of users. A successful example of such a service is the MOSIS facility provided by DARPA (through ISI) that enables members of the DARPA community to have their designs fabricated despite the lack of an in-house fabrication facility. This centralization has the benefit of localizing the choice of vendors and insulating the user from details of the fabrication process (to some extent). The emergence of such centralized silicon foundries is analogous to the development of university wide computing centers in the 60's and early 70's (in the absence of every department or research project having its own computing facility). A more geographically centralized example is the MACSYMA consortium, which provides access to symbolic computation facilities (located at MIT) to members of the consortium; these facilities are accessible through various international networks.

One obvious advantage of such centralized facilities is that the cost per user is reduced. Further, in some cases, the existence of a single or limited number of such centers either implicitly or explicitly imposes some community wide standards, e.g., the use of CIF files to describe fabrication masks. A potential disadvantage of this is the fact that undesirable features may creep into such standards prematurely, thus harming the community in the long run. The existence of such a centralized facility cannot obviously be used to pursue research in the service provided by that facility and therefore does not eliminate the need for research centers to explore improved fabrication methods, symbolic computation methods, etc.

5. DIFFERENCES AND SIMILIARITIES BETWEEN VLSI AND SOFTWARE ENGINEERING

The similarities and differences between software and VLSI Systems can be seen by examining what is underdeveloped in both areas and what is being done at present.

5.1 Similarities

The complexity of systems under development and the number of people participating in those developments are increasing. Subsequently, the costs of developing these complex systems are rising. How to best organize and perform these development projects with the people and resources at hand is not well understood. However, producing and cultivating such an understanding is a key factor in overall system development productivity [CAS 81, SCAC82]. Use of automated environments that support comprehensive system life cycle engineering are likely to be another factor as they become available for software and VLSI.

New system development environments for VLSI and software applications increasing rely upon formal notations or language-based system descriptions to support automated processing of each system life cycle activity. Because of this, a common set of automated tools that can be specialized to process these descriptions can be developed.

In general, there appear to be enough similarities

between the development process for complex software and VLSI systems that automated environments, engineering methodologies, and project management strategies tailored for one technology may be applicable to the other. However, differences in the development process for software and VLSI must be supported before comprehensive hardware-software "factories" can be built.

5.2 Differences

Although limited, we have more experience with software environments than those for VLSI. VLSI is a younger technology: tools and engineering environments for VLSI are still quite new. Software environments such as UNIX-PWB and Interlisp have a large user base [WASS81]. However, environments supporting the development of real-time software systems or complete system life cycle engineering are not widely used, if they are even available.[4] In addition, the importance of life cycle engineering efforts are not yet recognized throughout the VLSI development community.

More substantial difference between VLSI and software system development appear in later stages of their system life cycles. However, we should expect this since VLSI systems require a physical fabrication. This physical fabrication does not occur with software.

Clearly, there can be differences at each stage of the life cycle for VLSI and software systems. But these differences are subtle and usually specific to the system application domain or to the system development methodology in use.

With VLSI, preliminary circuit implementations must be made to test circuit operation with different fabrication constraints or circuit layouts to improve production yield. To minimize the chance of discovering fatal circuit design errors at such a late development stage, many VLSI simulation tools are used. Simulators for fabrication process characteristics are employed to either reveal electrical faults or verify circuit designs.[5] VLSI systems also undergo physical inspection and test upon fabrication and packaging. These evaluations are usually performed with expensive, special-purpose testing equipment. Since there can be fabrication or packaging variations (e.g., flaws) in individual copies of the same mass-produced circuit, statistical samples of production chips must be evaluated to determine current yield and ways to improve it. Widely used software systems are not tested in this manner.

---

[4]Real-time software systems often have performance requirements for timing behavior similar to those for VLSI systems.

[5]A current stumbling block in the use of VLSI simulation tools is the lack of a common language or engineering methodology that coordinates interaction between them.

Design libraries are used differently in the two disciplines. Some VLSI design methods (e.g., standard cell, gate arrays) consist of selecting the implementation of functions from a library and wiring them up to form the system. While software systems make extensive use of standard subroutine libraries, the design of the system is not influenced by the libraries to the same extent. Note however that early link and load systems were not unlike modern gate array systems, in that standard functions were selected from libraries and linked together to form an executable program.

In summary, the similarities between software and VLSI systems arise from the ways system engineering work is organized and performed. The development of either software or VLSI systems usually requires the articulation, transformation, and evaluation of various system descriptions within a single computational medium. On the other hand, the differences between VLSI and software systems arise because VLSI circuit descriptions must also be transformed (fabricated) and evaluated across computational and physical media.

NEAR TERM PROSPECTS AND FUTURE SCENARIOS

6.1 Available Now

For software systems, there already exist good operating and programming system environments. These include Bell Lab's UNIX [RITC78], the Programmer's Work Bench [DOLO78], and the InterLisp System [TEIT81]. Other systems supporting various activities in the software life cycle can be found in currently available surveys [HUNK81, WASS81]. A comprehensive, up-to-date survey on available software development methodologies can be found in [FREE82].

For VLSI, many integrated environments for circuit design exist, but these support a fixed, and often proprietary, methodology (e.g., IBM's Engineering Design System and various vendors design systems). These support the entire range of circuit design activities, but are often tuned for a particular implementation environment, thus limiting the transportablity of designs. To our knowledge, there is no integrated CAD environment that provides either complete system life cycle coverage or independence from circuit design methodology.

On the other hand, workstation-based systems are beginning to emerge that place complete sets of design tools in the hands of individual designers [SCHI82]. However, the tools are presented as a loose confederation, and frequently lack integration. Workstation system designers' are directing a great deal of effort towards building their tool sets around an integrated system development database to reduce these problems.

Except for the earliest and most strategic activities of the development cycle (product requirements, system specification, etc.), where the most commonality in development approaches is to be found, little has been done to combine the hardware and software development environments. As has been mentioned in section 3 above, an important need of the combined environment are tools to aid in partitioning a system into its hardware and software components. Fundamental research remains to be done to better understand the process of system partitioning.

6.2 Desired Future Capabilities

Expert systems technology as well as other artificial intelligence techniques will be applied in future development environments. The environment will not only adapt to the system developer/user as she/he progresses from novice to expert, but it will also take a more active role in aiding system development decisions. The system developer/user can concentrate on the higher level strategic issues of design, such as specification of functions to be implemented, while the environment does the low-level tasks, such as choosing detailed structures for implementing these functions. Additionally, the environment should be able to keep track of the developer/users interactions with various system components and provide a range of problem-solving or diagnostic help services if needed.

A major problem with current development environments is that there is little support for making system components reusable across a wide spectrum of applications. Examples of reusable components include technology-independent cell libraries for VLSI circuits and machine-independent subroutine packages for software. Continued research must be directed towards the issues of how to make portable systems. In particular, we must develop ways to specify the behavior of a system component in a technology independent manner.

Related to the issue of technology independence, is support for families of implementations and families of algorithms. Given a specification of the performance requirements of a system, a development environment will eventually be able to select among alternative implementations of the same functional unit. The environment should enable a designer to explore the space of alternative implementations of his design, with different combinations of performance metrics, such as area, speed, and power tradeoffs.

Finally, when all of these facilities are incorporated into the "ultimate" development environment, the question arises as to how to keep the whole thing manageable. The performance and usability of the system must remain reasonable, even as more powerful facilities are being added. An ability to tailor the development environment to specific projects and technologies should help to maintain adequate performance. Techniques for adapting the system to the expertise of system engineers, project managers, and other users must be developed, to avoid overwhelming them with the sheer complexity of the computational environment.

7. SUMMARY

Developing larger, more complex VLSI or software systems will remain very costly. Automated environments are costly and resource intensive [PREN81]. Accordingly, automated environments that support the life cycle engineering of complex systems will probably not reduce these costs; instead they may help keep them from rising too quickly. Substantial cost savings and productivity boosts are still elusive. Thus, we might look beyond automated system engineering tools to find the breakthroughs we seek. Perhaps the answers lie in discovering new ways to organize and perform system development work, and to manage the flow of production resources. Nonetheless, the tools we can identify are becoming more important.

In this report, we described the desirable features of environments for system (hardware and software) development. We emphasized the need for development environments to support the entire system life cycle, and discussed the significant events that constitute that life cycle. Important components of the environment were identified. We also described the large degree of similarity among development environments, and pointed out the few differences. Capabilities of existing development environments were reviewed, and we offered speculations about the future.

One of the goals of the workshop was to identify where VLSI and software engineering intersect. With respect to development environments, we discovered that the intersection was large, and that systems that support VLSI and software development share many of the same requirements and need to provide the same solutions. Development environments of the future will support complete system life cycle engineering, where components of the system can be realized as either hardware or software subsystems. Future environments will take a more active role in the development process, and will support families of alternative system implementations, with a greater emphasis on portability of designs. Builders of such environments will be faced with the challenge of providing a powerful, flexible system that is both easy to use and does the job with little overhead.

ACKNOWLEDGEMENTS

Many people contributed to the lively discussions that led to this report. The members of the Development Environments Working Group included Duane Adams, Marc Davio, Jacob Katznelson, John Kellum, Steven Reiss, Gilles Serrero, and Jack Thomas.

REFERENCES

[ALLE79] Allen, J., "Requirements for a Research-Oriented IC Design System," Proceedings of the Caltech Conference on Very Large Scale Integration, pp. 253-258. California Institute of Technology, (January 1979).

[ALLE81] Allen, J., P. Penfield, Jr., "VLSI Design Automation Activities at M.b;.i.T.," Proceedings of the 1981 IEEE International Symposium on Circuits and Systems, pp. 648, IEEE Circuits and Systems Society, (April 1981). IEEE Catalog No. 81CH1635-2.

[AYER78] Ayers, R., "A Language Processor and a Sample Language," Silicon Structures Project File No. 2276, Computer Science Department, California Institute of Technology, (June 1978).

[AYER79] Ayers, R., "IC Specification Language," Proceedings of the 16th Annual Design Automation Conference, pp. 307-309, (June 1979).

[BALZ81] Balzer, R. M., "Transformational Implementation: An Example," IEEE Transactions on Software Engineering SE-7(1):3-14, (January 1981).

[BATA80] Batali, J., A. Hartheimer, "The Design Procedure Manual," V.L.S.b;.i Memo 80-31, Massachusetts Institute of Technology, (September 1980).

[BOSC82] van den Bosch, F., J. Ellis, P. Freeman, L. Johnson, C. McClure, D. Robinson, W. Scacchi, B. Scheft, A. von Staa, L.L. Tripp, "Evaluation of Software Development Life Cycle Methodology Implementation," Software Engineering Notes, Vol. 7(1), pp. 45-61, (February, 1982)

[BRYA81] Bryant, R. E., A Switch-Level Simulation Model for Integrated Logic Circuits, LCS/TR-249, Massachusetts Institute of Technology, (1981).

[BUXT80] Buxton, J. N., "An Informal Bibliography on Programming Support Environments," SIGPLAN NOTICES 15(12):17-30, (December 1980).

[CAS 81] IEEE Transactions on Circuits and Systems, Special issue on Computer-Aided Design of VLSI Systems, (July, 1981).

[COHE76] Cohen, E., "Program Reference for SPICE2," Memorandum No. ERL-M592, Electronics Research Laboratory, University of California, Berkeley, (June 1976).

[DIJK76] Dijkstra, E. W., A Discipline of Programming, Prentice-Hall, N.J, (1976).

[DOD 80] Department of Defense, "Reference Manual for the Ada Programming Language," Proposed Standard Document July, 1980 edition edition, 1980. U.S. Government Printing Office, Order No. L008-000-00354-8.

[DOLO78] Dolotta, T. A., R. C. Haight, J. R. Mashey, "The Programmer's Workbench," The Bell System Technical Journal, V. 57, N. 6, (July-August 1978), pp. 2177-2200.

[FREE82] Freeman, P., A.b;.i. Wasserman, "Software Development Methodologies and Ada(tm)," technical report, University of California, Irvine, CA (1982)

[GOLD80a] Goldman, N., D. Wile, "GIST (Internal Report)," Unpublished, USC Information Sciences Institute, (September, 1980).

[GOLD80b] Goldstein, I. P., D. G. Bobrow, "A Layered Approach to Software Design," Xerox PARC CSL-5-80, (submitted for publication).

[GUTT78] Guttag, J., E. Horowitz, D. Musser, "Abstract Data Types and Software Validation," CACM 21:1048-64, (1978).

[HUNK81] Hunke, H. (ed.), Software Engineering Environments, North-Holland, New York, (1981)

[KATZ82] Katz, R. H., "A Database Approach for Managing VLSI Design Data," 19th ACM/IEEE Design Automation Conf., Las Vegas, Nv., (June 1982).

[KLIN79] Kling, R., W. Scacchi, "Recurrent Dilemmas of Computer Use in Complex Organizations," National Computer Conference, AFIPS Press, Vol. 48, pp. 107-115, (1979).

[KLIN80] Kling, R., W. Scacchi, "Computing as Social Action: The Social Dynamics of Computing in Complex Organizations," in M. Yovits (ed.), Advances in Computers, New York, Academic Press, Vol. 19, pp. 249-327, (1980).

[KLIN82] Kling, R., W. Scacchi, "The Web of Computing," in M. Yovits (ed.), Advances in Computers, Vol. 21, pp. 3-85, Academic Press, New York, (1982).

[KUNG79] Kung, H. T., "Let's Design Algorithms For VLSI Systems," Proceedings of the Caltech Conference on Very Large Scale Integration, pp. 65-90, Computer Science Department, California Institute of Technology, (January 1979).

[LEYK79] Leyking, L. W., "Data Base Considerations for VLSI," Proceedings of the Caltech Conference on Very Large Scale Integration, pp. 275-302, California Institute of Technology, (January 1979).

[MCCA79] McCarthy, J., "Comments on 'The State of Technology in Artifical Intelligence'", Research Directions in Software Technology, M.b;.i.T.Press, Cambridge, Mass., (1979), pp. 814-815.

[MCSW82] McSweeney, D. W., "Timing Verification of VLSI Logic Circuits," In Paul Penfield, Jr. (editor), Proceedings, Conference on Advanced Research in VLSI, pp. 63-66. Massachusetts Institute of Technology, Artech House, Inc., (January 1982).

[MEAD80] Mead, C. A., L. A. Conway, Introduction to VLSI Systems, Addison Wesley, Boston, (1980), pp. 115-127.

[OUST82] Ousterhout, J. K., "CAESAR: An Interactive Editor for VLSI Layout," Digest of Papers: CompCon Spring 82, pp. 300-301. IEEE Computer Society, (February 1982).

[PETI82] Petit, P., "Chipmonk: An Interactive VLSI Layout Tool," Digest of Papers: CompCon Spring 82, pp. 302-304. IEEE Computer Society, (February 1982).

[PNUE79] Pnueli, A., "The Temporal Semantics of Concurrent Programs," Semantics of Concurrent Computation, Kahn, ed., Springer Lecture Notes in Computer Science, pp. 1-20, Springer-verlag, (June 1979).

[PREN81] Prentice, D., "An Analysis of Software Development Environments," Software Engineering Notes, V. 6., N 4., (1981).

[RITC78] Ritchie, D. M., K. Thompson, "The UNIX Time-Sharing System," The Bell System Technical Journal, V. 57, N. 6, (July-August 1978), pp. 1905-1930.

[SCAC81] Scacchi, W., The Process of Innovation in Computing: A Study of the Social Dynamics of Computing, Ph.D. dissertation, Dept. of Information and Computer Science, University of California, Irvine, (1981).

[SCAC82] Scacchi, W., "Managing Software Engineering Projects: A Social Analysis," technical report, Computer Science Dept., University of Southern California, Los Angeles, CA (1982).

[SCHI82] Schindler, M., "Computer-Aided Engineering Comes of Age," Electronic Design, (November 11, 1982).

[SUBR80] Subrahmanyam, P. A., "A Basis for a Theory of Program Synthesis," Proceedings of the First Annual National Conference On Artificial Intelligence, pp. 74-76, AAAI, (August 1980).

[SUBR82a] Subrahmanyam, P. A., "Automatable Paradigms for Software-Hardware Design: Language Issues," J.Rader (editor), IEEE Workshop on VLSI and Software Engineering, IEEE, (October 1982). Also available as University of Utah Technical Report UTEC-82-096, (September 1982).

[SUBR82b] Subrahmanyam, P. A., "An Automatic/Interactive Software Development System: Formal Basis and Design," North-Holland, Amsterdam, 1982.

[SUBR82c] Subrahmanyam, P. A., "From Anna+ to Ada: Automating the Synthesis of Ada Package and Task Bodies," Technical Report Internal Report, University of Utah, (March 1982).

[SUBR82d] Subrahmanyam, P. A., "On Automating the Computation of Approximate, Concrete, and Asymptotic Complexity Measures of VLSI Designs," (to appear), Technical Report UTEC-82-095, Dept. of Computer Science, University of Utah, (October 1982).

[TEIT81] Teitelman, W., L. Masinter, "The Interlisp Programming Environment," IEEE Computer 14(4):25-33, (April 1981).

[VANC79] vanCleemput, W. M., "Hierarchical Design for VLSI: Problems and Advantages," Proceedings of the Caltech Conference on Very Large Scale Integration, pp. 259-274, California Institute of Technology, (January 1979).

[VLAD81] Vladimirescu, A., D. O. Pederson, "A Computer Program for the Simulation of Large-Scale-Integrated Circuits," Proceedings of the 1981 IEEE International Symposium on Circuits and Systems, pp. 111-113, IEEE Circuits and Systems Society, (April 1981).

[WASS81] Wasserman, A.b;.i., _Software Development Environments_, IEEE Computer Society Press, Los Alamitos, CA (1981).

[WILE80] Wile, D., "POPART: A Producer of Parsers and Related Tools, System Builder's Manual," Internal report, USC Information Sciences Institute, Marina Del Rey, CA, (June 1980).

CH1815-0/83/0000/0064$01.00© 1983 IEEE

THE RELATIONSHIP BETWEEN HDLs AND PROGRAMMING LANGUAGES

Gérard M. Baudet, Brown University
Melvin Cutler, The Aerospace Corporation
Marc Davio, Philips Research Laboratory
Arnold M. Peskin, Brookhaven National Laboratory *
Franz J. Rammig, University of Dortmund

Abstract

Hardware description languages (HDLs) are characterized, including development of a usable definition. The similarities and differences between HDLs and other computer languages are examined. Trends in HDL development are noted, especially in their pertinence to design of VLSI circuits. Some predictions are made of what progress may be expected in the next twenty years.

Introduction

This manuscript was spawned by discussions held during the VLSI and Software Engineering Workshop held in Port Chester, New York, in October of 1982. The workshop included the formation of working groups for gathering individuals with common interests. One of those working groups addressed itself to the relationship of hardware description languages (HDLs) for very large-scale integration (VLSI) design to programming languages. This paper was developed from the ensuing discussions and correspondence among members of that working group.

The first tasks of the group related to the characterization of HDLs, including development of a usable definition. This characterization appears below. A discussion follows of similarities and differences between HDLs and other computer languages, and how developments in each may benefit the other. This is followed by a discussion of trends in HDL development with some predictions of what the state-of-the-art holds for the next twenty years. The intent of these discussions is both to inform and to provoke ideas that may guide HDL development in positive ways.

The topic of hardware description languages is certainly crucial to VLSI design because the language and design method are intimately tied together. And, although the formal study of HDLs has been conducted for over a decade, it is surprisingly difficult to arrive at a serviceable consensus definition. The group defined an HDL as a class of representations which, given a known sequence of transformations, leads to a hardware realization.

This definition allows for several levels of abstraction or design hierarchy. The topmost level is a behavioral description. The bottom level is structural. Intermediate levels exist primarily as a convenience to ease the designer's and design automation tool developer's task. The most common instances of HDLs currently reside at these intermediate levels. The transformations from level to level may, in fact, be bidirectional so that a description may be compared with its progenitor for the purpose of design verification and tool validation. The definition itself can be refined by discussing the attributes which characterize an HDL and tend to distinguish it or render it similar to a programming language.

The study of HDLs and their relationship to programming languages can enhance understanding of important aspects of the design process. It may shed new light on the fundamental relationship of behavior and structure. It can promote comparison of a description with its progenitor and lead to development of formal verification techniques. And it has an obvious effect on the improvement of simulation tools, timing analysis, and similar testing aids.

The Influence of High Level Programming Languages on HDLs

Early HDLs like CDL and RTS were designed to describe relatively simple hardware systems just as early programming languages like FORTRAN, BASIC have been designed to program relatively simple algorithms. (The existence of enormous software packages written in FORTRAN is no contradiction, in fact FORTRAN is not well suited for complex problems.) The need to attack very large software problems efficiently has had remarkable impact on the design of high level languages (HLLs). As HDLs are faced today with a comparable complexity problem one should investigate which of the more or less recent developments in the HLL area are useful to be

---
* Work partially supported by the U.S. Department of Energy under Contract DE-AC02-76CH00016.

adapted in HDLs that are well suited for VLSI. Some examples follow.

a. Strong Typing
Strong typing is an underlying concept of PASCAL and was heavily requested in the design of Ada. It requires that an (data) object is of a single type whenever accessed. Any conversion has to be specified explicitly. Often, hardware is strongly typed; for each conversion there must exist a piece of hardware that carries it out. It offers a good opportunity to check hardware descriptions for consistency.

b. User Definable Types
The basic data object of an HDL is the single "bit" (more precisely an object of enumeration type with at least two different possible values). Such basic data objects are assembled in very different ways in hardware. An adequate tool to describe this variety is the existence of language constructs that allow the user to build his own types. Concepts of languages like PASCAL, at least, should be adapted in HDLs. Even more powerful is the concept of abstract data types.

c. Abstract Data Types (ADTs)
Usually these are given as a set of data objects and a set of operations on these data objects. The operations are specified in terms of algebraic equations. This conception reflects directly the notion of the instruction set processor, which is a basic concept in hardware for understanding noncombinational circuits. In order to implement an abstract data type one has to restrict oneself to previously defined (abstract) data types (e.g., by providing a carrier structure and a set of procedures containing only operations that are defined on this carrier structure). This again reflects very faithfully the way hardware is designed.

d. Generic Objects
Generic objects (compile-time scaleable objects) have become increasingly familiar with the development of Ada. They are also investigated in the ADT field as parametrized ADTs. In the hardware field generic objects are important, since objects with common principles and organization but different scalings and dimensions are standard.

e. Structured Programming
Structured programming (introduced by Dijkstra) was an early attempt to overcome complexity problems in programming. Of course, this strictly sequential concept cannot be introduced into HDLs without modification. The basic idea, however, to offer very few primitives for the description of an algorithm, fits very well. For an HDL this set of primitives has to be different (for example, concurrency must be included) but, as in modern HLLs, this set of behavioral primitives is reflected directly by special constructs in the language. One approach to this is an algorithmic state machine implementation of a digital system. Structured programming stresses the importance of systematic program transformations in view of achieving the decomposition of the control unit of a digital system. In fact, systematic and formal transformations from a general program to target programs written in terms of suitable sets of

instruction types will generally lead to interesting system decompositions. The introduction of some of these transformations within CAD packages would allow the designer to quickly investigate a number of interesting solutions. Furthermore, the above philosophy may be extended to more general situations, including in particular parallel or concurrent computation models. It is, for instance, possible to refine the design into a basic class of instructions from a more general instruction type describing, e.g., the behavior of a Petri Net.

f. Advanced Encapsulation Techniques
Encapsulation techniques (related to information hiding) are attempts to overcome complexity problems in programming (e.g., Ada, MODULA). This technique has a very good tradition in the hardware field. In fact, modular design without side effects, hiding of internal structures, precise interface descriptions (import/export lists) are basic design techniques for hardware. But one must distinguish between structural encapsulation (which is popular with hardware designers) and behavioral (which is not). A promising idea would be a symbiosis between the structural encapsulation tradition of hardware design with the behavioral encapsulation experience in the software field.

g. Monitors
Even in highly integrated systems where attempts are made to achieve a very high degree of parallelism there will still exist a lot of time-shared objects. These objects should be managed like bounded resources in the software field. Tools that have been used to successfully manage such problems in a highly complex environment (.e.g., Hoare's monitor) should be considered as basic language constructs in an advanced HDL. Combination with the ADT concept seems to be promising.

h. Functional Programming
Functional programming has been investigated at least since the development of LISP, but a functional language is not preferable in all cases. If an algorithm has to be described then an algorithmic language is adequate. However, this is not necessarily the most economic approach to specifying hardware. Often specifications at a lower level of abstraction are preferable.

i. Event Oriented Programming
Very different is the approach to substitute a global control structure by a set of local ones, each caused by specific events. This technique is standard in non-procedural HDLs, but can also be observed in the field of process control. This approach is comparable to Dijkstra's "guarded commands". It should be noted that Petri Nets are also a model based on local event driven transitions. As in the case of functional programming, the event oriented programming style has advantages for special applications, especially whenever the reaction to external events play a dominant role in the system.

An example is exception handling.

k. Exception Handling
Here we have to differentiate between design errors and faults of the system that can be tolerated with the aid of special reactions. The latter case of

exception handling (i.e., within fault tolerant systems) is a typical application of event oriented programming. Exception handling is of increasing interest in the HLL field (e.g., Ada). Future HDLs should include comparable language constructs explicitly in order to encourage the designers to design fault tolerant systems.

1. Formal Semantics

The outcome of any application of an HDL is of limited value if the semantics of the language are not defined formally. This may be done in different ways, by homogeneous or heterogeneous approaches. It does not matter whether the semantics are given by an operational, denotational or axiomatic method, or even by a mixture of the above. A uniform approach is preferable, however, especially if it is attempted to support verification.

m. Formal Verification

Formal verification implies a consistency check between different descriptions of a single object. In most cases an algorithmic description is checked against its functional specification. Of course this is possible only if the semantics of both languages are completely defined.

A sublanguage for the formulation of functional specifications can be used also to state assertions for a simulation bound verification technique. An advanced HDL should be designed in such a way that both approaches can be supported.

n. Pedagogical Languages

If things are already complicated they may be made even more complicated by an inadequate description method. But the best description can't transform an object that is complicated by nature into a simple one; i.e., a language that is well suited for VLSI may be too complicated to teach VLSI beginners its ideas and usage. Therefore, special pedagogical languages should be considered. Such languages may be limited in their field of application but can point out very clearly specific description and design methodologies. After acquiring experience it should be easy for a designer to switch over to a full power VLSI HDL.

Benefits to Programming Languages from Experiences with HDLs

Although the research and experience are much richer in the field of programming languages, there are at least three areas in which the programming language designers and users might benefit from the languages used to describe hardware. A resulting unified language would be applicable both to hardware and software.

1. Refinement of a design from structure to behavior is possible within one language.

2. The use of graphics is considered to be necessary in order to visualize the design, often at multiple levels of abstraction.

3. Time is an explicit or implicit method of aggregating concurrent processing from independently specified 'processing elements' or processes.

The first two characteristics grew out of the engineering technique of drawing based documentation. Though not machine processable, a formal record of the design - and changes to that design - was a major part of hardware design methodology. When automation began to be introduced to that methodology, the structural nature of the documentation evolved into a more formal hardware description language.

In fact, the resulting language was merely the union of the different languages that had been used for the different engineering disciplines involved in hardware systems design. For example, register transfer languages (RTLs) were included by computer architects, logic equation languages were introduced by logic designers, 'sticks' type graphics languages were introduced by circuit designers, and geometrically defined languages were introduced as an interface between VLSI designers and the mask fabrication companies. In order to test the design in a relatively efficient manner, simulators were developed for each level, and (at some places) integrated so that pieces of the design could be described and simulated concurrently at different levels of abstraction.

Some of these capabilities are provided by abstract data types in modern programming languages, perhaps more elegantly since the semantic domain is simpler and uniform. However, the abstraction in the control domain provided by multi-level HDLs is not paralleled by 'abstract control types'. This is currently a fruitful area for programming language research, especially for the description of concurrent processes.

The graphics attributes could readily be applied to software, as the software design methodologies often include the structural visualization of the software system at different levels of abstraction. While some methodologies have recognized graphics as a tool, none has utilized graphics as a design capture mechanism as formally as has been done in hardware design.

The third area of technology transfer is in timing. Real time programs development, with much the same characteristics as hardware development, still utilizes traditional programming language constructs that say nothing about timing requirements or characteristics. In HDLs, time is an ordering concept for concurrent computations and helps to specify the semantics of timing dependent functions.

The use of this characteristic in programming languages is predicated on the desire to write algorithm descriptions that transcend the von Neumann model of implementation. The maximum utilization of VLSI technology requires that a centralized locus of algorithm control be employed only at a local level (say, a chip), while distributed, concurrent, time ordering based control of large-scale computations provides high effective throughput. The algorithm description language is the key to this capability, and transfer of technology from HDLs is a critical input.

Toward a Common Description Language

Since one obvious goal is to have traditional programming languages (PLs) directly handling hardware description as an extension of their own original capabilities, rather than pinpointing the differences between HDLs and PLs, we will describe, in this section, additions and extensions that should be supported by a PL in order to be able to qualify as an HDL.

The following list is certainly far from being complete, but it proposes some initial suggestions for potential HDLs or future 'Circuit Description languages', as they may be better termed.

1. Data Objects

The basic object that is dealt with in an HDL is the 'bit' and, therefore, this should be considered the primitive data object of any HDL. The notion of a bit is very similar to the notion of a boolean in most PLs, but unlike PLs where the repertoire of boolean operations is often limited, HDLs should support a complete set of logical operations on bits. The operation (NAND x y z), or NAND (x,y,z), for example, has a perfectly well understood meaning and should be allowed as an integral part of any HDL.

'Integers' as existing in all PLs, with predefined operations such as addition, multiplication, etc., can hardly be regarded as composite objects or structured data types built from the bit data type since operations on integers (from a hardware description point of view) should not rely on a particular implementation predefined by the PL or HDL. In particular, there should be a way to specify the length of an integer and the way any operation on integers is to be performed. Binary addition, for example, could be implemented in a variety of ways: serially or in parallel, using a carry save method or a carry look ahead method, and any specific implementation should be perfectly acceptable and provided either directly by the language or through user specification.

A better way to look at this data object from an HDL point of view is to introduce the notion of a 'register'. Such a data type could be part of the language or could easily be built out of the bit data object in a way similar to the array construction in most PLs. Similarly, operations on registers could be directly part of the language, could be accessible through library defined operations, or could be user defined.

2. Constructs of the Language

Although the notion of integer, as it exists in PLs, cannot be assimilated with the notion of register, with its usual meaning in hardware or circuit design, integers should still coexist with registers in HDLs, but they will clearly serve a different purpose. While registers do realize a certain function in a hardware or circuit description, integers will help the user setting up or structuring this function. For instance, the register data type could be built from the bit data type using a construction similar to the array construct in many PLs; in this case, when a register is defined, integers can be used, for example, as indices, to refer to the structure.

Similar parallels do exist with other objects and constructs existing in PLs which are also useful in HDLs. Assignments, for example, have their usual meaning in PLs and can also be given an obvious meaning in HDLs. An instruction such as Z=X OR Y, for example, where X, Y, and Z are defined as bit variables, can be clearly understood as "the behavior of the signal implementing bit Z is obtained by or-ing the two signals implementing bits X and Y".

Generally speaking, the constructs that are specific to the HDL are to be used to define the structure of the hardware or circuit design under description, while the constructs that are specific to the PL are to be used to define the behavior of the design. We feel that this distinction between 'behavioral' and 'structural' interpretations is important.

Another distinction between the respective roles of HDLs and PLs stems from the distinction between space and memory, the two entities allocated by HDLs and PLs. The definition of a 'bit variable' or any other 'hardware variable' in a circuit design corresponds to a request to the HDL for some 'space' allocation which, in turn, will correspond to some physical allocation in the actual chip. Once space is allocated in this way by an HDL, it cannot be reused and, in that sense, an HDL can be said to use 'static allocation of space' as opposed to 'dynamic allocation of memory' in most current high level PLs.

3. Concurrency Control and Timing

One important language construct that is often neglected by PLs has to do with the possibility of expressing the concurrent flow of signals in a circuit design. 'Concurrency control' is a must in any HDL since computation in a circuit takes place inherently in parallel.

As mentioned previously, the related concept, 'timing', is usually completely ignored by PLs. The design of clocked circuits, however, requires this notion of timing, in contrast with the design of combinational circuits. 'Time', therefore, must be a notion present in any HDL as an abstraction of the 'clock'. This concept should be explicit as should the notion of 'phases' of the clock, therefore, allowing the user to specify actions that will take place on a particular clock phase or actions conditioned by some clock phase.

4. A Few Remarks

In addition to the clock signal mentioned in the previous section, there is a number of other signals that must be handled or dealt with by an HDL. In particular, although PWR and GND (i.e., power and ground) do not have to be explicit in the language, they have to be dealt with implicitly. For example, an instruction of the form X=0, where X is a variable of type 'bit' (as defined earlier), would probably have the following associated meaning or semantics: 'connect the signal that implements bit X to GND', and this, of course, should be perfectly acceptable.

This particular example brings about another issue which would deserve special examination. Consider the bit variable X. While it is meaningful to specify at some point in the description of a circuit an instruction of the form X=0 or X=1 to request that the signal implementing bit X be connected to GND or PWR, respectively, it should be considered an error to have both these instructions in the description of the same circuit, since this would correspond to a short. More generally, this example shows that once a 'behavior' has been specified for any 'hardware variable', that variable cannot be redefined, since this would cause a double specification. In other words, an HDL can be characterized as a 'unique assignment language', at least with respect to its 'hardware variables'. This relates very closely to the discussion of Section 2 between static and dynamic allocation of space and memory, and to earlier discussion of design verification.

Although we have raised a few issues that illustrate differences in interpretation between HDLs and PLs, we certainly do not feel that these will in any way preclude their integration, just as some graphic description langauges are fully incorporated into some programming languages.

The major change that this might require is probably our own way of thinking, since the usual von Neumann model of computation does not seem any longer adequate when dealing with VLSI computation.

Hardware Description Languages: 1990

The 1980s is likely to be considered the 'Golden Age' of HDLs, marked by extensive experimentation and some standardization. The experimentation will be driven by requirements of new technology, advancements - revolutionary and evolutionary - in design methodology, and innovation. Experimentation may be spread, feature by feature, over several languages. Pedagogical languages will be the fertile ground in which these ideas will germinate. We expect that new technologies, or evolving existing technologies, will enrich HDLs at the lower levels of abstraction.

A major enhancement will be the capability to describe timing dependencies and the concurrency of operation in a more explicit way. Both syntactic and semantic constructs will evolve to meet the needs of describing hardware at higher levels of abstraction, as well as at the lower levels of abstraction which are currently handled by contemporary HDLs.

Again, at higher levels of abstraction, the need to state explicit constraints on the design will drive the design and implementation of 1980s HDLs. These constraints will guide the design automation tools in their internal tradeoff heuristics/algorithms. Closely allied with this concept is the need to specify assertions about the behavior and timing of the design within its description. These are easily adapted from modern programming languages, and we expect them to appear in HDL in the 1980s.

This raises the possibility of formal algorithm transformation. While passing from the behavioral to the structural description, we encounter a number of degrees of freedom which can lead to a number of distinct resulting structures.

Formal transformations, as described by Davio, et al, allow one to reach a number of solutions and compare them. It becomes possible to leave to the program an important part of the usual trial and error process, and we can progress from iterated simulation to an actual design method.

We can also expect graphics based languages, rather than geometrically defined languages, to be developed. Instead of being an encoding of a picture, as are current VLSI oriented artwork description languages, these will provide semantic information.

Perhaps the key to the Golden Age will be the development of pedagogical languages, used for the teaching of VLSI design. As with programming languages, the academic laboratory for advanced concepts is necessary for the development of new features without the (often historically based) baggage of production oriented languages. This positive development has just begun to affect production languages, and we expect that its effect will continue.

The standardization pioneers are currently represented by the CONLAN project. Whether or not this working group is the developer of the standard, we will see some standardization in the 1980s. A purely structural language will become an accepted standard, and a government standard language will be (reluctantly) accepted. As with other standards, methods for escaping from the standard or by extending it will be cleverly developed. Macro processors and preprocessors will provide an extensibility that might weaken the standard, while making it more palatable.

Hardware Description Languages: 2000

In contrast, the 1990s are likely to be an era of HDL inertia, as the FORTRAN/COBOL syndrome takes effect. The large body of existing 'code', or machine descriptions, will stifle innovation because of the cost to rewrite those descriptions. This will be unfortunate, as the tremendous increase in the experience due to the writing of those descriptions will expose the weaknesses of whatever de facto standard HDLs emerge during the 1980s. The best that can be hoped for is that there will emerge a significant second tier language, analogous to PASCAL in the programming languages domain, which will also attain widespread use due to its fixing of the weaknesses of the existing languages.

Whatever positive developments occur in the 1990s will be due to evolutionary changes. An example from the programming languages field would be the development of structured preprocessors for FORTRAN. We would propose two possibilities.

One would be the disappearance, as far as the writer of machine descriptions is concerned, of the intermediate levels of representation. In our definition of HDLs, we emphasized that the key defining features of hardware description were the extreme (levels) of purely behavioral and purely structural, and that the other intermediate levels existed for the convenience of the automated design tools builders. This was motivated by the needs to reduce the cost of technology transfer and to handle large gaps in level of complexity. This requirement will be brought home in the 1990s, as the only designers who deal with descriptions at, say, the logic design level would be those who must hand optimize their designs for competitive or performance reasons.

The death of simulator based semantics would be another progressive change. The typical HDL user today has only the vaguest idea of the detailed semantics of the HDL, and discovers the nuances by running the "local simulator". Programming languages have come a long way in the careful, formal definition and specification of their syntax and semantics, and it is long overdue for HDLs to follow suit. We expect this to occur during the 1990s, as formalisms for defining timing and concurrency semantics are promulgated to the HDL world.

Finally, we concede the possibility, though slim, of revolution coming to the HDL area by 2000. What hardware has that is not available to software is the exponential growth in circuit density, its primitive 'operand'. This may not bind the community as tightly to a particular method of describing its behavior as if the difference in efficiency were not so great.

In short, the technology of HDLs will lag the technology of programming languages by about a decade. The merger of HDLs and PLs envisioned in a previous section will, if it occurs, close the gap. But this development certainly does not appear imminent and is considered by many to be unlikely in the next two decades.

Acknowledgment

The authors wish to acknowledge two other individuals who participated in the fruitful initial discussions at the VLSI/Software Engineering Conference; Surrendra Dudari of Honeywell, and Jacob Katzenelson of the Technion.

Bibliography

The following references have been included without direct citation in the text. The authors find this format most appropriate considering the wide scope and informal style of this report.

Bobrow, D., Raphael B.: New programming languages for artificial intelligence research, ACM Comp. Surv., Vol. 6, No. 3, Sept. 1974.

Chu, Y.: Introducing CDL, IEEE Computer, Dec. 1979.

Davio, M., Deschamps, J.P., Thayse, A.: Decomposition as a hardware design tool, Philips Research Laboratory, Brussels, Belgium.

Dijkstra, E.W.: Cooperating sequential processes in "programming languages", F. Genuys, Ed., Academic Press, London, 1968.

Foulk, P., The formal design of parallel hardware, 4th International Symposium on Computer Hardware Description Languages, pp. 162-168.

Frankel, R.E., and Smoliar, S.W.: Beyond register transfer: an algebraic approach for architectural description, 4th International Symposium on Computer Hardware Description Languages, pp. 1-5.

Hill, D.D.: ADLIB: A modular, strongly-typed computer design language, 4th International Symposium on Computer Hardware Description Languages, pp. 75-81.

Hoare, C.A.R.: Monitors: an operating system structuring concept, CACM, Vol. 17, No. 10, Oct. 1979.

Johnson, W.A., Crowley, J.J., and Ray, J.D.: Mixed-level simulation from a hierarchical CHDL, Computer Architecture News, May 1980, pp. 2-10.

Ledgard, H.: A language is born. Ada reference manual with an introduction, Springer, New York, 1981.

Liskov, B., Snyder, A., Atkinson, R., and Schaffert, C.: Abstraction mechanisms in CLU, CACM, Vol. 20, No. 8, Aug. 1977.

Meinen, P.: Formal semantic description of register transfer language elements and mechanized simulator construction, 4th International Symposium on Computer Hardware Description Languages, pp. 69-74.

Peterson, J.L.: Petri Nets, ACM Computing Surveys, Vol. 9, 1977.

Piloty, R., Barbacci, M., Borrionne, D., Dietmeyer, D., Hill, F., Shelly, P.: An overview of CONLAN - a formal construction method for hardware description languages, Proc. IFIP Congress 1980, Tokyo and Melbourne.

Preston, G.W.: Report of IDA summer study on hardware description language, October, 1981, Institute for Defense Analyses, ADA 110866.

Rammig, F.J.: CAP/DSDL, preliminary language reference manual, Forschungsbericht Nr. 129 der Abt. Informatik der Univ. Dortmund, W. Germany, 1982.

Wirth, N.: Modula: a language for modular multiprogramming, Software Pract. Exper., Vol. 7, No. 1, Jan. 1977.

Part II: Submitted Papers and Abstracts

Parallels between Software Engineering and VLSI Engineering

THE REVOLUTION IN VLSI DESIGN:
PARALLELS BETWEEN SOFTWARE AND VLSI ENGINEERING*

by S. Hirschhorn and A.M. Davis
Computer Science Laboratory
GTE Laboratories, Inc. Waltham, Massachusetts

ABSTRACT

The problems of VLSI design are discussed in the context of analogous software design issues. Current work in the areas of specification, methodology, support tools and environments for both disciplines are detailed. The trends in VLSI design seem to be similar to earlier and current software design trends in these areas.

INTRODUCTION

The purpose of this paper is to explore the similarities between the impending revolution in VLSI design and the revolution that has taken place over the past 15 years in software engineering. From this analysis it will become apparent that a significant portion of emerging VLSI design methodologies can be adopted or adapted from the software methodologies now in place. The synergy which results from the cross fertilization of ideas between the two disciplines will also lead to a better understanding of the software design process and enhance its own evolution.

As software systems have grown from hundreds of words of object code to millions of words of object code, a number of quite dramatic changes and trends have occurred:

o   A change from assembly coding to high level language programming to very high level language programming.

o   An increase in attention to formal requirements specification tools.

o   An increasing reliance on the compiler to produce optimized, correct code.

o   An increase in the number of software engineers involved in the design and implementation of software systems.

o   An increase in attention to, exploitation of, and need for formal, structured design methodologies.

o   An increase in the number of tools supporting the software life cycle.

o   An increase in attention to the reliability, maintainability, and robustness of software.

o   An increase in the number of software design constraints, especially for testability assurance.

o   A recognized need for the existence of extendable, integrated software development environments.

o   The birth of software engineering as a discipline itself.

The remainder of this paper will address these software trends and their counterparts in VLSI design. Important differences in trends will be noted where appropriate.

SPECIFICATION

Software specification levels have evolved from machine languages to assembly languages to procedural languages to abstraction-based languages. Each new wave of language genre brought with it a higher level of abstraction of the system under design. This has allowed the designer to more easily handle the growing complexity of the systems being engineered. Most software practitioners are programming in languages such as FORTRAN, PL/1, and COBOL. These general purpose procedural languages provide natural control constructs, complex data structures, and subroutines with formal parameters. Many software engineers are progamming in more modern abstraction-based languages, such as PASCAL, and soon, CHILL and ADA. These recently developed languages are characterized by their ability to hide implementation details of data and function through the use of data abstractions. They also catch many errors before execution through the use of strong type checking. Programs produced with such languages tend to be more resilient to change and easier to debug. The next ten years will probably show a continuance of this language level migration into the era of executable requirements languages[1], which are characterized by their ability to describe a problem to be solved in problem-domain terms rather than solution-domain terms. When using such languages, the requirements compiler generates an adequate solution (i.e., a program in the traditional sense) from a detailed specification of the problem to be solved. These advances have been accomplished by the maturation of language translation technology.

In the semiconductor industry, one also can

---

*This paper was presented at the Sixteenth Asilomar Conference on Circuits, Systems and Computers, Pacific Grove, CA, 11/8/82 - 11/10/82.

define a hierarchy of specification levels. These include physical, structural, behavioral, and requirements. The structural and physical levels of specification are still the most widely used. Netlist descriptions and computer graphics are still used predominantly during the design and implementation of LSI devices. The translation technology for hardware is not as mature as its software counterpart, though there is a new fervor of activity in the area.

One can characterize most IC specification languages as either data-oriented or procedure-oriented. A procedural description of a circuit is the encoding of an algorithm, using control constructs, expressions, etc., which when executed, creates the data necessary to construct the circuit. Data-oriented languages, such as the classical net list representation for interconnection data, specify the circuit data directly. Procedural languages are more flexible, easier to maintain, allow localization of concern and allow parameterization. Data-oriented approaches give designers a better feeling for the implications of their actions, are easier to use by current designers and are supported by the majority of CAD tools available today.

VLSI poses the same complexity challenge as very large software systems: the sheer number of modules and the complexity of their intercommunications have exceeded the conceptual capacity of the human brain. To overcome this problem, VLSI designers will be required to think in terms of much higher levels of abstraction (e.g., at the requirements and behavioral levels), utilizing languages and compilers which support such abstractions. Data-oriented VLSI languages clearly will not solve this problem. Data-oriented software languages (such as machine code) have not been used for many years. They have been replaced with the procedural and data abstraction languages; this will be the trend for VLSI as well.

There has been a great deal of attention focussed on the digital design language issue. The CONLAN work[2] attempts to standardize a hardware description language construction mechanism; ISPS[3] attempts to formalize the digital design process at the instruction set level; ALI[4] is a procedural language used to describe VLSI layouts; ADLIB[5] is a modular, strongly typed PASCAL-based language for defining the behavior of digital components; CTL[6] is a PASCAL-based template language which can be extended for each CAD application; even ADA has been suggested as a good design language for digital systems[7]. Ayers[8] gives a good case for the use of programming languages as IC design languages. He points out the need in such languages for automatic memory management, data type checking and coercions.

The problems with many of the efforts in VLSI specification languages are: attention to only a limited range of the IC development life cycle, avoidance of the performance specification problem, lack of a separate compilation feature, lack of constructs to specify parallelism and lack of use.

The maturation of a language translation technology for VLSI, as embodied in the current silicon compilation work, will probably change this. As software specification has evolved from the era of machine languages to the era of formal requirements languages, VLSI specification will evolve from graphical, data-oriented languages to procedural, compiled languages.

METHODOLOGY

Specification languages provide engineers with a medium in which to express a design. For large, complex systems, an engineer needs more than just a medium; he/she also needs a strategy, an approach, a disciplined technique that helps in the creation of a quality product. Methodology is the study of methods, specifically product development methods. As applied to software and hardware development, a method is a sequence of discrete, roughly sequential activities (called phases) which when followed transforms an idea into a product. Although there is little uniformity in naming these phases, most software engineers agree on the steps one must follow to arrive at a quality product. We have chosen the following names to define the phases of the software development life-cycle:

Requirements - The complete description of the features of the system to be built from a pure black-box perspective.

High-Level Design - The successive decomposition and refinement of the problem (starting with the requirements) into simpler subproblems or subfunctions and the definition of the interface among them.

Detailed Design - The assignment of algorithms and major data structures to each subfunction defined during high-level design.

Coding - The writing and debugging of programs (in some implementation language) which embody the algorithms and data structures.

Verification - The integration of implemented programs and the checking that such programs and their union perform their intended tasks.

A model of the VLSI development life cycle adapted from Penfield[9], is given by the following levels:

Requirements - The definition of the external behavior of the IC in terms of its function, speed, timing, area, topological constraints, etc.

Block - The definition of the architecture of the system in terms of its overall structure and behavior.

Logic - The definition of the interconnection of logic primitives which comprise the detailed structure of the system.

Circuit - The definition of the circuit elements (e.g., transistors, resistors, etc.) which comprise the logic primitives.

Symbolic - The definition of the chip's geometry in relative terms with flexible shapes.

Layout - The definition of the chip's absolute geometries for all devices, wires, contacts, etc.

Verification - The checking that the chip contains no manufacturing defects, that each component behaves in accordance with its specification, and that the union of all the components perform the intended task.

An analogy clearly holds between these two development life-cycles, as shown in Figure 1. The analogy is as follows: the requirements level of both disciplines define the external behavior of the system under development and are thus equivalent; the block level of VLSI and the high-level design of software each define the structure or architecture of the system; the logic and circuit levels of VLSI correspond to software's detailed design in that both define the logical details of components; and the symbolic and layout levels of VLSI define the two-dimensional geometric representation of the hardware and which correspond to the one-dimensional coding phase of software. Although not all phases have perfect correlations, there is enough similarity for us to apply similar methods to the two engineering disciplines.

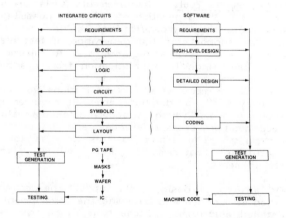

Figure 1. Comparison of IC and Software Development Life Cycles

Methodology applies not only to the taxonomy of phases, but also to the specific techniques used during any particular phase. As software engineering has developed as a discipline, the emphasis of software research has migrated from implementation (e.g., research into control constructs) in the 1960's to design techniques in the 1970's and now to requirements and verification in the 1980's.

With the ever-increasing size of software projects being undertaken, there has been a dramatic turn toward top-down design techniques such as data-driven decomposition, procedural decomposition, functional decomposition, and iterative refinement. This should not be surprising; definition of what you want to do before definition of how you are going to do it is an obvious necessity for large problems. Otherwise one can be trapped into producing a beautiful, elegant, maintainable piece of code which performs the wrong task. Similarly, early definition of interfaces among major functional components is essential for multi-person projects. These approaches allow the software engineer to think in "function," not in "code," and allow efficient use of the scarce human engineer resource. Pure bottom-up software design has not been considered a serious method for production software development since the 1960's.

On the other hand, bottom-up design techniques are still used predominantly today to implement LSI circuits. Consider, for example, the "standard-cell" approach utilized by many custom houses. Transistors are interconnected and packed together in small logical chunks, known as cells, and stored in a cell library. These cells are usually manually designed and optimized for area, typically with the aid of a color graphics terminal. A chip is formed, under this approach, by a layout tool such as FAMOS[10], which places the cells in horizontal rows and derives a routing scheme between the cells' IO's, the power and ground busses, and the chip's pads. This row-oriented layout approach is guided by the use of computer aided design tools. However, the layout is typically modified manually to complete routes or optimize area because the automatic aids don't perform sufficiently well, or because the designer enjoys getting "involved" with the design. The standard cell approach is essentially a two-level, bottom-up design approach. Chips on the order of five to ten thousand gates have been successfully implemented under this approach.

Clearly, this approach cannot work for systems with the complexity of VLSI. As in the software case, the building blocks (cells or program statements) are far too small to serve as a starting point in the design process. What is needed for VLSI are top-down techniques as used in software.

Just as the trend in the software research community has progressed from implementation and design to requirements and verification, the same trend is underway in VLSI. VLSI research has centered around the implementation stage (e.g., layout) but, as will be described in more detail later in the tools section, is starting to get more involved in design decomposition methodologies and tools which support these methodologies. The pioneering work of Carver Mead and Lynn Conway[11] is the best example of recent work in this area. They have developed a structured design methodology for VLSI which emphasizes hierarchy and exploits regularity. Under their approach, careful attention is given to the composition of hierarchical designs. Design constraints are imposed upon the designers to help solve the problems of complexity; only certain structures are permissible. This is analogous to the structured programming paradigm which is so pervasive in software today. VLSI activity in the requirements phase is still in utero; Dasarathy's work[12] in synthesizing architecture from specification may have application to the synthesis of block-level VLSI specifications from hardware requirements. The Carnegie Mellon University work on synthesizing a logic design from a behavioral description also holds promise[13].

It is expected that the fundamental concept of design, namely that of decomposition, is equally applicable in software and VLSI engineering. It is possible, but not completely demonstrated, that identical methods may work. In both cases, the engineer is required to define functions, which communicate via data (or data paths), and decompose the functions into subfunctions which communicate with each other via other data (or data paths). The only fundamental difference appears to be that in the software case, the functions and data occupy only a one-dimensional space which is fairly invisible during design; but in the VLSI case, the functions and data both occupy two-dimensional space, and consideration of that occupied space is essential during design (e.g., in the floorplan methodology[14]). An interesting approach towards design decomposition which makes explicit these types of concerns is the work at Xerox PARC and Stanford[15]. Certain levels of decomposition are defined along with the types of "concerns" one has at each level - such as event sequencing, clocking or digital behavior. At each level strict composition rules are enforced during design which ensure that certain classes of errors, related to these concerns, are avoided.

In coding, it is clear that the current hardware methods are equivalent to those software methods used during assembly language programming; Bit-twiddling (in software) and manual design of cells (in hardware) are roughly equivalent. As the specification level for VLSI increases to higher levels of abstraction, corresponding changes to methodology will occur. New methodologies will emphasize engineer efficiency and maintainability and reliability of the product instead of manual optimization of space or time.

Verification methodology in software is still in its infancy and thus perhaps fewer lessons may be learned in VLSI from software at the current time. Certainly the concepts of high cohesion and low connectivity[16] result in more resilient software. As programming languages start to be used for hardware specification, the same maintenance problems, and thus the same need for resilience will appear in hardware. Thus, these same heuristics may be applied to VLSI. However, the hardware verification problem is far more complex than its software counterpart. Hardware's behavior can change over time due to its environment and the failure of its physical elements. Even hardware, which is the result of "correct by construction" techniques, still may fail due to slight imperfections in manufacturing

or environment. We believe this is unique to hardware. Hence, design for testability, self-testing techniques, and redundancy have more applicability to hardware than software. It is likely that as these methods mature in the hardware community, they may be applied to software at a later date.

TOOLS

A good set of tools is required to support or automate any design methodology. The choice of tools should be governed to ensure that the methodology is followed, that enough designer flexibility is preserved to encourage innovation, that productivity is increased and that reliability of the product is increased. The level of automation support provided by the tools influences the degree to which a designer may concentrate on the more difficult, intuitive aspects of the design process and is critical to productivity. Use of appropriate tools can also ensure the correctness of the design.

Software Tools

Howden provides a good framework for discussing software tools[17]. He suggests a software tool taxonomy as follows: requirements tools, design tools, coding tools, and verification tools. In each category, he recommends that the level of sophistication of the selected tools be directly proportional to the complexity of the software under design. The following sections describe the state-of-the-art in software tools which support each phase.

Requirements Tools. Requirements tools provide support to the generation of complete, nonambiguous requirements specifications. They can also provide support for the generation of test plans based on a system's requirements. Requirements tools can range in sophistication from graphical non-automated approaches[18], to tools which carefully check requirements specifications for consistency[19] [20], to database oriented requirements analysis tools which support detailed problem decomposition, cross references, and configuration control[21]. The trend in this area is toward executable requirements and synthesis from requirements[1].

Design Tools. Design tools support the decomposition of function and data and the development of detailed algorithms. These tools range from text formatting languages[22], to tools which carefully monitor the decomposition of data and function[23], to tools which check for relative consistency between different views of a design in progress[24]. Most design tools generate cross references, check for consistent module interfaces, and extract document control and data flows. More recent research in design tooling concentrates on embedding design languages into programming languages and using modern programming constructs (e.g., abstraction) during design[25].

Coding Tools. Coding tools provide support for

the generation of source and object code. Chief among the coding tools is the programming language compiler. A compiler transforms a description of an algorithm in a high level language to a machine executable form. This transformation includes optimization steps which provide for highly efficient execution of the resulting code. Software compiler technology has matured to the point where parsers can be automatically produced from BNF descriptions of the language to be compiled. New optimization techniques result in code whose performance is comparable to manually generated assembler code. Integrated database-oriented compilation systems[26] provide front ends for several languages, code generation for several target architectures, sophisticated language dependent and language independent optimizations, and software development support tools. (It is interesting to note that when software compilers were first available, they were not used heavily; programmers were still too interested in playing with machine-level code.)

Verification Tools. Verification tools can be used to enhance the reliability and robustness of software. Until recently, most software verification has been limited to testing at the end of the software life cycle. However, when costs are analyzed, it becomes clear that the later one catches errors in the cycle, the more costly they are to fix[27] [28]. As a result, verification has become a more critical issue during the earlier phases of the software life cycle. As mentioned earlier, many requirements and design tools now routinely check for internal consistency. Tools are being developed to automate requirements test generation[29] and to automate test generation aimed at design and implementation[30]. Much effort has been devoted to measuring the completeness of coverage and the effectiveness of automatically generated tests[31]. On the other hand, testing is only one aspect of the verification problem. Far more effective, but also more costly and still experimental, are the formal verification methods such as proofs of correctness and correctness by construction[32]. Adrion, Branstad and Cherniavsky make a good plea for the integration of verification techniques throughout the software life cycle[33].

IC Tools

Our discussion of current IC design tools will concentrate on the levels of the IC development cycle that occur before the PG tape is built. Assumed tools include mask generators and other foundry tools which operate at the lowest levels. Most of the remaining tools currently available are either analysis tools, which provide support at a single design level, or extraction tools which feed back data to higher levels for comparison and verification. Most current tools used in production do not support a top-down or hierarchical approach towards design.

Requirements Tools. There is very little tool support in the area of IC requirements. Most current methods are ad hoc using informal requirements definitions and manual reviews. The

trend in software seems to point to application specific, executable requirements languages. Certainly one area of relevant research interest is the incorporation of performance constructs into VLSI requirements languages. These constraints should include area, timing, power and speed. Some work has been done in the specification of timing constraints for real time systems[34]. As with software, it is imperative that one defines what a system is to do, and under what constraints, before one defines how the system is to do it and with what structure it will be composed. Tools to support formal VLSI requirements are needed.

Block-Level Tools. At the block level, we start to find several tools in use. Block level (sometimes called functional level) simulation tools[35] [36] are now used to verify the behavior of designs during the initial decomposition stages. These tools can also be used to model the architecture of a design. Some more recent systems[37] [38] allow modularization of the hierarchical design structure with well-defined interfaces. In all but a few cases, the behavior of the system and the structure of the system at the block level are defined separately and verified separately. Some automation does exist at this level; in one approach[39] the control flow for a clocked digital machine is generated automatically from a parse tree of the dataflow for the machine.

Logic Level Tools. Logic level analysis tools have been in use for some time. At this level, we are concerned with the logic required to implement the block level design. Hence, this in analogous to the detailed design level of software development. The primary tool at this level is a schematic capture system and a gate level logic simulator. Some functional level logic simulators include gate level simulation and thus provide multilevel simulation capabilities. The logic itself is created manually, described by a netlist or a schematic, and then verified using these tools. The timing errors of a design are usually caught at this stage with the aid of accurate delay models, race detection, and hazard detection capabilities provided by most logic simulators. Timing analysis tools are also available to provide worst case path analysis and other critical timing data[40].

Circuit Level Tools. At the circuit and switch levels, unsized schematics are transformed into sized schematics. The major tools available are circuit level simulators[41] and the newer switch level simulators[42]. Accurate device models and accurate circuit descriptions are essential at this stage to achieve the correct sizing data. The algorithmic complexity of current circuit level simulation algorithms prohibits full simulation of the entire chip; however new results in this area, such as the work at Berkeley[43], look promising as a solution to this problem.

Layout Tools. The geometric level of abstraction is concerned with the actual shapes that will be used to produce the final mask set. Tools to support the geometric layout of a chip represent the largest set of available tools. This is not surprising, as this is where manual effort is still intensive and vendor competition intense. First and foremost of current tools in this area are interactive color graphics systems for defining and manipulating cell geometries. The trend appears to be to replace expensive systems with stand-alone cheaper workstations. These systems allow the layout technician to examine visually the geometric information, to interact with the display and to direct the layout manually with the aid of menus, light pens, joysticks, and data tablets. Symbolic layout tools[44] are now appearing on the market. These tools support a symbolic geometric description, where relative spacing is exploited to achieve productivity improvements. The automatic compaction of these symbolic layouts can be achieved with the aid of algorithms which attempt to minimize the cell area[45][46]. Compaction eliminates the need for stand-alone design rule checkers, as the compacted layout is design rule correct by construction. Compaction can also facilitate the translation of cell libraries when design rules change. However, stand-alone design rule checkers[47] are still widely used. Automatic placement and routing tools, such as FAMOS[10], are used to compose cells into chips. More modern automatic layout aids, such as channel routers, hierarchical placement tools, gate array layout tools and PLA generators, are now appearing. At this level, electrical checking can also be performed to locate electrical violations such as undriven transistors, signals with no loads, missing contacts, or pullup/pulldown violations.

Verification Tools. VLSI verification tools tend to traverse several levels of abstraction as do their software counterparts. Several of the more recent verification tools provide multilevel simulation capabilities. This approach allows a portion of a chip to be simulated at the transistor or gate level while the rest of the chip is simulated at the functional level. Hence, more accurate simulation can be obtained for critical portions of the design. Other new approaches to simulation include symbolic simulation and symbolic execution. Symbolic execution involves using symbols and expressions for input data, instead of waveforms, and then proving, for each path through an execution tree, that initial assertions lead to final assertions. This formal approach has been borrowed from software program verification and is discussed well by Darringer[48] and Kishimoto[49]. These approaches attempt to verify the functional correctness of the design.

Test generation to detect manufacturing faults, another dimension of the verification problem for VLSI, has been automated for circuits modeled at the gate level. The classical D-Algorithm[50] has also been extended to handle sequential circuits. However, there is no general purpose ATG algorithm at the behavioral level, though some interesting work is being done[51]. Fault simulation tools are utilized to indicate the fault isolation and fault coverage characteristics of a set of test vectors. The most promising fault

simulation method for VLSI is the concurrent method[52], which has been extended to the functional level from the gate level[53]. Most fault simulation tools are integrated with logic simulation tools. VLSI poses some other interesting problems for test generation, as the stuck at fault model is insufficient for VLSI. Other fault models to reflect new types of manufacturing faults (such as signal-to-signal shorts) are required.

Testability analysis tools[54][55] give the designer early feedback on the testability of the design. These tools provide testability measures of the design in progress and indicate to the designer which potential design changes would enhance testability. Unlike the LSSD approach[56], testability analysis does not impose any physical constraints on the design. The current focus of attention on testability analysis for VLSI is mirrored by the current attention given to software verification early in the design cycle.

Hierarchical Design Tools. Tools which support hierarchical design are also available. These include correctness by construction tools such as those which support logic driven layout. Logic driven layout prohibits the layout of a cell unless it conforms to a previously defined logical description. Thus, a whole class of errors is avoided. Floorplan tools are also in this category. With this set of tools, the plane is decomposed into templates for major functional units and the design proceeds to fill the floorplan with cells. This technique has given rise to stretchable cells which abut to achieve routing, instead of utilizing traditional placement and routing techniques. In this category are also the composition tools, described by Trimberger[14], which provide a formal method for joining together separately designed modules. In addition, some of the more classical tools, such as design rule checkers, are taking advantage of hierarchy, by checking only boundary violations during composition and by constraining cell overlap[57].

Silicon Compilation and Software Compilation

The trend in IC design tools and the analogy to software is probably best characterized by current work in silicon compilation. Although the definition of a "silicon compiler" has not been standardized, one can think of a silicon compiler as an IC design tool which takes as input a behavioral description of a chip (or a portion of a chip) and produces, automatically, the mask needed to fabricate it. Hence silicon compilation utilizes a textual description, not a graphical description, of the circuit. There is some question as to whether the input to a silicon compiler should describe structure or behavior; we feel behavior should be specified and structure synthesized.

Silicon compilers have several significant problems not shared by their software counterpart. As Rupp[58] points out, software involves a flow of sequential activity in the time dimension; hardware involves a set of concurrent operations in two spatial dimensions (perhaps three dimensions in the near future). However, by restricting cells to be rectangular with all connectors on the boundary, the two-dimensional problem can be transformed into two one-dimensional problems which are easier to deal with[14]. Also, communication costs (wire and wire space) are very high in hardware and much cheaper in software. Parameterization of symbols is useful in both disciplines; it allows an instantiation of a procedure to be customized to its calling environment. For VLSI, relative spacing can be handled by parameters which get bound to absolute dimensions when the call takes place. Both disciplines also share the same problem of composition, which is manifested in the software realm by the linking loader.

The two most important decisions one makes during the design of a software or a silicon compiler are the choice of input language and the choice of an intermediate form. The language should have a high degree of expression, be easy to learn, be concise, improve productivity, and be usable in a team-oriented approach. Current choices for silicon compiler languages include a LISP-based language[59], a C-based language[58], and a hierarchical, structural design language for gate array silicon compilation[60]. Although LISP and C are popular among some specialized groups of software engineers and have been effective at increasing programmer productivity, there is considerable evidence that these languages result in programs which are difficult to maintain over long periods of time. Hierarchical, highly structured, abstraction-based languages tend to produce more resilient programs.

The choice of an intermediate form is crucial because it determines the difficulty of translation and the ease of separate compilation. Compiling an input language immediately to transistors is too difficult because transistors are at too low a level and are technology dependent. A higher level intermediate form, which is technology independent, such as the binary decision trees used by Rupp[58] or the control/data path architecture chosen for MacPitts[59], seem to be achievable alternatives. The choice of intermediate form for a software compiler is equally important.

Rupp[58] gives a good description of the translation steps typically required for a silicon compiler. These include the mapping of a behavioral description into canonical logic equations; then, guided by a chip floorplan, switching equations are produced in a variable geometric form, and these are then hardened into final, fixed geometries (CIF format). It should be noted that this approach involves both technology dependent and technology independent stages, similar to the language and machine dependencies evident in typical software compilation systems. Silicon compilers also include aids for verification, area estimation, connectivity checking, and load factor analysis. Modern software compiling systems provide analogous tools such as data flow analyzers and interface checkers. Several different "wiring" stategies are used in silicon compilers. These include river routing in MacPitts[59] and cell abutment and cell stretching in Bristle Blocks[61].

Results achieved with silicon compilation systems are not well published, mostly because the technology is still in experimental form and has not been used in many chip designs. The bristle block approach has achieved layouts with area only 10% larger than manually, graphically designed efforts[61]. It is important to realize that as optimization techniques mature better results will be noted. The use of any tool is a trade-off decision. There are several major advantages to the use of a silicon compiler and as soon as these overshadow any loss of area or performance, they will be utilized more freely.

It is important to note that the existence of programming language compilers, for software or for IC's, does not obviate the problem of design. The high-level design and detailed design phases for complex software systems are the most time consuming; the coding step is now the shortest and easiest step in the process. Hence, silicon compilers are not a panacea, as Werner questions[62]. A complex software system of forty-five thousand lines of code can take over twenty man years for design, development and enhancement. The proper integration of silicon compilers into a design methodology for VLSI will, however, provide significant advantages over the traditional artwork approaches used today to design IC's. These will include: quick experimentation with alternate implementations, so as to test performance and area trade-offs effectively, easier enhancement and modification, easier design for testability, wirability and performance, facilitation of multiperson design efforts, localization of design concerns and avoidance of replication of effort.

ENVIRONMENTS

As software engineering has matured, many tools have been developed. However, the concept of software development environments is still somewhat new. A software development environment provides a cohesive system in which a user can interact with a wide variety of integrated tools, tools can easily be replaced with their more modern counterparts, and the software product being constructed is maintained under a consistent configuration control mechanism. Configuration control allows configurations (collections of modules) to be defined and retrieved, with version control to keep track of the dynamic status of the modules as they evolve. These environments usually include a central database which serves as a repository for the design components during their development. A good environment must support the entire software development life cycle by providing assistance to the builder of a deliverable product through the requirements, design, implementation and maintenance phases. Environments ranging from few interactive tools to many automated tools integrated around a central database have been constructed or proposed[63]. Instead of translating between the input languages for each tool or transferring files among tools, the database approach allows each tool to extract their specific input needs from a common database of objects. This approach provides a medium for integration without forcing a strict interrelationship among tools. As one author[17] puts it, to achieve a more flexible approach, it is better to build bridges into the database than bridges between tools. A good example of recent research in the area of programming environments is given by Rudmik[64]. In a related paper[26], he points out the advantage of a central database to the separate compilation of very large software systems (a problem shared certainly by VLSI design).

Extendable systems have been around for a long time (the American Constitution comes to mind). The rapid growth in design technology demands that systems grow, and that new tools can be integrated gracefully. Such systems should also provide a cost effective approach to preserve old data when a new tool is integrated with the environment. The trend toward extendable software environments supporting a robust software approach is apparent.

The integrated approach toward VLSI design environments is just starting to receive a great deal of attention. Although central database systems for digital design data have been used by large mainframe manufacturers for a decade or more, IC design systems with central databases are just now appearing on the market and are still unproven technologies. The same rationale used for database-oriented software environments applies equally well in the hardware case. In contrast, there is some effort in the decentralized database approach[65]. In this particular system, a stand-alone database for hierarchical schematic data is provided, but is not integrated with any (other) tools; netlists are extracted from the database, translated, and fed to simulators running on different databases.

It is interesting to note that one of the university leaders in the exploitation of software concepts to VLSI, California Institute of Technology, does not support the central database concept for VLSI design[14]. Instead they advocate simple interchange standards between tools. They argue that because a university environment is experimental by nature, adhering to outdated data structures would be intolerable. In an industrial environment, however, one relies on the stability of a data structure, and so the central database concept is well accepted there. In fact, some of the newer database systems allow for dynamic restructuring of the database, and hence provide for the graceful acceptance of change.

SUMMARY

We have explored the current state of software and VLSI development technologies to examine their similarity. There seems to be a significant degree of commonality in the areas of specification, methodology, tools and environments. The emerging VLSI design approaches borrow significantly from their more mature software counterparts. The two disciplines are both rapidly advancing.

Recognition of the parallelism between the two is important to provide a framework for study and an avoidance of past mistakes. As the trend in VLSI design marches forward towards synthesis and structure, it behooves us to learn about its origins. The problems of design will not be solved by this observation alone, but the synergy which could result from the meeting of these traditionally separate camps, could enable some of the efforts to reach critical mass.

ACKNOWLEDGMENTS

The authors wish to thank Mary Walsh for her excellent typing of this manuscript.

BIBLIOGRAPHY

1. Zave, P., and R. Yeh, "Executable Requirements For Embedded Systems," Fifth IEEE International Conference on Software Engineering, March 1981, pp. 295-304.

2. Piloty, R., and D. Borrione, "The CONLAN Project: Status and Future Plans," Nineteenth Design Automation Conference, June 1982, pp. 202-212.

3. Barbacci, M., and J. Northcutt, "Application of ISPS, an Architecture Description Language," Journal of Digital Systems Vol.4, No. 3, pp. 221-239.

4. Lipton, R. J., et al., "ALI: A Procedural Language to Describe VLSI Layouts," Nineteenth Design Automation Conference, June 1982, pp. 467-474.

5. Hill, D. D., "ADLIB: A Modular, Strongly-Typed Computer Design Language," Fourth International Symposium on Computer Hardware Description Languages, October 1979, pp. 75-81.

6. Miller, T. J., and J. H. Vellenga, "A High Level Language for VLSI Design," IEEE Phoenix Conference on Computers and Communications, May 1982, pp. 41-44.

7. Haynes, C. L. F., "The Use of ADA as a Design Language for Digital Systems," IEE Electronic Design Automation Conference, September 1981, pp. 139-143.

8. Ayres, R., "IC Specification Language," Sixteenth Design Automation Conference June 1979, pp. 307-309.

9. Penfield, P., Presentation to GTE, Inc. Southbury, Connecticut, April 1981.

10. Mattison, R. L., "A High Quality, Low Cost Router for MOS/LSI," Ninth Design Automation Workshop, 1972, pp. 94-103.

11. Mead, C. A., and L. A. Conway, Introduction to VLSI Systems, Addison Wesley Reading, Massachusetts, 1980.

12. Dasarathy, B., D. Prerau, and J. Vellenga, "The System Compiler," submitted to the 1983 IEEE International Symposium on Circuits and Systems, May 1983.

13. Parker, A., et al., "The CMU Design Automation System: An Example of Automated Data Path Design," Sixteenth Design Automation Conference, June 1979, pp. 73-80.

14. Trimberger, S., et al., "A Structured Design Methodology and Associated Software Tools," IEEE Transactions on Circuits and Systems, Vol. 28, No. 7, July 1981, pp. 618-634.

15. Stefik, M., et al., "The Partitioning of Concerns in Digital System Design," MIT Conference on Advanced Research in VLSI, January 1982, pp. 43-52.

16. Yourdon, E., and L. Constantine, Structured Design, Prentice Hall, Inc., Englewood Cliffs, New Jersey, 1979.

17. Howden, W., "Contemporary Software Development Environments," Communications of the ACM, Vol. 25, No. 5, May 1982, pp. 318-329.

18. Ross, D., and K. Schoman Jr., "Structured Analysis for Requirements Definition," IEEE Transactions on Software Engineering, Vol.3, No. 1, January 1977, pp. 6-15.

19. Davis, A. M., et al., "RLP: An Automated Tool for the Automatic Processing of Requirements," COMPSAC '79, IEEE Computer Society, Los Alamitos, California, 1979, pp. 289-299.

20. Bell, T. E., et al., "An Extendable Approach to Computer-Aided Software Requirements," IEEE Transactions on Software Engineering, Vol. 3, No. 1, January 1977, pp.49-60.

21. Teichroew, D., and E. Hershey III, "PSL/PSA: A Computer-Aided Technique For Structured Documentation and Analysis of Information Processing Systems," IEEE Transactions on Software Engineering, Vol. 3, No. 1, January 1977, pp. 41-48.

22. Caine, S., and E. Gordon, "PDL - A Tool for Software Design," National Computer Conference, Vol. 44, AFIPS Press, Montvale, New Jersey, 1975, pp. 271-276.

23. Romanos, J., "The Software Design Processor," COMPSAC '79, IEEE Computer Society, Los Alamitos, California, 1979, pp. 380-383.

24. Smith, D. G., Autoidefo: A New Tool for Functional Modeling, Softech Inc. Technical Report TP-125, Waltham, Massachusetts, 1981.

25. Rudmik, A., B. Casey, and H. Cohen, "Consistency Checking Within Embedded Design Languages," 6th IEEE International Conference on Software Engineering, September 1982, pp. 236-245.

26. Rudmik, A., and B. Moore, "An Efficient Separate Compilation Strategy for Very Large Programs," ACM SIGPLAN 82 Symposium on Compiler Construction, and SIGPLAN Notices, Vol. 17, No. 6, June 1982, pp. 301-307.

27. Boehm, B., "Developing Small-Scale Application Software Products: Some Experimental Results," IFIPS Conference, October 1980, pp. 321-326.

28. Daly, E., "Management of Software Engineering," IEEE Transactions on Software Engineering, Vol. 3, No. 3, May 1977, pp. 229-242.

29. Dasarathy, B., and M. Chandrasekharan, "Test Generation for Functional Validation of Real-Time Systems," 6th IEEE International Conference on Software Engineering, Poster Session, September 1982.

30. Huang, J. C., "Detection of Data Flow Anomaly Through Program Instrumentation," IEEE Transactions on Software Engineering, Vol. 5, No. 3, May 1979, pp. 226-236.

31. Miller, E., "Program Testing: Art Meets Theory," IEEE Computer, Vol. 10, No. 7, July 1977, pp. 42-51.

32. Leinwand, S. M., "Logical Correctness by Construction," Nineteenth Design Automation Conference, June 1982, pp. 825-831.

33. Adrion, W. R., et al., "Validation, Verification, and Testing of Computer Software," ACM Computing Surveys, Vol. 14, No. 2, June 1982, pp. 159-192.

34. Dasarathy, B., "Timing Constraints of Real-Time Systems: Constructs for Expressing Them, Methods of Validating Them," IEEE Real-Time Systems Symposium, December 1982.

35. Hirschhorn, S., et al., "Functional Simulation in FANSIM3 - Algorithms, Data Structures and Results," Eighteenth Design Automation Conference, June 1981, pp. 248-255.

36. Wilcox, P., "Digital Logic Simulation at the Gate and Functional Level," Sixteenth Design Automation Conference, June 1979, pp. 242-248.

37. McWilliams, T. M., and L. C. Widdoes, Jr., "SCALD: Structured Computer-Aided Logic Design," Fifteenth Design Automation Conference, June 1978, pp. 271-277.

38. Duke, K. A., and K. Maling, "ALEX: A Conversational, Hierarchical Logic Design System," Seventeenth Design Automation Conference, June 1980, pp. 318-327.

39. Evangelisti, C. J., et al., "Using the Data-flow Analyzer on LCD Descriptions of Machines to Generate Control," Fourth International Symposium on Computer Hardware Description Languages, October 1979, pp. 109-115.

40. Hitchcock, R. B., "Timing Verification and the Timing Analysis Problem," Nineteenth Design Automation Conference, June 1982, pp. 594-604.

41. Nagel, L. W., "SPICE 2: A Computer Program to Simulate Semiconductor Circuits," Electronics Research Laboratory Memorandum ERL-M520, University of California, Berkeley, May 1975.

42. Bryant, R. E., "MOSSIM: A Switch Level Simulator for MOS/LSI," Eighteenth Design Automation Conference, June 1981, pp.786-790.

43. Lelarasmee, E., and A. Sangiovanni-Vincentelli, "Relax: A New Circuits Simulator for Large Scale MOS Integrated Circuits," Nineteenth Design Automation Conference, June 1982, pp. 682-690.

44. VLSI Design, Vol. 3, No.1, January/February 1982, p. 54.

45. Hsueh, M., "Symbolic Layout and Compaction of Integrated Circuits," Ph.D. dissertation, University of California, Berkeley, 1980.

46. Weste, N., "Mulga - An Interactive Symbolic Layout System for the Design of Integrated Circuits," Bell System Technical Journal, Vol. 60, No. 6, July - August 1981, pp. 823-857.

47. DRC User Guide, NCA Corporation, Sunnyvale, California.

48. Darringer, J., and J. King, "Application of Symbolic Execution to Program Testing," IEEE Computer, April 1978, pp. 51-59.

49. Kishimoto, Z., and K. Son, "Symbolic Evaluation for VLSI Design Verification," IEEE Workshop on the Engineering of VLSI and Software, October 1982.

50. Roth, J. P., "Diagnosis of Automatic Failures: A Calculus and a Method," IBM Journal of Research and Development, Vol. 9, No. 10, October 1966, pp. 278-281.

51. Son, K., and J. Fong, "Automatic Behavioral Test Generation," Cherry Hill Test Conference, November 1982.

52. Ulrich, E., and T. Baker, "The Concurrent Simulation of Nearly Identical Digital Networks," Design Automation Workshop, June 1973, and IEEE Computer, Vol. 7, No. 4, April 1974, pp. 39-44.

53. Crowder, D. E., and N. P. Goodall, "An Implementation of a Concurrent Algorithm for Functional Level Digital Fault Simulation," IEE Electronic Design Automation, September 1981, pp. 198-202.

54. Goldstein, L. H., and E. L. Thigpen, "SCOAP: Sandia Controllability/ Observability Analysis Program," Seventeenth Design Automation Conference, June 1980, pp. 190-196.

55. Fong, J. Y. O., "A Generalized Testability Analysis Algorithm for Digital Logic Circuits," IEEE International Symposium on Circuits and Systems, May 1982, pp. 1160-1163.

56. Eichelberger, E. B., and T. W. Williams, "A Logic Design Structure for LSI Testability," Fourteenth Design Automation Workshop, June 1977, pp. 462-468.

57. Tucker, M., and L. Scheffer, "A Constrained Design Methodology for VLSI," VLSI Design, Vol. 3, No. 3, May/June 1982, pp. 60-65.

58. Rupp, C., "Components of a Silicon Compiler System," VLSI 81 Conference, August 1981, pp. 227-236.

59. Siskind, J. M., et al., "Generating Custom High Performance VLSI Designs from Succinct Algorithmic Descriptions," MIT Conference on Advanced Research in VLSI, January 1982, pp. 28-40.

60. Gray, J. P., et al., "Designing Gate Arrays Using a Silicon Compiler," Nineteenth Design Automation Conference, June 1982, pp. 377-383.

61. Johannsen, D., "Bristle Blocks: A Silicon Compiler," Sixteenth Design Automation Conference, June 1979, pp. 310-313.

62. Werner, J., "The Silicon Compiler: Panacea, Wishful Thinking, or Old Hat?," VLSI Design, Vol. 3, No. 5, September/October 1982, pp. 46-52.

63. Stenning, V., et al., "The Ada Environment: A Perspective," IEEE Computer, Vol. 14, No. 3, March 1981, pp. 51-62.

64. Rudmik, A., and B. Moore, "The CHILL Compiling System: Towards a CHILL Programming Environment," IEE Fourth International Conference on Software Engineering for Telecommunication Switching Systems, July 1981, pp. 187-190.

65. Jenne, D. C., and D. A. Stamm, "Managing VLSI Complexity: A User's Viewpoint," VLSI Design, Vol. 3, No. 3, March/April 1982, pp. 14-20.

A Comparison of Design Strategies for
Software and For VLSI[*]

Connie U. Smith and John A. Dallen

Duke VLSI Research Laboratory
Duke University
Durham, N.C. 27706

Abstract

A structure is developed and used for the
comparison of the VLSI and software design processes. The comparison reveals both similarities and
differences in the two disciplines and in their
evolution. Several possible implications are presented which contribute to an understanding of the
processes and provide insights into appropriate
directions for future research. Finally, some areas with high potential gains through technology
transfer are discussed.

---

[*] Full paper appears in Proc. IEEE Compcon, San
Francisco, March 1983.

SOFTWARE ENGINEERING LESSONS FOR VLSI DESIGN METHODOLOGY *

Wm. Randolph Franklin

Electrical, Computer, and Systems Engineering Dept.
Rensselaer Polytechnic Institute
Troy, New York, USA, 12181

ABSTRACT

There are several lessons that VLSI designers can learn from the recent history of software engineering. They include 1) the need for the widespread dissemination of existing tools and techniques in addition to the development of new ones, 2) the need for standardization efforts in software and database formats, and 3) the difference between the interests of the manufacturers and the users. This paper presents examples to illustrate these points.

INTRODUCTION

In this paper, we will see several areas where design methodologies from software engineering and computer graphics can teach us lessons for VLSI. In fact, the term "Software Engineering" was coined to express the need for some logical engineering methodology in software development. That field has been very slow to learn, billions of dollars have been wasted, and as Boehm[3] shows, rules formulated over 20 years ago, such as testable requirements, and defensive programming, are still often ignored. We have the opportunity to avoid much of this wasted effort in VLSI design. Some of the areas where design methodology transfer can occur SWE and VLSI that are considered here include:

i) the need for dissemination of existing tools,
ii) the need for standardization, and
iii) the difference between the interests of users and the interests of the manufacturers.

We will now consider them individually.

KNOWLEDGE DISSEMINATION

In this section, we will argue that there is a need for a organization whose job is to take research quality software used in VLSI research and development which has demonstrated a general

usefulness, prepare it for public distribution, and support it. There must be a mechanism to disseminate software tools once they have been shown to work at one research location.

This has not happened in software engineering, where there is an enormous difference between the current state of the art and what the average programmer is forced to use. Some of the techniques in software engineering that are slow to propagate are:

i) very high level languages such as Lisp and Smalltalk,
ii) interactive debuggers, and
iii) abstract databases.

In the real world, by comparison, IBM Assembly Language is one of the most widely used languages in the USA, and many people still debug programs in batch mode with hexadecimal core dumps.

Software development is becoming a capital intensive industry in the sense that a large investment in tools is necessary to achieve high programmer productivity[21]. However, organizations that will buy a $250,000 midi-computer system without qualms refuse to buy a powerful screen-oriented programmable text editor for $5,000, or a good document formatter for $10,000. They see software as an insubstantial item that cannot be compared to hard money.

This preparation of tools for public use will not happen unless someone is paid to do this. According to Brooks[6], there is a three to one ratio in cost between a program, suitable for its author to use, and a programming product, suitable for public use. The programming product has not only a working program, but also

i) extensive error checking for invalid input,
ii) help files,
iii) user documentation,
iv) a humane user interface,
v) an internal logic and maintenance manual to help the user customize it, and
vi) a set of test cases that so that the user can do regression testing after a change.

One attempt to create a public set of useful software was the software tools project[17]. This was a project to increase Fortran programming productivity by writing a front end preprocessor adding block structure and macros called Ratfor[12],

---
* This material is based upon work supported by the National Science Foundation under grant ECS 80-21504.

and then a set of programs ranging up from character manipulation and I/O to an editor and document formatter. With these, a user can move from any computer (that has Fortran) to another while working in the same environment. What makes this project unique is that all the source code is freely available so that users are encouraged to modify it. Modifications that appeared to be generally useful might be distributed to everyone later. Scherrer at Lawrence Berkeley Labs made a valiant effort to use DOE seed money to start a volunteer group to manage this process, i.e. answer user queries, accept mods, test them, combine them with other mods of the same program, and then distribute them. Although everyone involved with the process agreed that the result was useful, no organization wanted to allow its people to volunteer sufficient labor for a long enough period to ensure continuity.

The lesson for VLSI is that there will need to be a funded clearinghouse to handle generally useful software. On a simple level, is it more useful for each institution that receives a large program from another to spend several man-months (at least) bringing it up, or is it more cost effective to have one organization whose job it is to bring that software up to public distribution standards?

In another example, Bernard[2] has studied cooperative computing arrangements that span several independent organizations. (His lessons would also apply to cooperative arrangements involving VLSI research.) These arrangements involved either:

i) a shared application, such as an airline reservation system,
ii) shared processing, such as several institutions buying a supercomputer among them,
iii) shared data, such as the National Crime Information Center,
iv) shared software, such as the Health Education Network, or
v) a general purpose combination of the above, such as the Arpanet.

He identified five common problems:

i) the need for a central authority,
ii) conflicts of interest among participants,
iii) loss of local autonomy,
iv) separate perception of costs and benefits, and
v) coordination and user support.

His lesson was that a network organization, separately funded and separate from any of the nodes of the network, is necessary.

Finally, although it is necessary to have generally useful software distributed, it would be better to have it done by a separate funded organization than as a commercial enterprise, because preparation of software for public use is different from commercialization for sale in several ways. In a commercial system:

i) The source code is often not released,
ii) modifications and extensions by the user are not encouraged, and
iii) the software is not designed to interface with other packages that would be considered as competitors, even though this would benefit the user.

Thus in summary, unless an organization is established to take the best research ideas in VLSI software and prepare it for unrestricted public use, progress in the field will suffer.

STANDARDIZATION

In VLSI design, as ever larger databases of circuits are created and modified, and as more complex design programs are created that must interface with each other, there arises a need for standardization in data structures and program interfaces. We already see CIF with assorted dialects, and other languages. This parallels some of the problems that have occurred in computer graphics concerning standardization and compatibility between different graphic devices. Some of the standardization that resulted includes:

i) the SIGGRAPH Core standard[1] and GKS, the Graphics Kernal System[16], in graphics, and

ii) IGES in CAD[10,14,20].

That different E-beam systems take input in different formats, such as raster scan, random vector, and rectangle, is similar to the problem of different graphics output devices. There it has been found possible to have common display files in spite of the apparent incompatibilities. It is worthwhile to consider the SIGGRAPH Core effort since it involved a large, fast growing discipline of both academic and industrial importance. (GKS is a European graphics standard similar to the SIGGRAPH core. It has been adopted by the ISO and may be adopted by ANSI as the US standard.)

The Core report states that "a successful design activity requires essential ingredients": a body of knowledge and a design methodology or set of strategies and codes of practice for the designer to follow. Thus, before the committee could present a standard graphics package, they had to formulate a graphics standards design methodology.

The purpose of the standardization effort was not only program portability, but also programmer portability, i.e. the ability of people to move from one installation to another with minimal retraining. There are three levels of program portability:

i) No changes required,
ii) Only editorial changes required, such as changing routine names, and
iii) Structural changes required such as when the program assumes multiple segments or subpictures but the new installation does

not allow them.

The first is ideal for porting programs, while if the program adheres to the second level, porting is still reasonably easy to achieve. However, if the program is at the third level, then porting is difficult and error-prone. It is also possible to define a subset of the standard such that programs that adhere to it are easier to port.

All of these general rules concerning graphics program portability also apply to VLSI database portability, and to VLSI program portability when the programs must interface to common data. These are some of the problems that are being addressed by the IGES (Initial Graphics Exchange Specification) effort. It is designed to exchange CAD/CAM geometrical model data between dissimilar systems using commercially standard pre- and post-processors. It is now an ANSI standard, and has been demonstrated to work in practice. It preserves a manufacturer's proprietary internal database by allowing him to write processors to read or write the data onto a tape in the public IGES format. Some variant of this standard might be useful for graphic VLSI databases.

DIFFERING INTERESTS OF MANUFACTURERS AND USERS

In the dynamic field of VLSI development, the various contending parties of the manufacturers and the users have different interests, sometimes possibly to the extent of hindering the development of the field as a whole. This has also happened in several forms in software engineering and graphics:

a) Non-standard extensions to standard languages: Almost every Fortran-66 compiler has extra features added, such as END= in READ, generalized array subscripts, and free-format I/O. These help the user somewhat, at least in the short term. However, software endures longer than hardware; there are probably programs written for IBM1401's still being run on emulators. Thus in five or ten years, people may want to move the programs to a new machine, but non-standard extensions will prevent this. This is especially true when the program is poorly documented and the author has vanished.

There is a related problem of a manufacturer who implements "most" of a language. We see this with some micro-computer implementations of Fortran that may have everything but, say, double precision. Sometimes difficult features to understand, such as nested parentheses in format statements, are simply implemented wrong.

ADA, the common DoD language that is being developed[4,5,7,18,19,22], attempts to counteract this by forbidding any subsetting or supersetting. Nevertheless at least one company is now advertising an "ADA compiler" that the fine print reveals to lack most of the features that make ADA interesting.

The lesson for VLSI developers is that once standards are agreed upon, if certain manufacturers add extra features, to ignore them.

b) Proprietary databases to lock in users: Every CAD/CAM workstation manufacturer has his internal data structure format for the customers' data, and the customers are required to keep that format secret. These formats do not generally advance the state of the art in database design. However, they do

i) prevent add-on packages written by others, and

ii) prevent the user from changing to other equipment.

A user reaction to this has been the IGES effort mentioned above. This effort has been hindered by the need to avoid compromising the security of proprietary data formats. The lesson for VLSI development is to avoid a similar entrapment.

c) Software independent of hardware: In spite of efforts to lock users in, it is possible to build portable interfaces on top of non-portable features such as operating systems. This was the point of the software tools project. Another example is the UNIX (R) operating system,[8], originally written for internal use that grew essentially on its merits without any user support and against competing operating systems designed by the manufacturer of the hardware that it is most commonly used on. As a mark of success, in the last few years many other versions have sprung up that call themselves "extensions" or "UNIX-like". Of course most of them are incompatible, so we have another standardization effort ahead.

Pascal[11,13] is another example of a software product that grew without any initial hardware manufacturer support because it was well designed, implemented and documented.

Thus VLSI researchers and designers must realize that although marketing the products is necessary for the field to survive, their interests do not always match. Thus the VLSI researchers and designers must make an attempt to keep formats portable and standard independent of the hardware.

SUMMARY

We have seen several areas in which design methodology in VLSI can learn from the history of software engineering.

REFERENCES

1. Assoc. for Computing Machinery. "Status Report of the Graphics Standards Planning Committee", Computer Graphics, a Quarterly Report of SIGGRAPH-ACM 13, 3, (August 1979), 1 – V-10.

2. D. Bernard. "Management Issues in Cooperative Computing", ACM Computing Surveys 11, 1, (March 1979), 3-17.

3. B.W. Boehm. "Software Engineering – As It Is", 4th International Conference on Software Engineering, Munich, 1979, sponsored by the IEEE and ACM, 11-21.

4. C.L. Braun. "Guest Editor's Introduction: ADA – Programming in the 80's", IEEE Computer 14, 6, (June 1981), 11-12.

5. R.F. Brender and I.R. Nassi. "What is ADA?", IEEE Computer 14, 6, (June 1981), 17-25.

6. F. Brooks. The Mythical Man-Month, Addison-Wesley, (1975).

7. W.E. Carlson. "ADA: a Promising Beginning", IEEE Computer 14, 6, (June 1981), 13-16.

8. T.H. Crowley et al. (the whole issue), Bell System Technical Journal 57, 6 part 2, (July – August 1978), 1897-2312.

10. IGES Y14.26M Response Committee. Final Draft Sections 1,2,3, and 4 Proposed American National Standard, Engineering Drawing and Related Documentation Practices, Digital Representation for Communication of Product Definition Data, Approved as an American National Standard, September 21, 1981, (January 1982).

11. K. Jensen and N. Wirth. Pascal User Manual and Report (2nd edition), Springer-Verlag, (1978).

12. B.W. Kernighan and P.J. Plauger. Software Tools, Addison-Wesley, (1976).

13. B.W. Kernighan and P.J. Plauger. Software Tools in Pascal, Addison-Wesley, (1981).

14. M.H. Liewald and P.R. Kennicott. "Intersystem Data Transfer via IGES", IEEE Computer Graphics and Applications 2, 3, (May 1982), 55-63.

15. National Bureau of Standards. A Technical briefing on the Initial Graphics Exchange Specification (IGES), Automated Product Technology Division, Center for Manufacturing Engineering, National Engineering Lab, US Dept. of Commerce, National Bureau of Standards, Washington DC 20234. NBSIR 81-2297, (July 1981).

16. H.K. Quigley, Jr. "The Standardization of Computer Graphics", Computer Graphics News 2, 4, (November/December 1982), 4.

17. D. Scherrer. "Editorial", Software Tools Communications, 7, Newsletter of the Software Tools Users Group, Lawrence Berkeley Lab, CSAM-50B/3238, University of California, Berkeley, CA, 94720. (November 1981), 1-5.

18. V. Stenning, T. Froggatt, R. Gilbert, and E. Thomas. "The ADA Environment: A Perspective", IEEE Computer 14, 6, (June 1981), 26-36.

19. United States Department of Defense. Reference Manual for the ADA Programming Language, (July 1980), revised (Summer 1982).

20. J. Wellington (ed). IGES Newsletter, National Bureau of Standards, Bldg. 220, Rm. A-353, Washington, DC, 20234.

21. P. Wegner. "Reflections on Capital-Intensive Software Technology, (Draft: 17 Sepember 1982)", Software Engineering Notes, An Informal Newsletter of the ACM-SIGSOFT 7, 4, (October 1982), 24-33.

22. M.I. Wolfe, et al. "The Ada Language System", IEEE Computer 14, 6, (June 1981), 37-46.

TRANSFORMATION SYSTEMS FOR SOFTWARE-HARDWARE DESIGN: LANGUAGE AND SYSTEM DESIGN ISSUES
(Extended Summary)

P.A.Subrahmanyam

Department of Computer Science
University of Utah
Salt Lake City, Utah 84112

1. Introduction

The possibility of implementing reasonably complex special purpose systems directly in silicon using VLSI technologies has served to underline the need for design methodologies that support the development of systems that have both hardware and software components. In this context, we have been investigating two (somewhat related) design paradigms that use automated program synthesis/transformation systems as a basis: one proceeds from an abstract, representation independent specification of a problem and aids the development of efficient "executable" programs and/or VLSI structures, while the other proceeds from more-or-less representation dependent specifications in a high level language (specifically, Ada) and is geared to aid the design of a hardware implementation of an interacting ensemble of state machines.

Our preliminary explorations along these directions have been quite encouraging [23, 20]. (An example of realistic proportions that is being used to test the methodology involves the specification and hardware realization of a module implementing the DOD Internet Protocol (IP) [16], [12], [13], [14].) However, they have served to emphasize the need for a common framework for system design that provides for both specification options, and that facilitates a smoother transition between such specifications. Further, we have uniformly observed that two of the factors that are crucial in formulating an overall design strategy for guiding details of the system synthesis are: (i) the performance requirements of a system, and (ii) the characteristics of the global environment a system is designed to function in. It is therefore necessary to incorporate into the design paradigm ways to specify and reason about performance characteristics. Towards this end, we have developed the rudiments of a theory designed to support synthesis and verification, and that explicitly allows for a discussion of the performance criteria of systems [23].

In this paper, we outline briefly the two approaches to integrated system design that we have found promising, and discuss how they can be fruitfully reconciled. Proposed annotations to high level languages (e.g. Ada) that aid (1) the formal specification of synchronization properties by using algebra/temporal logic based constructs, as well as (2) the specification of performance criteria desired of modules along relevant dimensions are discussed.

We then elaborate on some of the language and systems related issues that have come to light as a result of our preliminary investigations. In particular, we consider a central implementation issue that is relevant to transformation systems and, not too co-incidentally, compilers: intermediate tree representations. We indicate why parse trees are inappropriate for this purpose, and delineate an alternative that uses abstract syntax trees. Such abstract syntax tree generator- generators have been designed both in Lisp and in C (as augmentations to YACC and LEX).

2. Perspectives on Software-Hardware Design

We view both software and hardware design as the process of representing the abstractions of objects and operations relevant to a given problem domain using primitives that are already available.

- When synthesizing programs, the primitives used are those provided by the lower-level abstractions: these may either be chosen from an available library, or be explicitly supplied.

- When synthesizing hardware implementations, the "primitives" available during conventional (i.e., printed circuit board) logic design are in the form of off-the-shelf chips: this is quite analogous to synthesizing programs. On the other hand, considerable flexibility in the number and nature of the primitives is available when doing special purpose VLSI design: this potentially enables the structure of the problem to be more directly mirrored in silicon.[2]

2.1. Design Paradigms

The need for design paradigms wherein the choice of a final implementation medium —hardware or software— is not fixed *a priori*, mandates that a uniform perspective be adopted both in the specification of the problem to be solved and in the development of an implementation. Ideally, a problem specification must be representation independent, and as close to the user's conceptualization of the problem as possible. However, there is sometimes a trade-off involved between the use of completely representation independent (axiomatic) specifications (e.g., [7], [3] [15]), and the use of conventional high level languages as "specification" languages that yield specifications which are more or less representation dependent. While there are promising axiomatic specification techniques being investigated, the average (current day) system designer is not yet adept at writing formal specifications; in fact, most tend to be put off by the mere presence of formalism, although there are notable exceptions. A second —and more technical— issue is that it is sometimes not easy to specify a desired behavior axiomatically because of inadequate understanding about the problem domain. In such cases, it may not always be feasible to invest the extra effort required to acquire such an understanding due to project deadlines to be met. Consequently, an alternative problem statement technique that is viable in such circumstances is useful as a practical alternative— this can generally take the form of an understandable "specification" in a high level language e.g., GIST [5] Ada [1].

---

[1]This research was sponsored in part by the Defense Advanced Research Projects Agency, US Department of Defense, Contract No. MDA903–81–C–0414

[2]In the solution of a *specific* problem using *specific* technology, however, the number of primitives is usually quite small (e.g., pass transistors, boolean logic gates, flip flops, multiplexors). This is partly necessary to reduce the complexity of the design process at this stage: such primitives are at a very low level, their correct implementation depends critically upon the technological "design rules" and usually require substantial effort to be "debugged". It is somewhat fortuitous that a small number of carefully chosen primitives suffices for a large class of problems.

90

Corresponding to these two options available in specifying a problem, there are two approaches to system design that one may adopt:

1. We can attempt to synthesize special purpose (software/VLSI) systems proceeding from abstract, representation independent specifications of problems. This paradigm can potentially mirror the structure intrinsic to a problem directly in an implementation structure in silicon, and thus provide a way of tailoring machine architectures to specific problems. As a consequence of the modularization inherent in such specifications at different levels, parts of the system may either be in software or hardware.

2. Alternatively, a (more or less representation dependent) specification of the problem in the form of a program can be transformed into a hardware implementation and/or more efficient software implementation.

We have been experimenting with the use of (i) axiomatic specifications of problems [21], as well as (ii) the use of Ada as a high level language for "specification" of special purpose systems [13, 14].

.2. Accomplishments

We now summarize our major accomplishments along the two lines of research mentioned above.

1. We have developed the rudiments of an algebraic framework to aid in the synthesis and verification of special purpose VLSI systems, proceeding from high level specifications. It allows for abstract specifications of the syntax, semantics, temporal and performance requirements particular to a given problem. The characteristics of the environment the system is embedded in can also be specified and are used in the synthesis process. In addition, the framework allows several of the constructs in existing languages to be modelled, including nondeterminism, concurrency, and data/demand driven evaluation. This allows the infrastructure to be (1) applied to situations wherein the problem "specification" is in the form of a program in a conventional high level language and (2) used to model the lower level synchronous/asynchronous nature of implementations. Topology and circuit layout geometry can also be expressed by using the algebraic primitives available. Examples that demonstrate the use of the proposed basis in synthesizing various classes of algorithms have been worked out. In particular, we have shown how (families of) systolic algorithms may be obtained as a special case. The concept of the propagation of computational loci arises naturally in course of the development, and serves to generalize the commonly used notion of a "wavefront" of computation for 2–dimensional architectures. MOS circuits can be modelled using the primitives available, and the algebraic derivation of Bryant's simulation algorithm used in MOSSIM II has been illustrated.

2. A part of the DOD Internet Protocol (IP) [16] has been chosen as a relevant example of realistic proportions as a candidate for mapping into hardware. An Ada program intended to serve as a specification of the system has been written. We have transformed, using transformation rules that are mechanizable, one of the modules into a hardware description of a state machine executing an environment that is defined by the data structure definitions. A prototype transformation system written in Interlisp, and running on the DEC–20 is being used to experiment with the mechanized version of the transformations. This system has recently been ported over to the Vax, because of address space limitations on the DEC–20. The output of this phase forms the input for a program that converts the hardware control unit description into a layout using PPLs (Path Programmable Logic Cells) automatically [2]. The output produced by this program can also be directly in terms of masks in either Caltech Intermediate Form (CIF) or Computervision EXDB format. These masks can be used for direct fabrication.

3. Directions Toward Unified Paradigms: Annotating High Level Language Programs

In order to implement the unifying framework that we have argued for above while maintaining the ability to write programs in high level languages (HLLs), it is necessary to augment the HLLs (e.g. Ada) with the ability to specify problems formally. This will then enable us to:

1. Translate abstract specifications directly into special purpose VLSI structures;

2. Translate abstract specifications into software implementations (in the form of Ada programs, for example);

3. Translate Ada program fragments into silicon implementations.

As a consequence of the ability to do the above, it then becomes possible to implement selected parts of a problem in hardware (i.e., design specialized machines for these parts), and the remaining parts in software (executable on either a special purpose or general purpose machine),

The existence of formal specifications for a problem can greatly increase the reliability of software developed for it by (i) precisely defining the interfaces of the programs developed; (ii) aiding both manual and/or automated verification; and (iii) enabling the development of automated tools for synthesizing implementations of the specifications. Motivated by these considerations and others, an extension of Ada that provides for formal *annotations* to Ada (ANNA) has been proposed by Krieg–Bruckner and Luckham.

We have proposed further extensions to ANNA that aid (1) the formal specification of tasking features in Ada by using temporal logic based constructs, as well as (2) the specification of performance criteria desired of modules. The techniques we have delineated in [21] above can be used by a transformation implementation system for automatically/interactively obtaining the implementations of Ada packages bodies *directly* from the formal specifications of the visible annotations of a package. Techniques for automating the synthesis of task bodies are outlined in [22].

In this section, we summarize the suggested augmentations to ANNA that facilitate formal descriptions of tasks using temporal logic based constructs. It is possible to automatically synthesize code for such formally specified tasks [18]. We now briefly review the annotations for packages in Ada presented in [9] before delineating our proposed annotations to aid in the specification of temporal and performance characteristics.

3.1. Package Annotations in ANNA

The *visible annotations* of an Ada package describe properties that characterize the visible operations on a package. The visible portion of the package (along with the annotations in ANNA) serves to specify the syntax and semantics of the operations defined on the package. Of these, the syntax is, for the most part, already embodied in the Ada program; it is mainly the semantics of the operations that are given by the annotations. The semantics of the visible functions are usually expressible as universally quantified algebraic identities, and correspond more or less to the algebraic axioms characterizing the operations [6, 7].

(Of less direct concern to this paper are the "hidden annotations" in a package, serving to describe the relationship between the visible operations and their implementation: such annotations can be automatically generated as a by–product in course of the synthesis.)

3.2. Annotations for Formally Specifying Concurrent Systems

Depending upon whether the synchronization of a system of concurrent processes is achieved by message passing or by sharing a common pool of resources, the primitives that enable one to best specify a problem may vary somewhat. The properties that are usually germane in this context include mutual exclusion (of resource access), invariant behavior of the shared resource, sequencing access to resource (in accordance with some constraints), priorities of access, fairness in servicing and scheduling requests, and time taken to respond (in real time systems).

The primitives that are useful for formally expressing the desired behavior in such contexts can be obtained by building on the primitives available in temporal logic. Temporal logic is ordinary (first order) predicate logic extended to include temporal operators (e.g., "eventually", "always" etc.) that facilitate reasoning about sequences of concurrent programs. It provides a convenient tool to express both invariant and time–dependent properties of software systems [18, 10]. Use of temporal constructs such as "henceforth", "eventually" and "until", along with the constructs derivable from them, result in intuitive specifications for synchronization problems. These constructs can independently express properties such as scheduling constraints, priority of operations, mutual exclusion of operations, invariance of resource state, absence of starvation and other relevant properties e.g., fairness criteria.

Real time behavior may be specified using using timer interrupts. However, if one desires an abstraction to express events such "n time steps hence", it is possible to make use of constructs expressible in extended temporal logic [25] (which permits regular expressions in specifications). A set of primitives rooted in algebra that allows the above in a more unified framework is discussed in [23].

The example given below illustrates some (but not all) of the features of the annotation primitives that are afforded by temporal logic. We omit detailed semantics of the specification primitives here.

3.3. An Example

A fixed number of similar resources is managed by an Operating System. User processes acquire a resource by executing the operation "acquire", and the operation "release" releases the resource. The number of resources free at any given time is maintained in "free". "Max" gives total number of resources. The operation Release is given priority over the operation acquire.

Both the (skeletal) annotated specification and the synthesized task body are shown in figure 3–1. We omit the discussion of the synthesis of task bodies in this paper.

3.4. Annotations for Performance Specifications

The operations defined on a module can be associated with performance specifications which can be used in two ways:

1. *Before an implementation exists:* The performance specification of an operation can be interpreted to mean

the minimum performance that is required of any (manually or automatically) synthesized implementation. This information is important in deciding amongst possible implementation strategies at intermediate points in the synthesis process.

2. *After an implementation exists:* The performance specification of an operation can be interpreted as characterizing the existing implementation. This information can then be used in other contexts. In particular, it can be used when computing the performance characteristics of some other implementation that uses this operation i.e., in the synthesis of a "higher level" module.

The example in figure 3–2 contains annotations for indicating performance specifications along the space and time dimensions.

3.5. Environmental Characteristics

Quite often, the characteristics of the global environment in which a module is designed to operate in influences the design of its implementation. For instance, consider the operations defined on a Set package. These might typically consist of: Insert (an element into a set), Delete (an element from a set), Member?, etc., with the functions having the obvious semantics. Obviously, the frequency of application of these operations, in conjunction with the desired performance will influence the choice of the internal data structures used to implement a set. Thus, the implementation synthesized may be a linked list (if inserts are frequent, and searches infrequent), a sorted array (if searches are frequent and inserts infrequent), a bit vector (if the size of the set is approximable), etc. The example below illustrates how annotations can be used to indicate such characteristics of a packages environment. Each implementation synthesized assumes (rather, is tailored to,) some implicit or explicit function application patterns.

On the other hand, it is sometimes necessary for the environment to adhere to some constraints if a system is to meet its specifications. For example, if a specified of software module (i.e., one whose visible specifications are formally specified in, say, ANNA, but whose "body" is cast in Silicon) is implemented as an asynchronous hardware module, then one of the requirement is that the input wires be "held" at their levels as long as it takes for the outputs to stabilize: this may therefore be construed as a constraint that the environment of a system must obey. Somewhat more typically, the arguments supplied to a function being invoked must be legitimate in order for the implementation to respond properly. Such constraints can again be specified axiomatically; see figure 3–3.

3.6. Specification Primitives for Hardware

We have experimented with using both the algebraic and the temporal logic primitives to specify hardware configurations at lower levels. The basic "logical" data values are 0, 1 and $\bot$. Other values are formed as vectors of these basic elements. Equality of signal values at the commencement of, during, and at the end of a temporal interval can then be easily expressed. Stability, liveness, and fairness issues at the low level can be handled expressed by building on the basic primitives. For example, the notion of a signal that marks the successful completion of one computation sequence triggering a second signal that commences another computation sequence (temporal dependency) can be easily expressed.

4. Discussions of Empirical Explorations

We now outline some of the important issues that have come to light as a result of our investigations so far. These can roughly be categorized into:

– Implementation/systems issues

```
task limited–resources is
 entry release;
 entry acquire;
—| for all  a : Acquire; r : Release;
—| RESOURCE–STATE–INFORMATION:
—| RESOURCE–STATE–SPECIFICATION
—| max : CONSTANT Integer 10;
—| free : [0,max] INITIALLY max;
—| RESOURCE–STATE–CHANGES
—| Acquire : free <— free — 1;
—| Release : free <— free + 1;
—| RESOURCE–STATE–INVARIANCE
—| (free <= max ) & (free=>0);
—| SERVICING CONSTRAINTS
—| ALWAYS (Start(r) ONLYIF Request(r) );
—| ALWAYS (Start(a) ONLYIF Request(a));
—| OPERATION EXCLUSION
—| Acquire EXCLUDES Release;
—| MULTIPLE Release EXCLUDE EACH OTHER;
—| MULTIPLE Acquire EXCLUDE EACH OTHER;
—| INTER CLASS  PRIORITY AMONG  ENABLED OPERATIONS
—| Release > Acquire;
—| end
end;

— The synthesized task body is the following:
— reserved words have been capitalized, to highlight them.

task body limited–resources is
 max : CONSTANT INTEGER := 10;
 free : integer range 0..max := max;
begin
loop
select
 when (free < max AND request(release)'count > 0)
  =>
   accept release do
    — code for release —
   end;
   free := free + 1;
 when (free > 0 and request(acquire)'count > 0 and
       (free = max OR request(release) = 0))
  =>
   accept acquire do
    — code for acquire —
   end;
   free := free — 1;
 end select;
end loop;
end limited–resources;
```

Figure 3–1: An Example of Synchronizer Specification in ANNA +

```
generic
 Size:Natural; type Elem is private;

package Set is
 ...
procedure ADD(E: in Elem) ;
 ...
— We omit all "normal" ANNA annotations

—| PERFORMANCE SPECIFICATIONS:
— An auxiliary function SIZE is defined in terms of the visible
— operations of the Set package, and is used in the performance
— specifications.
—| for all s in Set, let SIZE(s) be
—|    begin
—|       SIZE(InitializeSet) = 0;
—|       SIZE(Add(s,x)) = SIZE(s) + 1;
—|    end;
— Now the performance specifications.
—| TIME(INSERT(s,x)) = 0(1);
                     — INSERT must be done in constant time
—| TIME(DELETE(s,x)) = 0(SIZE(N));
                     — DELETE takes time that is a linear
—|                   — polynomial in the SIZE of the set.
—| SPACE(INSERT(s,x)) = 0(1);

package body Set is

....

end;

....
—| TIME(Lock–In–Radar–Data(t)) = 15 milliseconds;
           — an example of real time performance specifications;
```

Figure 3–2: Performance Specifications in ANNA +

```
package Set if
....
—| ENVIRONMENTAL CHARACTERISTICS
.—| FUNCTION APPLICATION PROBABILITIES AND FREQUENCIES:
—| FREQUENCY–OF(InitializeSet) = 1;
—| FREQUENCY–OF(INSERT) > FREQUENCY–OF(DELETE);
—| FREQUENCY–OF(MEMBER?) APPROXIMATELY THE SAME AS
—|                              FREQUENCY–OF(INSERT);
....

end Set;

— An example constraint on inputs that exhibits "Weak"
— conditions on asynchronous hardware modules
—| CONSTRAINTS ON INPUT:
—| there exists i in INPUT such that DEFINED(i)
—|    BEFORE there exists o in OUTPUT such that DEFINED(o);
....
```

Figure 3–3: Specification of Function Application Patterns

– New tool development

– Conceptual/theoretical issues

which are in turn germane in the context of

– Language related issues

– Transformation System issues

– Conceptual/theoretical issues relating to specification, synthesis (in particular, strategy guidance) and verification.

The above classification is not meant to be exhaustive. Moreover, the last 3 classes are not necessarily independent; however, they serve to indicate the thrust of the directions along which further research needs to be pursued. We now elaborate upon these in turn. Before doing so, however, it is useful to summarize the common implementation paradigms that are evidenced. Most of our subsequent discussion is in terms of the our experimentation with high level language programs into state machine transformations.

We have found that a typical transformation scenario can be thought of in terms of two "phases": (1) an *analysis* phase, wherein some global information relating to the program/specification needs to gathered; and (2) a *synthesis* phase wherein the implementation is built up. The analysis phase typically requires an examination of the *entire* program; this is usually done by traversing the parse tree. The synthesis phase is typically incremental in nature, and involves the use of the information gathered in the analysis phase and (optionally) further information of a more specific nature (i.e., not computed in the analysis phase) which may involve non–local analysis.

In essence, therefore, there is a common set of global properties needed for the transformations which is profitably gathered in the analysis phase, and a set of more specific properties that are better computed if and when needed. This separations into two phases, albeit somewhat nebulous, allows for

– Conceptual clarity

– Improved efficiency (because global traversals tend to be comparatively expensive)

– Added flexibility in "global" decision making, since one is not forced to make an implementation decision too prematurely.

Development Environment: Automated Tool Generation

A suitable "development environment" is needed to facilitate the activities in these phases. We already have implementations of the beginnings of such a development environment [24, 20] that includes tools such as grammar driven, parsers, pattern matchers, pretty printers, complexity computation routines etc. There are some further components that we would like to have in such an environment that currently are not implemented, but are planned in the future e.g., flow analysis tools, more elaborate complexity computation packages, etc. Additionally, there is a class of tools which we would like to have, but whose proper construction would seem to require some further basic research. Finally, the tools in all of these classes can be improved: in general, every piece of software can stand improvement in its interface, if not in its reliability and efficiency. It has been manifest that large address space is indispensable, fast machines are useful, and good graphics certainly helps.

Transformation System Issues

Two of the main features that are needed in course of experimenting with transformations are: (1) the ability to experiment with varying source and target languages; and (2) the ability to experiment with the transformation paradigms used.

While the need for a good development environment that aids these tasks cannot be overstated, it is important that this environment not intrude upon the user. For instance, we currently have the ability to automatically generate syntax directed editors and pattern matching packages tailored to a grammar: this has been found to be very useful (although one can always imagine embellishments that improve any editor). However, we are strongly convinced that the grammar used for defining the language should impose as few idiosyncratic constraints on the user as possible i.e., it should require minimal "massaging" in order to ensure that the automatically generated grammar based tools work.

As a specific example, the tool generator we use generates parsers, editors, and pattern matchers for grammars that are specified in a variant of BNF (and that allows for regular expressions). However, since the parser generated is a recursive descent parser with limited backtracking, it can sometimes be quite tricky to get the grammar into a form such that the parser in fact "works". (Although, it is perhaps as simple to work with as with other parser generators such as YACC. Another parser generator MINI is somewhat more flexible, but imposes a less rigid interface on the user —this may be construed as a drawback in some sense.)

Efficiency. Incremental Tool Generation

Efficiency becomes an important concern for the size of systems we are working with, along both the space and time dimensions. We are already pressing the limits of the DEC–20 address space; unfortunately the implementations available on the VAX/750 and VAX/780 are considerably slower.

An *incremental* tool generator set is therefore important for two reasons: (1) when working with a non–trivial language, the initial generation of tools consumes non–trivial computing resources (e.g. 10 minutes of CPU time on a 2060 for each startup for the grammar defining all of Ada): it is best to minimize this exorbitant expense in as far as is possible by using incremental tool generators; (2) since the 10 minutes of CPU time translate into about 30 minutes of real time, the slow system response is a psychological deterrent for interactive system development (this is particularly manifest when incrementally debugging the grammar to ensure that the tools are generated properly). This slow response is an irritant for very much the same reasons that debugging Pascal programs in a batch environment is, as opposed to debugging in an Interlisp–like programming environment.

Performance Issues

Among the characteristics that affect the strategic decisions during design are (1) desired performance criteria along various dimensions e.g., space, time, chip area, response time, pin count and throughput; (2) function application patterns, which can be expressed as probability distribution functions or approximations to such probabilities in the form of partial orders on function application frequencies; (3) cost characteristics of the target primitives.

It is necessary to be able to specify and reason about such characteristics in a uniform fashion. Further, the concepts involved need to be formalized, methods of computing the properties of interest defined, and automated tools to aid the complexity computations along various dimensions of interest constructed. The developments in [23] are geared towards the former end. A companion paper discusses the detailed performance evaluation tools needed. In particular, we mention that we have a prototype complexity computation package [17] for data type implementations that uses REDUCE [8] for its algebraic manipulations.

Temporal Characteristics of Systems

It is important to develop linguistic primitives that enable specification of temporal (e.g., liveness and fairness) and performance characteristics of systems. Further, it is preferable that the number of conceptual primitives be minimal, and capable of specifying both the low–level and high–level temporal characteristics of systems. For instance, high level algorithmic concurrency as well as low level fine grain concurrency (at a state machine instruction level) should be specificable with equal facility. Our augmentations to Anna are a step towards this end (see also [23]). We have shown elsewhere how the primitives developed in [23] are capable of succinctly specifying weak conditions of Seitz [19] for self–timed circuits.

Data Flow Analysis: Specification and Implementation

It is necessary to have a way to specify a list of global properties that are needed. Further, it is necessary to have a way to indicate their semantics, without giving a detailed algorithm for their computation. In essence, what is needed for the most part is a succinct specification of a data type that accepts a program (or some representation of a parse tree), and provides for accessing some specified list of data flow properties. It is then envisioned that the computational routines that perform the actual computation will be mechanically generated, given a set of standard flow analysis algorithms. Thus, while the actual computation of the data flow properties is a language issue, *which* properties are required/useful in course of synthesis is a transformation issue. We intend using attribute grammars evaluator generators to aid in some of the flow analysis computations.

4.1. Intermediate Representations: Parse Trees vs. Abstract Syntax Trees

One of the aspects that has proven to be somewhat problematic in our empirical explorations is that of parse tree representations. The problem stems basically from the fact that the complete parse tree in all of its gory detail is extremely unwieldy, expensive to store and traverse. Fortunately, it is seldom necessary to store the entire parse tree. As a consequence, there is an attempt made by the various tools generated to reduce the amount of irrelevant detail that is in fact stored. For example, there is a facility in the transformation system for specifying certain compactions in the representations of the parse trees generated: the amount of such compaction is limited by the effect on the pattern matching tools and the need to retain "relevant" features that may be used by other tools, in particular, the transformation routines.

The major tools that are affected by the representation are: the parser, the pattern match/search routines, and the transformation routines. Unfortunately, we find that each of these tools that are used in course of the transformations need to be cognizant of different levels of detail in the parse tree corresponding to a program. We find each of three routines needs details (not completely overlapping) relating to the underlying grammar/parse tree, and, ideally speaking, different accessing techniques. Further, it has become evident that if the transformation process is to work mainly on the parse trees, then a lot of the compaction that is otherwise feasible can no longer be achieved. Even worse, it appears that the details of the relevant portions of the parse tree depend upon the actual transformations. And finally, the amount of compaction that can be specified has some subtle interplays with the pattern matching routines.

The current version of our transformation system enables the fields of the parse tree to be accessed in a relatively representation independent manner. (This has indeed proven useful, since the underlying parse tree representation has been changed twice without affecting the programs that access the fields of interest.) Unfortunately, there are some non–uniformities in the way the parser tree is used by the pattern matching functions and the parser view; as a result of this, it is sometimes necessary to actually to manipulate the data structures, although we have been able to do this in a fairly modular fashion whenever needed. This deficiency is one that needs to be remedied in a future versions. The issue of the interaction between the nature of the transformations used and the portions of the parse tree that need to be retained is a more technical question, and needs further experimentation to be answered succinctly.

4.1.1. Abstract Syntax Trees as Intermediate Representations

As mentioned above, parse trees have proved to be inappropriate as the major intermediate data structure for experimenting with transformation systems. Parse trees are dependent not only on the concrete syntax chosen for expressing a concept (e.g., "Multiplication of 2 integers" can be expressed as a * b, *(a,b), ab*, (TIMES a b), (MULTIPLY a b), MultiplyAfterDecodingPrimePowers($2^a 3^b$) etc.), but on the parsing method that is chosen. The parsing method chosen is related to the grammar; this grammar is in turn related to the external concrete syntax. In view of the fact that there are several possible context free grammars (CFGs) that can derive a chosen language, and a parse can be ambiguous, it is important to isolate the underlying concept that is of interest from the intervening obfuscations in as far as possible.

In order to achieve the above isolation to a high degree, and, equally important, to do so in a automatable manner, we have augmented existing parser generators to enable automatic generation of abstract syntax tree (AST) generators. (This modification has not yet been incorporated into the overall transformation system.)

Not surprisingly, as there is a reasonable commonality between ordinary compilers and the somewhat more general transformation systems we are discussing, there are analogous advantages to using abstract syntax trees as the primary interface between the syntactic and semantic phases of compilers. As we have just delineated, these reasons are practical, theoretical, and "aesthetic"! All of the transformation routines are concerned with operating on "semantically significant" entities, and these are the only ones that preserved in the ASTs. It can therefore be argued that is more natural to assign semantics to abstract syntax trees than parse trees. This has the further advantage of enabling semantics to be given to non–context free grammars that generate "context–free" ASTs, generalizing some of the results in [4] (section 3).

The generation of ASTs is conceptually rather straightforward. The input to the AST generator is an annotated grammar in a BNF variant, where the annotations indicate the "semantically significant" terminal and nonterminal symbols associated with every production.

The nature of the basic annotations associated with the grammar productions are summarized below:

1. A CFG production that has a semantically significant terminal t (e.g. an identifier) yields an AST that has a single node labelled with the terminal t.Empty productions and semantically insignificant terminal symbols (e.g., "(", ")") do not contribute to the AST.

2. A nonterminal production that contains a significant operator symbol f (indicated by an appropriate annotation) yields an AST that has f at the root node; the subtrees of this AST are the AST's corresponding to the sub–parse trees of the same node. All empty subtrees are discarded.

3. A nonterminal production that does not contain a significant operator symbol yields a *list* of ASTs. This set of of ASTs subsequently become the subtrees of a superior node at some future point in the parse.

In the case of lookahead grammars e.g. LL(1), the annotations associated with a production need to indicate the number of (lookahead) operands still expected by an operator. While it is possible to given the formal translation of parse trees into abstract syntax trees, we do not do so here due to lack of space. The algorithm has been implemented as an augmentation to (1) LEX and YACC in C and (2) the MINI parser generator [11] in Lisp.

4.2. Optimization

Optimizations of a design are possible at all of the levels in the design hierarchy:

- At the very lowest level, it is possible to increase system performance by redesigning individual transistor layouts (e.g. changing Width/Length ratios) to increase speed etc.

- At a somewhat higher level, performance improvements can be obtained by using specialized circuits to achieve certain functions instead of using a standard cell set.

- At the next level, symbolic version of layouts can be locally "manipulated" in order to improve efficiency e.g., this may involve swapping adjacent columns (or rows) of PPLs etc., while ensuring that logical function is not impaired.

- At the state machine level, performance improvement can affected by state minimization, improved parallelism, etc.

- Finally, the high level architecture of the implementation can be juggled in order to improve performance, while maintaining consistency with the the abstract, representation independent, specifications of the problem.

It is important to note that these levels have rough analogs in the realm of standard language translation/machine architecture: faster/more powerful instruction sets, peephole optimization, flow analysis on intermediate compiler code, and algorithm improvement. Further, the overall improvement is typically greater the closer the optimizations are to the initial stages of development of an implementation: it is therefore more advantageous to attempt to design an appropriate architecture (/algorithm), rather than spend time optimizing channel layouts.

References

1. *Reference Manual for the Ada Programming Language, Proposed Standard Document.* July, 1980 edition edition, United States Department of Defense, 1980. For sale at U.S. Government Printing Office, Order No. L008–000–00354–8.

2. Carter, T.M. ASSASSIN: An Assembly, Specification and Analysis System for Speed–Independent Control–Unit Design in Integrated Circuits Using PPL. Master Th., University of Utah, Department of Computer Science, June 1982.

3. E.W.Dijkstra. *A discipline of Programming.* Prentice–Hall, N.J, 1976.

4. J.Goguen, J.Thatcher, E.Wagner, J.Wright. "Initial Algebra Semantics and Continuous Algebras." *JACM 24* (1977), 68–95.

5. Goldman, Neil and Wile, Dave. GIST(Internal Report). Unpublished, USC/ISI, September 1980

6. J.V.Guttag. *The Specification and Application to Programming of Abstract Data Types.* Ph.D. Th., Computational Sciences Group, University of Toronto, 1975.

7. J.Guttag, E.Horowitz, D.Musser. "Abstract Data Types and Software Validation." *CACM 21* (1978), 1048–64. Alsso Technical ReportISI/RR–76–48, USC ISI, August 1976

8. A.C.Hearn. REDUCE Users Manual. University of Utah, 1973.

9. B.Krieg–Bruckner and D.Luckham. ANNA: Towards a Language for Annotating Ada Programs. Proc. of the ACM–SIGPLAN Symposium on the Ada Programming Language, Boston, Mass., SIGPLAN, December, 1980, pp. 128–138.

10. Z.Manna and P.Wolper. Synthesis of Communicating Processes from Temporal Logic Specifications. Proc. of the Workshop on Logics of Programs, Yorktown Heights, NY, Springer Verlag Lecture Notes in Computer Science, 1981.

11. Marti, Jed. B.; Hearn, Antony C.; Griss, Martin L.and Griss, Cedric. "Standard LISP Report." *SIGPLAN Notices 14*, 10 (October 1979), 48–68.

12. Organick, E.I., and Lindstrom, G. Mapping high–order language units into VLSI structures. Proc. COMPCON 82, IEEE, Feb., 1982, pp. 15–18.

13. Organick, E.I., Carter, T.M., Lindstrom, G., Smith, K.F., Subrahmanyam, P.A. Transformation of Ada Programs into Silicon. SemiAnnual Technical Report. Tech. Rept. UTEC–82–020, University of Utah, March, 1982.

14. Organick, E.I., Carter, T., Hayes, A.B., Lindstrom, G., Nelson, B.E., Smith, K.F., Subrahmanyam, P.A. Transformation of Ada Programs into Silicon. Scond SemiAnnual Technical Report. Tech. Rept. UTEC–82–103, University of Utah, November, 1982.

15. Pnueli, A. The Temporal Semantics of Concurrent Programs. in Kahn (ed.), Semantics of Concurrent Computation, Springer Lecture Notes in Computer Science, June, 1979, pp. 1–20.

16. Postel, Jon: editor. Internet Protocol: DARPA Internet Program, Protocol Specification. Tech. Rept. RFC 791, Information Sciences Institute, USC, Sept., 1981.

17. Ramachandran, R. A Complexity Computation Package for Data Type Implementations. Master Th., University of Utah, Department of Computer Science, June 1982.

18. Ramamritham, K.and Keller, R.M. Specification and Synthesis of Synchronizers. Proc. 1980 International Conference on Parallel Processing, Aug, 1980.

19. C.L. Seitz. Self–timed VLSI systems. Procedings of the Caltech Conference on Very Large Scale Integration, January, 1979.

20. Subrahmanyam, P.A. and Rajopadhye, S. Automated Design of VLSI Architectures: Some Preliminary Explorations. Tech. Rept. UTEC # 82–067, University of Utah, October (Revised), 1982.

21. P.A. Subrahmanyam. An Automatic/Interactive Software Development System: Formal Basis and Design. In H.J–Schneider and A.I.Wasserman, Ed., *Automated Tools for Informations System Design and Development*, North–Holland, Amsterdam, 1982.

22. Subrahmanyam, P.A. From Anna + to Ada: Automating the Synthesis of Ada Package and Task Bodies. Tech. Rept. Internal Report, University of Utah, March, 1982.

23. Subrahmanyam, P.A. An Algebraic Basis for VLSI Design. Draft of a Research Monograph, April 1982. Available from the Department of Computer Science, University of Utah.

24. Wile, Dave. POPART: A Producer of Parsers and Related Tools, System Builder's Manual. Unpublished, USC/ISI

25. P.Wolper. Temporal Logic Can be More Expressive. Proc. of the 20th Symposium on the Foundations of Computer Science, SIGACT, October, 1981.

SOFTWARE METRICS AND LOWER BOUNDS

by R. Cuykendall

California Institute of Technology/Jet Propulsion Laboratory
Pasadena, California

One of the major concerns in the construction of computational systems is the controlled introduction of complexity. The design of software systems has typically been based on purely qualitative guidelines, such as module independence or information hiding. However, recent interest in software quality assurance has motivated research efforts to develop and validate quantitative metrics to measure the complexity of software computational structures. If the measurement can be made from the specifications generated during the design phase, the system designer could use the metric evaluation in selecting between alternative designs or in altering poorly structured system components before a sizeable investment is made in the implementation of these components. In addition, quantitative metrics permit tradeoffs in the allocation of critical project resources, e.g. scheduling and cost vs. quality.

Much of the recent work in software engineering has explicitly recognized a fundamental relationship between complexity and software quality. Reducing costs and increasing quality are compatible goals that can be achieved when the complexity of the software is properly controlled. For example, the use of structured design methodologies allow the controlled introduction of complexity through levels of abstraction, virtual machines or layered hierarchies. By establishing an ordered discipline during the design phase, these techniques have had significant impact on the production of higher quality, lower cost software. The common principle shared by these design methodologies is the careful structuring of the connections among the components of a system.

Research in software metrics can generally be divided into two categories: lexical metrics and connectivity metrics. The lexical metrics focus on the individual system components (sub programs, modules and procedures) and require a detailed knowledge of their internal mechanisms. Examples are Halstead's software science metrics derived from counts of operators and operations; its subsequent development, McCabe's cyclomatic complexity related to the count of the number of branch points in a program; and Thayer's measure of software reliability factors based on the occurrence of various statement types. The common principle in these methods is the counting of lexical tokens without specific regard for the structure created by those tokens. The lexical measures are easy to calculate, and have been surprisingly robust in evaluating reliability aspects of computational structures comprised of independent modules.

Connectivity metrics, on the other hand, attempt to measure the degree of interaction between components of amodular computational structures. Examples of this type of metric are Yin and Winchester's inter-level metrics, which observe the information flow across major levels in large hierarchic structures; the semantic entropy measures of Channon, based on the idea that the connection between components is determined by their shared assumptions; the partitioning formula of Belady and Evangelisti derived from circuit clustering considerations in laying out chip designs; and the fan-in/fan-out technique of Henry and Kafura which observes all communication patterns within a structure, rather than just those across level boundaries[2,5].

One of central problems in VLSI is the determination of the minimum amount of area required to lay out a network on a chip. In VLSI chips the computation is distributed over the chip, and the various processing elements must communicate via wires. These wires generally occupy more space than the computational elements themselves, and have become the principal factor in determining cost and performance. Both the number of wire crossings and wire area are worth minimizing when designing a chip. Chips with a large number of crossings may have problems with capacitive coupling (interference with overlapping wires), whereas chips with high wire densities are more likely to be ruined in fabrication by localized random errors.

The relationship between communication requirements and complexity of computational structures has received much attention lately. Information transfer can be regarded as a measure of inherent modularity: a computation is inherently amodular if any way of partitioning the computation demands highly interacting parts. This amodularity entails tradeoffs among critical resources such as chip area, computation time and energy dissipation in circuits.

A number of metrics have appeared in the literature for measuring VLSI layout complexity[1,6,7]. The bisection-width technique initially

CH1815-0/83/0000/0097$01.00 © 1983 IEEE

developed by Thompson observes the necessary flow of information between two sides of an arbitrary partition of a circuit into nearly equal parts. Hong and Kung on the other hand obtain lower bound results corresponding to the limitations due to the I/O requirements of VLSI circuits, based on the computation graphs of specific operations. Baudet accounts only for the memory required by a circuit in order to encode the input that has already been read before the output has been released completely, while Brent and Kung account for memory as well as information transfer. Vuillemin's measure accounts for information transfer and the period of computations in pipelined chips. Chazelle and Monier's metric assumes the time for propagating information is linearly proportional to distance, rather than a constant, and accounts for information transfer. They also consider a more restrictive metric tailored to NMOS technology which additionally assumes the current density of electrical power supplied through wires to a circuit is bounded by a constant. Leighton uses crossing number and wire area arguments to find lower bounds on layout area and maximum edge length (length of the longest wire in any layout of a network on a chip).

As can be seen, a fair degree of similarity appears between the software metrics and the VLSI measures. Whereas the development of software metrics was primarily driven by reliability concerns, the driving force behind the VLSI measures was interest in determining lower bounds on the difficulty of computation. Under appropriate mappings*, the VLSI measures therefore provide some degree of insight into software design complexity on an absolute rather than relative scale[3]. However, both software and VLSI metrics permit evaluation of computational structure, and useful trades in critical resources to be made early in the design phase. As the use of high-level languages[4] for designing chips increases, combined with the possibility of larger integration and bigger chips, the asymptotic properties of these metrics will become indistinguishable.

---

* For example, if procedure p has fan-in m (the number of local flows into p plus the number of data structures from which p retrieves information) and fan-out n (the number of local flows emanating from p plus the number data structures which p updates), the number of distinct information paths connecting p to its environment is mn. A collection of procedures p forms a program P computing a function f. If f is computed by a VLSI circuit with bisection-width w and area A, then

$$\left[\sum_p (mn)\right]^2 = \Omega(w^2) = A$$

and every lower bound technique for the bisection-width of a graph is also a lower bound technique for the software metric $\left[\sum_p (mn)\right]^2$ and layout area A.

If the total amount of information that must flow across the bisection boundary during the entire computation is I, then the time taken must satisfy

$T > I/w$. Thus a measure which arises naturally within this model is $AT^2 = \Omega(I^2)$. If h is an upper bound on the total information transferred among procedures of P, then every lower bound for the VLSI measure of difficulty AT^2 of f is also a lower bound for the interconnectivity metric

$$\left[h \sum_p (mn)\right]^2$$

for computing f.

References

[1]   G. Baudet, On the Area Required by VLSI Circuits, Conf. VLSI Systems And Computations, CMU Oct. 1981.

[2]   L.A. Belady and C.J. Evangelisti, System Partitioning and Its Measure, J. of Systems and Software 2, 23-29 (1981).

[3]   R. Cuykendall, Relations Among Software Interconnectivity Metrics, VLSI Lower Bounds, and Programming Primitives, Computing Memorandum No. 490, Jet Propulsion Laboratory, California Institute of Technology (Sept. 13, 1982).

[4]   C.A.R. Hoare, Communicating Sequential Processes, Comm ACM   V.21, No. 8 (1978) pp 666-677.

[5]   D. Kafura and S. Henry, Software Quality Metrics Based on Interconnectivity, J. Systems and Software 2, 121-131 (1981).

[6]   F.T. Leighton, New Lower Bound Techniques for VLSI, FOCS Nov. 1981.

[7]   R. Lipton and R. Sedgewick, Lower Bounds for VLSI, Proc. 13th Ann. ACM. Symp. Theory of Computing, May 1981 pp 300-307.

A LANGUAGE-INDEPENDENT ENVIRONMENT
FOR SOFTWARE ENGINEERING

Walt Scacchi
Dept. of Computer Science
University of Southern California
Los Angeles, CA 90089-0782

INTRODUCTION

Software engineering environments consist of an ensemble of software tools and a methodology organizing their use for producing large software systems. Together with the recent support for the development of programming support environments for the ADA programming language, a major research and development activity is emerging throughout the software industry aimed at producing such environments.

We are interested in investigating three questions:

- what environment is most appropriate for developing and maintaining large software systems

- what methodology is most appropriate for developing and maintaining large software systems

- how to manage the life cycle of large software systems with the package of resources available in an environment and structured according to a methodology.

Our research is directed at identifying how to answer these questions within various complex organizational settings [Scacchi, Gasser, Gerson and Strauss, 1982]. We expect that no single development methodology or engineering environment can ultimately be considered the best. Rather, we assume that the use of such methodologies and environments is situated within a variety of slowly changing workflows among participants in particular settings [Kling and Scacchi, 1978; Scacchi and Kling, 1978; Scacchi, 1982]. Therefore, what we seek is to discover the kinds of answers that reflect the actions that participants follow in life cycling well-engineered software products [Scacchi, 1982].

There is much apparent excitement about the potential of personal computing workstations and their impact on the software development process. But how these systems will be adopted, implemented, used, and evolved in real-world organizations is unclear and complicated [cf. Kling and Scacchi, 1978, 1980, 1982]. It is clear, however, that a web of technological, social, and economic arrangements into which such systems are fitted are likely to impact the software development process. Personal workstations are expected to not only change the work habits of individual programmers, but also the structure and operation of software and VLSI system development organizations [Gutz, Wasserman, and Spier, 1981; CAS, 1981]. Similarly, the adoption and implementation of the accompanying methodologies and software environments are likely to affect how software will be produced with personal workstations. But how will people determine what methodology or environment is appropriate for developing different kinds of software systems? What technological and organizational resources will they consume in producing software under these new arrangements? Will software production costs be greater or less than expected? Will the benefits be less or of a different kind than expected? How will people define and act toward the costs, benefits, organizational impacts of software development on personal workstations? Answers to these questions require observational studies of people at work with personal computing workstations.

We want to understand what accounts for variation in the way people develop software life cycle products and how the local software engineering infrastructure aids or constrains their production [Scacchi, 1982].

OUR APPROACH

We propose a two-track research approach. The first focuses on conducting comparative case studies of the use of existing distributed workstations for developing software products. Such systems are likely to be in use in other software development organizations (be they academic or industrial sites) and in VLSI system development organizations. These are field studies directed at observing and identifying patterns of interaction between participants, their systems, and the organizations where they perform their work. The field studies serve to better inform our understanding and implementation of a software engineering system on personal workstations. Such case studies require systematic research designs to ensure the comparability and generalizability of the findings [cf. Scacchi, 1981;, van den Bosch, et al., 1982].

The second research track is directed at implementing a language-independent environment for software engineering. This effort further pursues our prototype implementation of such an environment on a large time-sharing computer system. This environment is intended to serve as testbed for experimenting with and evaluating the practice of software development as performed in other organizational settings. We envision these two research thrusts as concurrent rather than sequential investigations. However, to be consistent with the focus of the VLSI and Software Engineering Workshop, we limit the remainder of this digest to briefly elaborate the software engineering environment (SEE) we have developed.

A SOFTWARE ENGINEERING ENVIRONMENT

During spring 1981, we undertook the development of a full-scale software engineering environment. This prototype environment was implemented by a project team of 53 graduate students, based on a design specified by the author. More than 25000 lines of PASCAL were implemented, debugged, and tested while 2500 pages of system requirements, specification, design, implementation, testing, user manuals, and maintenance analysis (ie, "documentation") were produced in 8-10 weeks (averaging 12 hours per person per week) time. All of the development work and supporting life cycle documentation were developed on a DECsystem-10 here at USC.

During the fall 1981, 26 undergraduate students participated in redeveloping some of the software components while also adding others. During the spring 1982, another 45 graduate students participated in redeveloping the existing components in the environment while adding others deemed necessary. The current environment now represents over 40K lines of working subsystem code and over 4K pages of supporting development analysis and user documentation. Further, the production environment and development analysis are designed to be portable and reusable. We are now beginning to move these products to a VAX-VMS and VAX-UNIX facility, and then to a network of UNIX-based personal computing workstations.

The SEE represents a collection of automated software tools useful for supporting the development and evolution of software applications throughout their life cycle [Katz, Scacchi, and Subrahmanyam, 1982]. The tools we choose are, in general, language-independent; they can be specialized to a system description language of the engineer's choice so long as it can be defined within the tool's language range. This means it is possible to generate a software tool set that can process alternative language-based descriptions for a particular software application. Similarly, it is possible to specialize a set of tools to support a single language, as well as to specialize a family of tools supporting each software description occurring at each system life cycle stage.

Each of the tools contained in the SEE contains a set of its own life cycle engineering documents. This means each has requirements analysis, system specifications, architectural design, detailed design, implementation (in PASCAL unless otherwise noted), test plans and results, user manual, and maintenance guide. All of these life cycle documents exist in machine-readable form. Further, most contain, or are based upon, language-based descriptions: for example, documents on architectural design of a component are organized around the use of a "architectural design" (aka module interconnection) language.

Environment Tools

The SEE consists of the following automated tools we have developed through a complete life cycle:

Syntax-directed editor A syntax-directed editor is an editor that utilizes knowledge of the language being edited to construct syntactically-valid descriptions. A user constructs code fragments in the language the tool has been specialized for through individual editting commands. The program outputs a either an attributed syntax tree and a processable software description. If this description is a system "specification" stated in a specification language, then the description can serve as input to a functional simulator or other system prototyping facility [cf. Davis, 1982]. If this description is "code", then it can be compiled without syntax errors. If a code generator is interfaced to this tool, this would produce a simple programming environment [Feiler and Medina-Mora, 1981; Teitleman and Reps, 1981]. Two implementations exist: one targeted for TOPS-10 and interfaced to the translator writing system; the other targeted to VAX-VMS and interfaced to the flow analyzer.

Translator Writing System A translator writing system takes in a formal definition of a language's syntax (as does the syntax-directed editor), and generates a set of parsing tables and driver for that language. Also known as a parser generator and compiler-compiler. This is a LR(1) translator based on the Pager algorithm [Wetherell and Shannon, 1981]. Its implementation is targeted to TOPS-10.

Module Interconnection Language compiler This "compiler" processes a description expressed in a module interconnection language It supports "programming in the large" [DeRemer and Kron, 1975; Tichy, 1979]. That is, system modules are the compilation unit, and the compiler checks the consistency of module interfaces and calling sequences. It also can be extended to perform type-checking between separately-compiled modules. Its output is a system configuration (or architectural design) that can be interfaced with a link/loader, as well as a graphic display. The MIL81 implementation is targeted to TOPS-10, while the MIL82 is interfaced to the testing system and targeted to a Honeywell series 6 computer.

Relational Data Base Management System This is a single user, data base management system that supports the relational data model. This RDBMS can be used in either stand-alone or interfaced to other tools to provide file services and data base management. This RDBMS supports a "Query-By-Example" user-friendly screen interface [Zloof, 1977,1981]. Current implementations exist for TOPS-10 and TOPS-20. A procedural query language based on SEQUEL-2, which can be embedded within application programs, is planned and being implemented [Chamberlain, et al. 1976]. In addition, a separate "Office Procedures By Example" interface is implemented for TOPS-10 which interfaces the QBE system to electronic mail and other office automation facilities [Zloof, 1981, 1982].

Configuration Management System This is a special-purpose file management system that serves as a file system interfaced to a link/loader. As a file system, it can manage the configuration of files across different versions, independent of file contents. Thus, it can be used to maintain configuration control over system life cycle documentation as well as source/executable code [Feldman, 1979; Huff, 1981; Oldhoeft, Ralph, and Tindall, 1981]. The current implementation is targeted to TOPS-10.

Testing System This testing system takes in source code in a language defined externally. It then generates assertions about the code's behavior (ie, static analysis) which are added to the code locally, then check them against the program's execution (dynamic analysis) selected test data inputs [Osterweil, Brown, and Stucki, 1978; Voges, et al. 1980]. The test data itself can be generated through either extension to the syntax-directed editor, or through the testing system itself. Current implementations are targeted to TOPS-10 and Honeywell series 6 computers.

Flow Analyzer The flow analyzer processes the attributed syntax tree that describes the code's behavior. It checks for the completeness of the code (control-flow analysis) as well as the consistency (data-flow analysis) of the use of variables [Brown and Johnson, 1978; Munchnick and Jones, 1981; Osterweil, 1981]. This tool is usually interfaced to the syntax-directed editor or translator writer system to provide its input, and it can also be interfaced to either a code generator (as an optimizer) or a RDBMS for traceability analysis or program explanation. Current implementations are targeted to VAX-VMS.

Shell Processor The shell processor provides the same functionality as does the one operating in the UNIX programmers workbench. It allows users to build shells containing programs that can communicate via "pipes" [Ash, 1981; Kernighan and Mashey, 1979]. The current implementation is targeted to TOPS-10.

Macro-Preprocessor The macro-preprocessor supports a user's desire to extend the surface form of a language-based software description [Comer, 1979]. It also supports a conditional compilation facility. The current implementation is targeted to TOPS-10, although a redeveloped version coded in FORTRAN for VAX-VMS is under development.

Source-to-Source translators These translators support a simple rewriting of the surface form of PASCAL into ADA and FORTRAN into ADA [Albretch, et al 1980; Freak, 1981]. The current

implementations are not comprehensive source-to-source translators (ie, compilers). The PASADA translator is targeted for TOPS-10, while the FORTADA translator is targeted to VAX-VMS.

General-Purpose User Interface This "front-end" allows a user to run multiple programs/tools through a dual-window display manager and command processor [Bass and Bunker, 1981; Carlson and Metz, 1980]. It maintains a log file of all valid user commands. It also provides capabilities similar to the Shell processor. The current implementation is targeted to a VAX-VMS system.

Program Documentation Facility This facility supports the definition of program or documentation "templates". The data base routines interpreting these templates help to maintain the configuration of structured system development documents. A report generation subsystem allows any subset of template elements to be selected and assembled into a formatted document. The current PL/1 implementation is targeted to large IBM-type of systems.

The ability to configure an integrated set of these tools to support different software life cycle activities is under user control and facilitated through common interfaces [Katz, Scacchi, and Subrahmanyam, 1982]. Most of the tools are table-driven and can be specialized to support different language-based descriptions of software through augmented-BNF grammar initialization procedures. This means that software life cycle products such as system requirements, specifications, architectural designs (system configuration), detailed designs, testing plans, executable program code, and structured diagrams can be processed by the tools in this environment as long as they can be stated in a language described via an augmented-BNF formalism. In fact, we produced processable descriptions for the products documenting each tool in the environment. These kind of software descriptions are therefore amenable to automated manipulation to support system maintenance and evolution.

Finally, it is fair to say that none of these tools exist in a "production-quality" form. However, sufficient development progress has been made on each so that further development or evolution would bring them to this form. Thus, each tool varies in distance from this goal. However, the tools are sufficiently developed to support research and pedagogical investigations into software engineering (and now "silicon engineering") environments [Katz, Scacchi, and Subrahmanyam, 1982].

FUTURE DIRECTIONS

What we would like to do next is to move the current environment onto a network of personal workstations to (a) continue its refinement and evolution toward production-quality, (b) experiment with the use of the environment in developing and maintaining large software systems (including itself), (c) extend the environment to support VLSI circuit development applications, (d) examine the use of this (or similar) environment in different organizational settings, and (e) continue to train people in the development and use of environments for software engineering. In particular, we believe that extending our SEE to support VLSI system life cycle engineering is within reach if we employ hardware (silicon) descriptions languages such as:

- ISPS/RTL to describe system functional specifications [Director, et al 1981]

- Intermediate Circuit Description Language [Weste and Ackland, 1981] or Linked Module Abstraction [Conway, Stefik et al, 1982] to describe system architectural design (ie, circuit "floor plan")

- Design Procedure Language [Batali, et al, 1981] or ALI [Lipton, Sedgewick and Valdes, 1981] to describe the detailed circuit design layout implemented in CIF formats, and

- verification of circuit functions and layout based on use of syntax-directed environments employing these languages for circuit development [cf. Foster, 1981].

In total, this agenda forms the basis of our current research plans.

REFERENCES

Albretch, P., P. Garrison, S. Graham, R. Hyerle, P. Ip, B. Kreig-Bruckner; "Source-to-Source Translation: Ada to Pascal and Pascal to Ada," SIGPLAN Notices, Vol. 15(11), 183-193, (1980)

Ash, W.; "MXEC: Parallel Processing with an Advanced Macro Facility," Communications ACM, Vol. 24(8), pp. 502-510, (1981)

Bass, L. and R. Bunker; "A Generalized User Interface for Applications Programs," Communications ACM, Vol. 24(12), pp. 796-800, (1981)

Batali, J., N. Mayle, H. Schrobe, G. Sussman, and D. Weise; "The DPL/Daedalus Design Environment," in VLSI 81, Academic Press, New York, pp. 183-192, (1981)

van den Bosch, F., J. Ellis, P. Freeman, L. Johnson, C. McClure, D. Robinson, W. Scacchi, B. Scheff, A. von Staa, and L. Tripp; "Evaluation of Software Development Life Cycle Methodlogy Implementation," Software Engineering Notes, Vol. 7(1), pp. 45-61, (Jan. 1982)

Brown, J.C. and D.B. Johnson; "FAST: A Second Generation Program Analysis System," Proceedings 3rd International Conference on Software Engineering, pp. 200-206, (1978)

Carlson, E.D. and W. Metz; "A Design for Table-Driven Display Generation and Management Systems," IBM report RJ2770(35325), IBM Research Laboratory, San Jose, CA (1980)

CAS;"Special Issue on Computer-Aided Design for VLSI," IEEE Transactions on Circuits and Systems, Vol., CAS-28(7), (1981)

Chamberlain, D., M. Astrahan, K. Eswaran, P. Griffiths, R. Lorie, J. Mehl, P. Riesner, and B. Wade; "SEQUEL-2: A Unified Approach to Data Definition, Manipulation, and Control," IBM J. Research and Development, Vol. 20(6), pp. 560-575, (1976)

Comer, D.; "MAP: A Pascal Macro Preprocessor for Large Program Development," Software - Practice and Experience, Vol. 9, pp. 203-209, (1979)

Davis, A.M.; "The Design of a Family of Application-Oriented Requirements Languages," Computer, Vol. 15(5), pp. 21-28, (1982)

DeRemer, F. and H. Kron; "Programming-in-the-Large vs. Programming-in-the-Small," IEEE Transactions Soft. Engr., Vol. SE-2(2), pp. 80-86, (1976)

Director, S., A. Parker, D. Siewiorek, D. Thomas; "A Design Methodology and Computer Aids for Digital VLSI Systems," IEEE Trans. Circuits and Systems, Vol. CAS-28(7), pp. 634-644, (1981)

Feiler, P.H. and R. Medina-Mora; "An Incremental Programming Environment," IEEE Trans. Soft. Engr., Vol. SE-7(5), pp. 472-482, (1981)

Feldman, S.I.; "MAKE: A Program For Maintaining Computer Programs," Software - Practice and Experience, Vol. 9(4), pp. 255-265, (1979)

Foster, M.; "Syntax-Directed Verification of Circuit Functions," in H.T. Kung, B. Sproull and G. Steele (eds.), VLSI Systems and Computations, Computer Science Press, Rockville, MD (1981)

Freak, R.; "A FORTRAN to PASCAL Translator," Software - Practice and Experience, Vol. 11, pp. 717-732, (1981)

Gutz, S., A.I. Wasserman and M.J. Spier; "Personal Development Systems for the Professional Programmer," Computer, Vol. 14(4), pp. 45-53, (1981)

Huff, K.E.; "A Database Model for Effective Configuration Management in the Programming Environment," Proceedings 5th International Conference on Software Engineering, pp. 54-62, (1981)

Katz, R., W. Scacchi, and P. Subrahmanyam; "Development Environments for VLSI and Software Engineering," VLSI and Software Engineering Workshop, (in these proceedings), (1982)

Kernighan, B.W. and J.R. Mashey; "The UNIX Programming Environment," Software - Practice and Experience, Vol. 9, pp. 1-15, (1979)

Kling, R. and W. Scacchi; "What will the Actual Impacts of a Common Higher Order Programing Language Be?" Proceedings of the Irvine Workshop on Alternatives for the Environment, Certification, and Control of the DoD Common High Order Language, University of California, Irvine, (June 20-22, 1978)

Kling, R. and W. Scacchi; "Assumptions about the Social and Technical Character of Production Programming Environments," Proceedings of the Irvine Workshop on Alternatives for the Environment, Certification, and Control of the DoD Common High Order Language, University of California, Irvine, (June 20-22, 1978)

Kling, R. and W. Scacchi; "Computing as Social Action: The Social Dynamics of Computing in Complex Organizations," in M. Yovits (ed.), Advances in Computers, New York, Academic Press, Vol. 19, pp.249-327, (1980)

Kling, R. and W. Scacchi; "The Web of Computing," in M. Yovits (ed.), Advances in Computers, Vol. 21, Academic Press, New York, pp. 3-87, (1982)

Lipton, R., R. Sedgewick, and J. Valdes; "Programming Aspects of VLSI" Proceedings 1981 Principles of Programming Languages Conference, ACM, pp.92-101, (1981)

Munchnick, S.S. and N.D. Jones; Program Flow Analysis, Prentice-Hall, New York, (1981)

Oldehoeft, R.R., W.D. Ralph, and M.H. Tindall; "An Interactive Manager for PASCAL Software," Software - Practice and Experience, Vol. 11, pp. 867-873, (1981)

Osterweil, L.; "Using Data Flow Tools in Software Engineering," in S. Munchnick and N. Jones (ed.), Program Flow Analysis, pp. 237-263, (1981)

Osterweil, L.J., J.R. Brown, and L.G. Stucki; "ASSET: A Lifecycle Verification and Visibility System," Proceedings COMPSAC 1978, pp. 30-35, (1978)

Scacchi, W. and R. Kling; "DoD's Common Programming Language Effort: The Work Environments of Embedded System Development," Proceedings of the Irvine Workshop on Alternatives for the Environment, Certification, and Control of the DoD Common High Order Language, University of California, Irvine, (June 20-22, 1978)

Scacchi, W.; The Process of Innovation in Computing: A Study of the Social Dynamics of Computing, Ph.D. dissertation, Dept. of Information and Computer Science, University of California, Irvine, CA (1981)

Scacchi, W.; "Managing Software Engineering Projects: A Social Analysis," (submitted for publication), (May, 1982).

Scacchi,W., L. Gasser, E. Gerson, and A. Strauss; "Understanding the Development, Use, and Evolution of Advanced Computing Technologies: A Research Proposal," technical report, Computer Science department, University of Southern California, Los Angeles, CA (1982)

Teitlebaum, T. and T. Reps; "The Cornell Program Synthesizer: A Syntax-Directed Programming Environment," Communications ACM, Vol. 24(9), pp. 563-573, (1981)

Tichy, W.; "Software Development Control Based on Module Interconnection," 4th. International Conference on Software Engineering, pp. 29-41, (1979)

Voges, U., et al.; "SADAT--An Automated Testing Tool," IEEE Transactions on Software Engineering, Vol. SE-6(3), pp. 286-290, (1980)

Weste, N. and B. Ackland; "A Pragmatic Approach to Topological Symbolic IC Design," in VLSI 81, Academic Press, New York, pp. 117-129, (1981)

Wetherell, C. and A. Shannon; "LR--Automatic Parser Generator and LR(1) Parser," IEEE Trans. Soft. Engr., Vol. SE-7(3), pp. 274-278, (1981)

Zloof, M.M.; "Query-By-Example: A Data Base Language," IBM Systems Journal, Vol. 16(4), pp. 324-323, (1977)

Zloof, M.M.; "QBE/OBE: A Language for Office and Business

Zloof, M.M.; "QBE/OBE: A Language for Office and Business Automation," Computer, Vol. 14(5), pp. 13-32, (1981)

Zloof, M.M.; "Office-By-Example: A Business Language that Unifies Data and Word Processing and Electronic Mail," IBM System Journal, Vol. 21(3), pp. 272-304, (1982)

VLSI Design and Engineering

INTELLIGENT ASSISTANCE FOR TOP DOWN DESIGN OF VLSI CIRCUITS

G. SAUCIER - G. SERRERO

Laboratory IMAG BP 68 - 38402 St Martin d'Hères (FRANCE)

ABSTRACT

A classification of software top down design tools for VLSI is proposed according to their decision, validation and synthesis power. This leads to the more general concept of intelligent assistants for the design of VLSI circuits. Examples of such tools, especially for the architectural and layout design, developed at the University of Grenoble are presented.

I - TOP DOWN DESIGN AND TOP DOWN DESIGN TOOLS

1.1. It is very common to emphasize the necessity of a safe top down design methodology based on stepwise refinements for VLSI circuits [1][2][3][4]. The goal is to minimize the probability of design errors by efficient validation between two successive levels.

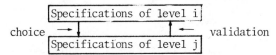

Most of the research efforts deal with the definition of the tools allowing to go safely and efficiently from a level i to the following one, j. These tools may be classified according to several criteria, the most common of which being :

(i) The original and the destination levels

Examples : most of the tools go from logic specifications to layout specifications (symbolic or micron levels). The M.I.T. Lincoln lab's tool [5] starts from a NOR gate network to get a structured layout (Weinberger layout). The University of Grenoble developed OASIS [6] processing a logical description through a symbolic layout, to obtain a micron level layout (TRADUC).

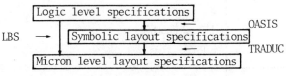

Some tools also exist, that produce directly the layout from architectural specifications. As an example, Siskind's tool [7] starts from a bit-slice architecture to get the layout.

Very few tools start from specifications of higher level, except the case of control automata whose synthesis is brought out from a functional description to the layout.

(ii) The number of considered solutions between two levels

. It may not exist any design choice or decision between level i and level j
. There is an "enumerable" set of solution for the design choices between levels i and j
. The set of solutions is considered as "non enumerable".

(iii) The selection of the solutions (design choices) can be made or guided by the top down design tool or left to the designer.

(iv) The top down design tool is a synthesis tool or not

In the first case, the top down design tool generates or constructs the solution of lower level.

(v) The top down design tool is a validation tool or not

According to a solution, the top down design tool is able to claim the conformity of the solution with respect to the origin level specifications.

1.2. Simulation, compilers and intelligent assistant

Simulators, extractors, checkers are commonly used as validation tools (to validate level j according to the previous levels). They are widely used at the structural levels. Formal proof techniques, symbolic execution tools are used for higher levels.

"Silicon compiler" is a term commonly used to designate a sequence of tools leading to the silicon mask level. The successive tools are usually automatic production ones.

Tools which help to optimize the design choices especially if they are non enumerable, and which generate the solution by construction (automatic layout tools) show features very different compared to the previous ones. They look rather like intelligent assistants and can be designed as expert systems.

More generally, a good notion for top down design tools would be the notion of intelligent assistant. These tools can be classified according to their ability to provide one or several of the following functions :

. validation functions : they validate specifications of level j according to the previous level.
. Selection functions : they guide the choice of the solutions of level j.
. Creative functions : the create the solution of level j.

1.3. A top down design and intelligent assistant

A safe top down design methodology has been developed at the University of Grenoble to several test cases. Its steps are sketched on the following figure. Its extension to top down design tools or intelligent assistants, will be discussed in the following section.

It will more precisely concern two steps : the first one, the CADOC system, that leads to the architectural specifications, starting from the algorithmic ones, and the second one, the SEPIAC system, that generates topological specifications from the logic ones.

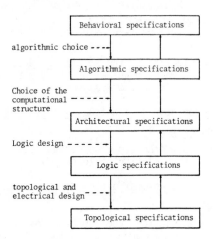

II - FROM ALGORITHMIC SPECIFICATIONS TO THE ARCHITECTURE OF THE CIRCUIT : THE CADOC SYSTEM [7]

Starting from algorithmic specifications, the designer has to choose the operators, the data path, the controllers to be laid out on the silicon. At this point, the questions are : is it reasonable to look for a powerful intelligent assistant generating an architectural solution ? Or is it more adequate to let the designer propose some architectures and to look for an intelligent assistant who, at least, validates and compares the solutions with respect to several constraints (timing, chip area, etc..) and, at most, guides his choices ? In the CADOC system developed at Grenoble both solutions are explored.

2.1. Automatic production or very creative assistant

Let us suppose that the designer has expressed his solution in terms of a high level language (PASCAL,

ALGOL, ADA, et..). The functions of the circuit are expressed in terms of primitives like (For i:=1 to n do .., while.. do.., if.. then.. eslse, etc.) A hierarchical approach is then feasible. To each algorithmic primitive is associated a list of hardware structures or hardware solutions. To each microoperations is associated a hardware "box". If this microoperation is not a hardware "primitive", an algorithmic description is treated again.

Example 1
Primitive "For i:=1 to N do OP(X) ;" if N is fixed five solutions can be exhibited for the designer·

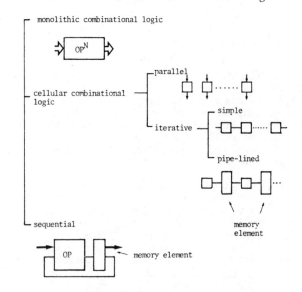

Example 2
Primitive "while X<L do X:= OP(X) ;" three solutions can be exhibited for the designer·

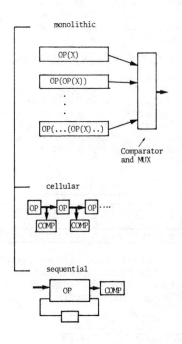

It is obvious that a set of structures may be proposed automatically. If a non combinational solution is chosen for a primitive, a portion of the hardware is dedicated to the control functions (counter, memory elements, ...). If two non combinational primitives are embedded, the designer can either choose two hierarchical levels of control or one centralized control level. In the second case, only one controller controls all the sequencing of the operators. At a first step, one can imagine that no minimization is made on the number of operators, memory elements, and at a second step, compaction of the circuit can be done by minimizing the necessary resources. Comparative evaluation can be performed (area, time,..) for each primitive and for the whole circuit. All the solutions generated by such an approach have been studied for a square root extractor circuit as a testcase at the University of Grenoble [8].

2.2. CADOC system : an intelligent "consultant" assistant

CADOC system under development at the University of Grenoble suggests to let the designer propose himself the architectural choices and to provide him with a flexible validation tool to check if his solution meets the higher levels requirements. CADOC describes a circuit as a set of coordinated functional resources. A resource is described by the transformation of its input data (mathematical or algorithmic description) and its timing protocol. Specification of the timing protocol means the description, with respect to time reference of the way this resource can be activated and validated. Some uncertainty can be described in the use of this resource. Composition of resources, and hierarchization of resources are described. A resource can be declared as a controller type resource whose function is to synchronize lower level resources. Graphical representation is provided to the user and looks like "Petri net" representation (coordination graph of controllers and activation graphs for the elementary resources). CADOC is therefore a functional specification and a simulation tool. It can deal with more and more precise timing information and can afford timing validation especially for parallel VLSI. The designer will verify for instance if, with an adder working within a given time range or given by his precise control timing diagrams, his whole circuit will work.

CADOC is accompanied by an automatic synthesis tool for the controller. CADOC can therefore be seen like a "semi-intelligent" assistant which stores and validates architectural choices through their functional description. Chip area and first floor plan evaluation can help to choose the good solution. We shall see that a more active and more intelligent assistant has been chosen as a solution for the layout problem in the next section.

III - AUTOMATIC LAYOUT AND EXPERT SYSTEM

3.1. Previous experience

Several automatic layout systems have developed in the University of Grenoble at the IMAG Laboratory for several technologies.

✱ OASIS [6] is an automatic layout system for N-MOS circuits using the MD-MOS [9] and an original symbolic representation. The different placement procedures (constructive placement and iterative improvement) and routing procedures are parametrized so that the designer might define the placement constraints, choose or modify the cost vector to be optimized, select the set of the exchanges to be carried out (for iterative improvement). The designer modifies the cost vector and the exchanges domain interactively according to the layout result. This flexibility in the use of the placement routines increases notably the algorithm efficiency. Many cells made of about 60 gates (i.e. 300 transistors) have been processed through OASIS. They were laid out in less than one hour whereas many days are necessary if manually performed. The area increase varies from 10 to 30 % when compared to an entirely manual layout. OASIS has been implemented within CASSIOPEE, a large CAD environment developed by the french telephone company.

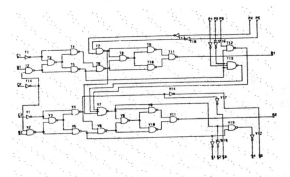

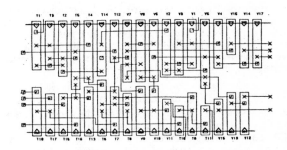

* IACA [10] is an automatic layout system for the ACE family of Uncomitted Logic Arrays showing the structure described in the following figure. The blocks (nodes of four cells) are separated by two metal layers of interconnection channels of fiwed capacity. The blocks placement is performed with the uniformization of the predicitive density of the connections in the channels. The connections are assigned to the channels so that saturation is avoided, length is minimized and the global density of the net is uniformized. The actual routing is performed by a modified "dogleg channel router" [11]. IACA is now working as a part of the DELILA CAD system of the RTC Caen Society.

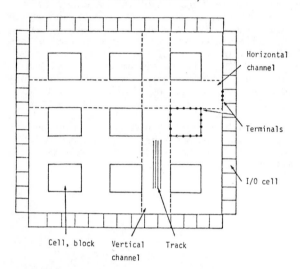

* The authors are currently developing a third automatic layout system for Ferranti's CML-ULA's. This layout procedure is seen like an embedding algorithm of a logic gate network into an array made of elementary cells. Each cell is characterized by its capacity (gate and feed-through capacities). The algorithms assigns the gates and the connections with respect to the resource capacity of the Uncomitted Logic Array.

With regards to this three recent experiences, an universal intelligent assistant for automatic layout seems to be necessary. This assistant must know anything about the experience in the field, and must be able to cope with any technology and future complexity.

3.2. Towards an expert system

The diversity of the tools we have developed leads us to define an organization of an expert system (SEPIAC) whose objectives are to be an intelligent assistant for any type of technologies for both following situations :

(i) for computer aided interactive layout of complex circuits,

(ii) for computer aided design of an automatic layout software package for a given technology.

SEPIAC includes the three classical parts of an expert system : the knowledge base, the cognitive system and the interface.

The *knowledge base* consists of a set of parameterized layout primitives or elementary layout procedures (constructive placement primitives, placement improvement primitives, single layer routing primitives, channel routing procedures,..). The parameters define the element of the network to be laid out as well as the target structure, the cost vector to be optimized.

The *cognitive system* helps the designer to construct and to optimize a solution. It can propose layout strategies which link (forward search and backtracking) the layout primitives or elementary procedures. It provides a complexity evaluation (it can warn the designer about the processing time it needs), a memory requirement evaluation before the execution of the primitives. It can suggest cost vectors to optimize the layout.

IV - CONCLUSION AND GENERAL STRUCTURE OF A VLSI CAD ENVIRONMENT

The recent years have seen a very rapid evolution in the area of VLSI CAD tools. The most common tools have been, till now, the verification tools (simulator , checker, etc..). Faced with too complex circuits, more sophisticated tools are now necessary. The first idea was to look for automatic top down synthesis tools (silicon compiler). These tools are given not flexible enough with regards to the design decisions. A more general approach leads to the notion of intelligent assistant which is in fact made of several sub-assistants, specialized in different areas (layout, test and diagnosis). Indeed, their experience or knowledge base will be distinct. The general block diagram of a CAD VLSI environment will then be the following one.

BIBLIOGRAPHY

[1] R.W. DUTTON, *Standford overview in VLSI research*, IEEE trans. on C.A.S., July 1981.

[2] A.R. NEWTON et al, *Design aids for VLSI : the Berkeley perspective*, IEEE trans. on C.A.S., July 1981.

[3] J. ALLEN and P. PENFIELD, *VLSI design automation activities at MIT*, IEEE trans. on C.A.S., July 1981.

[4] S. TRIMBERGER et al, *A structured design methodology and associate software tools*, IEEE trans. on C.A.S., July 1981.

[5] J.R. SOUTHARD et al, *LBS - Lincoln Boolean Synthesizer*, technical Report 622, MIT Lincoln Laboratory (1982).

[6] R. MALLADI and G. SERRERO, *OASIS - An automatic design tool for symbolic layout*, ESSCIRC 1981, Friburg (RFA).

[7] G. SAUCIER et al, *CADOC - Un outil de spécification et de simulation fonctionnelle*, Grant Report DAII n° 82 35 064 00 790 75 00, March 1983.

[8] G. MAUPETIT, *Top down design of a circuit : square root extractor*, Research Report 302, IMAG Laboratory, May 1982.

[9] J. MAJOS and J.C. LARDY, *The multidrain MOS transistor*, ESSCIRC 1978, Amsterdam.

[10] A. BELLON, G. DUPENLOUP and G. SAUCIER, *Routing algorithms for cell-arrays in IACA system,* to be published.

[11] D.N. DEUTSCH, *A dogleg channel router*, Design Automation Conference 1976, San Francisco, California.

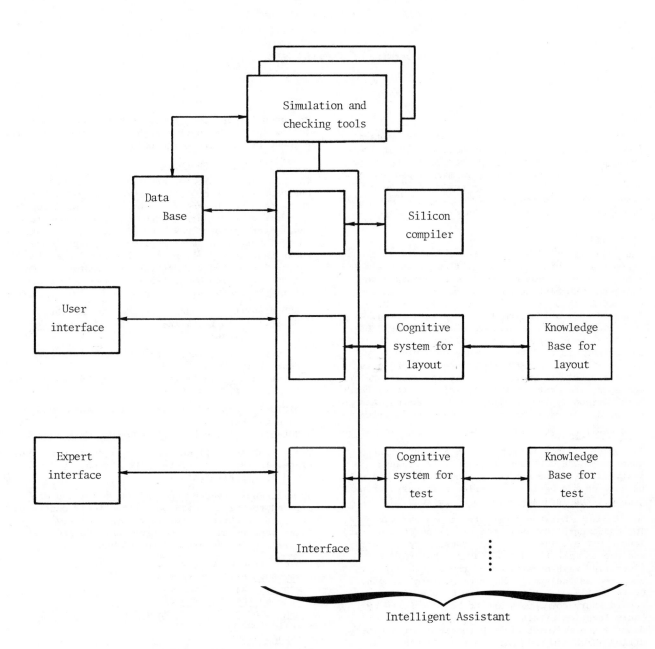

Hierarchical Modular Description of VLSI Systems

Franz J. Rammig

University of Dortmund, Abt. Inf. I

Abstract

In this paper it is shown how the design process from functional specification down to the discrete transistor level can be supported by a single CHDL named CAP/DSDL. The language is based upon a single semantical model: Timed Interpreted Petri Nets. Language concepts that are general or dedicated to specific levels of abstraction will be discussed.

1. Introduction

Language design always has been an important aspect of software engineering. After first rather simple approaches of Hardware Description Languages now relatively sophisticated languages have been developed in this field. They are more or less influenced by results from software engineering. As an example of such a language may serve CAP/DSDL which has been designed and implemented by the author and his collegues and has been used very successfully by SIEMENS AG in numerous projects since a couple of years. The language makes use of concepts like Abstract Data Types, Monitors, Petri Nets, Strong Typing, Structured Programming, Assertions, all originating from software engineering.

2. General Remarks

This paper is not intended to be a general introduction to CAP/DSDL but only specific language features are to be discussed. However, as this will be done on the basis of examples some basic principles of the language have to be introduced.

We deffer between constants, types and variables. The basic data object is the bitstring of arbitrary length $bit(n)$. The basic type constructors (array and record) are taken from PASCAL. Records are identified with bitstrings of the length which is computed as the sum of their components' length. Consequently each bitstring can be viewed as a record where components are to be identified by their location within the record, e.g. $a.(7:0)$ denotes the leftmost eight bitposition of a bitstring which has to be at least of length 8. As operators we have logical ones (PL/1 notation) &, |, ¬, ¬&, ¬|, ⊕ (exor), ¬⊕ which also may serve as reduction operators, relational ones =, <>, <, >, <=, >=, arithmetic ones +, -, *, /, mod and concatenation || . Relational and arithmetic operators interpret arguments as two's complement integers as long as they are not enclosed in bars; e.g. + means a two's complement addition while |+| means an

unsigned integer one. Expression and assignments follow the PASCAL syntax with an "if then else" and a "case of" construct included.

3. Algorithmic constructs

The basic principle for behavioural descriptions in CAP/DSDL is that of Timed Interpreted Petri Nets. These nets may be specified by a designer directly or indirectly via structured concurrent constructs. The latter approach has some limitations but has to be favoured whenever applicable. Experience has shown that nearly all practical control structures can be formulated with structured constructs. For convenience three basic types of transitions are offered by CAP/DSDL:

- AND transition (usual Petri Net transition)
  Notation: on $(in_1 \& in_2 \& ... \& in_k)$ do mark $(out_1 \& ... \& out_n)$

- OR transition (place with backward conflict in usual Petri Nets)
  Notation: on $(in_1 | in_2 | ... | in_k)$ do mark $(out_1 \& ... \& out_n)$

- DECIDER transition (place with foreward conflict in usual Petri Nets)
  Notation: on (in_1) do if cond then mark (out_1)

The variables involved are special objects of type place. In their declaration their capacity may be bound to a finite value.

By well known reasons special net templates are offered to the user via own syntactical constructs. If a user restricts himself to use exclusively these constructs it is ensured that the resulting net is 1-safe, deadlock free and reusable.

The constructs offered are the following:
- seqbegin $S_1; ...; S_n$ end
- conbegin $S_1; ...; S_n$ end
- if cond then S_1 else S_2
- case cond of $S_1; ...; S_n$ end
- while cond do S
- repeat S until cond
- for a := i seqto f do S
- for a := i conto f do S

The seqbegin construct corresponds to the begin construct in PASCAL (with same differences that shall not be discussed here) while conbegin means the concurrent execution of the included statements S_1 to S_n. The complete statement will be terminated when all included statements are terminated. In the for statements we allow only constants as bounds. The reason becomes clear immediately if one considers the conto alternative. This means that all statements S_a (S with the proper index value) have to be executed concurrently. It should be noted that we don't have a loop in this case.

The advantage of the structered approach can be seen immediately with the aid of a small example: The control structure to be described may consist of two concurrent branches, where one may be a loop. Such a control structure is reflected by the following CAP net:

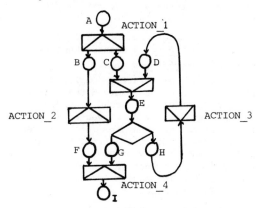

This net may be described directly:

```
var A, B, C, D, E, F, G, H, I : place;
net
    on(A) do mark(B & C)  ACTION_1;
    on(B) do mark(F)      ACTION_2;
    on(C | D) do mark (E);
    on(E) do if CO then mark(H)
                 else mark(G);
    on(H) do mark(D)      ACTION_3;
    on(F & G) do mark(I)  ACTION_4
end
```

Much easier to understand is the following description of the same net:

```
seqbegin
    ACTION_1
    conbegin
        ACTION_2;
        while CO do ACTION_3
    end
    ACTION_4
end
```

It should be noted, that up to now no timing concept has been introduced, neither via delay operators nor via clocking. These possibilities will be discussed later. In an early design phase the CAP/DSDL user can be liberated from these implementation details. He only has to specify a concurrent causality structure as indicated in the above example.

4. Data driven control

In the above section the basic ideas of CAP/DSDL in order to support the algorithmic RT level have been presented. To describe the flow of data through the combinational parts of a hardware system an other concept is offered by CAP/DSDL.

A data variable that is declared with attribute explicit (or without attribute) is interpreted as device with storing capability (e.g. register). It gets a new value if and only if it is ordered to do so explicitely by the control structure. (An assignment statement is executed due to the control structure.)

Variables that are declared with the attribute implicit are interpreted as non storing devices (e.g. wires, outputs of combinational logic). They are allowed to stand on the left side of exactly one assignment statement. It gets a new value implicitly whenever one of the variables within the expression on the right hand side of this assignment statement gets a new value. These statements have to be grouped in a special section of a CAP/ DSDL description.

It should be noted that this is a single assignment rule for implicit variables. In fact, CAP/DSDL descriptions may be restricted completely to implicit variables leading to a functional programming style.

The following small example may give an idea about this capability of CAP/DSDL. It describes a gate level solution of a 16 bit wide RS register:

```
var R, S, Q, NQ : implicit bit(16);
impdef
    Q  := R nor NQ;
    NQ := S nor Q
```

Of course the lexical ordering of the assignment statement within the impdef section of a CAP/DSDL description has no influence on the meaning of the description.

This language feature seems expecially adequate for gate level descriptions of systems or parts of a system within more abstract descriptions. In section 5 it will be shown how the discrete transistor level (switching level) can be covered with the aid of this technique, too. In section 6 we will introduce timing and will show how this concept also offers the framework for the structural (nonprocedural RT level).

5. MOS specific features

MOS introduces a bidirectional point of view into the language. This level of abstraction is covered using the techniques of data driven control. CAP/ DSDL offers three builtin procedures for this purpose:

pullup(A) and pulldown(A) with an obvious meaning and transfer (techn, gate, left, right) in order to model transistors. The parameter "techn" controls whether a nMOS or pMOS transistor is described. The parameter "gate" is a unidirectional input while the parameters "left" and "right" are bidirectional ones. Variables that are mentioned as such bidirectional parameters of transistors are interpreted as seven valued ones (per bit) with the meaning: low impedance one and zero, medium impedance one and zero (pulled up or down), high impedance one and zero (charged and then isolated), uncharged. Uncertain values are described by the subset of this set that contains exactly the possible values (so we are working with a 128 valued logic for this purpose). Such variables are restricted on implicit variables. In their declaration a charge decay time can be given. So dynamic storage elements and dynamic logic can be described precisely.

As an example may serve the description of a dynamic nMOS RAM cell:

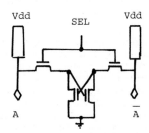

```
const nMOS = "1";
var A, NOTA, SEL, LEFTMEM, RIGHTMEM: implicit bit
                                     decay(1ØØ);
impdef
    pullup(A);
    pullup(NOTA);
    transfer(nMOS, SEL, A, LEFTMEM);
    transfer(nMOS, SEL, NOTA, RIGHTMEM);
    transfer(nMOS, RIGHTMEM, LEFTMEM, "Ø");
    transfer(nMOS, LEFTMEM, RIGHTMEM, "Ø");
```

6. Timing and clocked systems

Timing in hardware design usually is expressed either by counting clock signals or by the real time behaviour of the envolved actions. In many causes both methods are used and therefore both are supported by CAP/DSDL.

Every assignment statement and every empty statement may include delay specification. The actual delay time may be specified via an arbitrary expression of type integer (bit(n)). So it is very easy to specify delays that are dependent on actual values, states, histories. Intervals of uncertaincy may be specified, too. By delay is meant in CAP/DSDL the period between the evaluation of the arguments of an assignment and the assignment of the resulting value. Within a sequential control structure the statement following the delayed one is initiated after the specified delay time.

Example

```
var R, S : bit; Q, NQ : implicit bit
impdef
     Q := NQ var R delay (up 5 to 7, down 4 to 6);
    NQ := Q var S delay (up 6 to 8, down 3 to 6);
seqbegin
    R || S := "Ø1" delay (if S = "1" then 1Ø else 5Ø);
    R || S := "1Ø" delay (5Ø)
end
```

In order to describe clocked systems in CAP/DSDL first a clock generator has to be defined. This is usually be done via an implicit variable which is defined as its own complement with a proper delay.

Example

```
CLK := not CLK delay (up 5, down 45)
```

Now the edges or the levels of such clock signals may be interrogated by the at resp. when prefix. Any statement may be prefixed with these constructs. If this is done within the explicitly given control part this logical control specification remains

unchanged. Only concerning timing it is synchronized with the clock signals.

Example: (see section 3, now synchronized with clock signals)

```
seqbegin
    at SLOWCLOCK do ACTION_1
    conbegin
        at SLOWCLOCK do ACTION_2;
        while CO do at FASTCLOCK do ACTION_3;
    end
    at SLOWCLOCK do ACTION_4
end
```

It should be noted that the at prefix is not restricted to clock like signals.

When used within the impdef part of a CAP/DSDL description the at resp. when statements constitute the main control structure.

The prefix may initiate arbitrarily complex operations in this case. It can be observed that now we have a data driven control of "second order". The isolated control part now may be viewed as a data driven system while the whole system may be viewed as a system triggered by control events. But this is the classical point of view of RT languages. In order to clarify the difference we usually call it structural RT level to distinguish it from the algorithmic RT level described in section 3.

Example: (usual finite state machine, LAMDA and SIGMA are user functions)

```
var CLK: implicit bit; STATE: bit(2); X,Y: bit(16);
impdef
    CLK := not CLK delay(50);
    at STATE = "ØØ" & CLK do conbegin
                                Y    := LAMDA(X,STATE);
                                STATE:= SIGMA(s,STATE)
                              end;
    at STATE = "Ø1" & CLK do ...
    .
    .
    .
```

7. Modularization concepts

CAP/DSDL offers one basic concept for modularization: The procedure. But this single concept has been designed in such a way that the concepts of
- Modules
- Abstract Data Types
- Generic Objects
- Monitors (management of critical sections)
  can be subsumed.

First of all a CAP procedure is a procedure in the sense of PASCAL. It constitutes a context with the scope of variables rule from PASCAL. The only difference is that all variables are static ones (own in ALGOL terms). I.e. they maintain their value after the deactivation of a procedure and may be used after a reactivation of it. There may be a formal parameter list. Here in, out and inout parameters are distinguished. Parameter passing is always by reference. However if an actual parameter is a constant or an expression that consists of more symbols than a single variable, the value of the actual parameter is first copied to a dummy variable that is passed by reference (i.e. de facto parameter passing by value).

Like in PACAL also a function procedure is offered using the PASCAL notation.

There is a strong type checking of the formal parameters against the actual ones. This is true also in the case of separately compiled procedures and functions. A separately compiled procedure or function has to be declared like an internal one with the difference that its body is substituted by the keyword external. So the type checking between the formal parameters and the actual ones can be carried out by the compiler while the check whether the declared procedure is compatible with the referenced one is done by the binder.

Example

```
procedure PROCEDURE_DEMO;
    var F,G : bit(16); H : bit(17);
    procedure SWAP (inout A,B : bit(16));
        conbegin
            A ‖ B := B ‖ A
        end;
    function SUM (in A,B : bit(16)): bit(17);
        external
    conbegin
        SWAP(F,G);
        H := SUM(F, F & G)
    end.
```

A procedure or function must contain an explicit control part (i.e. a compound statement). It remains active after a activation until this control part terminates. If a never ending control part is used and implicit variables are used as parameters then procedure are well suited to modularize combinational circuits, too. The "calling" in the main program then has the meaning of a "power on".

Example

```
procedure FULLADD (in A,B,C,CIN : implicit bit;
                   out S, COUT  : implicit bit);
    const NEVER = "∅";
    procedure MAJORITY (in A,B,C : implicit bit;
                        out D    : implicit bit);
        impdef
            D := A & B | A & C | B & C ;
        seqbegin at NEVER do end;
    procedure PARITY (in A,B,C   : implicit bit;
                      out D      : implicit bit);
        impdef
            D := (exor) (A ‖ B ‖ C);
        seqbegin at NEVER do
    conbegin
        MAJORITY (A,B,CIN,S);
        PARITY   (A,B,CIN,COUT)
    end.
```

Of course in reality nobody would modularize such a small circuit.

Every procedure or function includes a monitor mechanism. I.e. at one point of time a procedure or function can be active only once. All additional activations are delayed until the actually served one has terminated. Concurrent activations are served according to a fixed priority scheme by an arbiter. By this feature a procedure or function in CAP/DSDL models a once existing piece of hardware that may be requested concurrently but is allocated to requests in a time shared manner.

Procedures and functions may not be not declared as single objects but also as types of objects. Instances of such a type may be generated in the usual

way using var declarations. It should be noted that a module concept is introduced into CAP/DSDL simply by overcoming a PASCAL restriction (absence of type: procedure). The module concept offers its benefits especially in regular structures. Presently such regular structures became more and more popular in VLSI design. Another important feature of CAP/DSDL modules (i.e. procedure types) is that they may be generic. In the type definition there may be a list of formal attributes standing for constants or types. By these attributes any objects within the procedure type definition may be attributed. In the var declaration these formal attributes have to be substituted by actual attributes.

Example:

```
procedure GENERIC_AND_MODULE_DEMO;
    type ADDER =
        procedure ADDER [WORD: type]
                        (in A,B: WORD, CIN : bit;
                         out SUM: WORD; COUT : bit);
            conbegin
                COUT ‖ SUM:=if CIN then("∅"‖ A)+("∅"‖B)+1
                                   else("∅"‖ A)+("∅"‖ B)
            end
    var ALU_ADDER : ADDER [bit(16)];
        ADR_ADDER : ADDER [bit(24)]
    .
    :
```

Generic objects are especially suited to be stored in a data base for multiple use   various designs. Structures like systolic arrays are supported by arrays of objects of type procedure.

A last (but especially powerful) concept that is included in CAP/DSDL procedures is that of Abstract Data Types (ADT). An abstract data type is defined as a carrier data structure (that may be an ADT as well) and a set of operations on this carrier. A user of an ADT has access to the data structure only via the offered operations. This idea is followed by export procedures in CAP/DSDL. An export procedure has no own control part (so it is the only exception to the rule started above). It consists of a local data structure (carrier data structure) and a set of procedures and functions that manipulate this carrier structure (offered operations on the carrier structure). These procedures and functions have to be listed in an export list in front of the procedure head. So just following the usual scope of variables the internal carrier data structure is hidden from the outside while the operations on it are made available (well controlled encapsulation technique). As an example may serve a very simple ALU that is able to carry out the operations add, sub, and, or, not. The result is stored into an internal register in any case. This register can be read by an additional operation read. This internal register is one bit longer than the used wordlength. In the leftmost bit the carry is stored in. In the example a generic solution is demonstrated.

```
type ALU = export (ADD,SUB,AND,OR,NOT,READ);
                   procedure ALU [WORDLENGTH: const];
    type WORD = bit (WORDLENGTH);
    var  BUFFER : bit (SORDLENGTH + 1)
    procedure ADD (in A,B : WORD; in CI : bit);
        external;
    procedure SUB (in A,B : WORD; in CI : bit);
```

```
        external;
    procedure AND (in A,B : WORD);
        external;
    procedure OR  (in A,B : WORD);
        external;
    procedure NOT (in A : WORD);
        external;
    function READ : bit (WORDLENGTH + 1);
        external;
    end;
 .
 .
 .
var ADR_ALU : ALU[16];
    DATA_ALU : ALU[24];
 .
 .
 .
conbegin
 .
 .
 .
  DATA_ALU.ADD(REG[1], REG[O], REG[2].(O));
 .
 .
 .
  ADR := ADR_ALU.READ.(23 : O);
 .
 .
 .
end
```

The concept of ADT's is especially valuable at the
level of functional specification. Here typically a
set of ADT's is specified from which operations are
requested. This closes our discourse through the
levels of abstraction. It has been shown by which
language features different levels of abstraction
are supported. These levels are (top down):
- Functional Specification
- Algorithmic Register Transfer Level
- Structural Register Transfer Level
- Gate Level
- Discrete Transistor Level.

Though being so powerful the language is easy to
learn and to use as it is based on very few principles. This is reflected by a very good acceptance
both in industry and at our university. It turned
out that neither design engineers (in most cases
with EE background) nor CS students had problems to
understand these few principles (i.e. PASCAL + Timed
Interpreted Petri Nets + Data Driven Control).

8. Additional language features

Two main features of the language have not yet been
discussed: Assertions and Interrupts.

CAP/DSDL allows the user to formulate per procedure
or function a set of assertions that must hold
throughout the procedure's execution. It should be
noted that there is a strict distinction between
hardware description and description of certain
features of this hardware (requested behaviour).
Assertions are used either for formal verification
purposes or in the case of simulation as tool that
liberates the designer from the neccessity to read
same inches of print out. Instead of looking for
somewhat in the simulation result he formulates as
assertion for what he looks and let the simulator
do this job.

Interrupts are very suitable for the specification
of highly event oriented systems like telecommuni-
cations or industrial control systems. The interrupt concept of CAP/DSDL allows to specify interrupt
systems where concurrent algorithms are partially
interrupted or that partially wait for interrupts.

While assertions are a levelindependent tool, the
interrupt constructs are mainly designed in order
to support the functional specification level.

9. References

We avoided references in the text but prefer a re-
ferencing annex.

A language reference manual for CAP/DSDL is given by
/RA1/. As an introduction into the theory of Petri
Nets may serve /PE1/. The idea of classical RT lan-
guages is explained very well in /DD1/. For monitors
see /HO1/ while /LS1/ may serve as reference to ADT's.
The RAM cell of section 5 can be found in /CL1/.
Modularization techniques are presented in /WI1/.

/CL1/: W. A. Clarke: "From electron mobility to
        logical structure: A view of integrated
        circuits". ACM Comp.Surv.Vol.12# 3 (1980)

/DD1/: J. Duley, D. Dietmeyer:
        "A digital systems design language (DDL)"
        IEEE ToC, Vol. C17, # 9 (1968)

/HO1/: C. A. R. Hoare:
        "Monitors: An operating system structuring
        concept"
        CACM, Vol. 17, # 1O (1979)

/LS1/: B.Liskov, A.Snyder, R.Atkinson, C.Schaffert:
        "Abstraction mechanisms in CLU"
        CACM, Col. 2O, # 8 (1977)

/PE1/: J. L. Peterson:
        "Petri Nets"
        ACM Comp. Surveys, Vol. 9 (1977)

/RA1/: F. J. Rammig:
        "CAP/DSDL, preliminary language reference
        Manual"
        Univ. Dortmund, Abt. Inf., Techn. Report
        # 129 (1982)

/WI1/: N. Wirth:
        "Modula: A language for modular multipro-
        gramming"
        Softw. pract. Exper. Vol. 7, # 1 (1977)

A Decision-Based Framework for Understanding Hardware Compilers

Jack Mostow

USC Information Sciences Institute
4676 Admiralty Way, Marina del Rey, CA. 90291[*]

Abstract

This paper argues that "hardware compilers" (broadly construed as systems that automate any part of the VLSI design process) should be classified not simply by their input and output languages, but by how they treat the various kinds of decisions made in the design process. It examines several aspects of decision-making and attempts to classify some silicon compiler efforts with respect to this framework.

1. Introduction

There now exist, in various stages of implementation, a growing number of systems that automate one or more of the decisions made in the course of developing a VLSI design. These systems are often described in terms of their input and output languages. This is informative but provides an inadequate characterization of what the systems actually do. For example, some systems that accept a seemingly abstract input language, such as Ada, LISP, or Algol68, predefine a fixed hardware implementation of the high-level constructs, so that the user must encode in the input relatively low-level decisions about timing and sharing, that one might not ordinarily consider bound at such a high level of representation.

Thus in order accurately to characterize what a hardware compiler does and does not do, one should classify it according to how it treats the decisions made at successive design levels.

This paper begins by exploring several aspects of design decisions:

- selecting a design method versus applying it (Section 2)

- division of labor: who decides what, and when (Section 3)

- scope: global versus individual decisions (Section 4)

- search: exploring the design space (Section 5)

- level: form(s) of description involved (Section 6)

[*]This research was supported by DARPA Contract MDA-903-81-C-0335. The views and conclusions contained in this document should not be interpreted as representing the official policies, either expressed or implied, of the Defense Advanced Research Projects Agency or the US Government. This paper has benefited from comments by David Wile and Neil Goldman and discussion with Matthew Morgenstern. The errors, of course, are my own.

Section 7 enumerates the decisions made in the design process. Section 8 places several current research efforts in this conceptual framework based on how they treat each of these decisions. The paper concludes with a snapshot of the field summarizing this framework-based survey.

2. What is a Design Decision?

In order to classify hardware compilers by the decisions they make, we must first of all define what we mean by a design decision. We view a design decision as *selecting a particular transformation from a set of alternatives* [1]. The transformation *elaborates* a design description at some level of abstraction into a more detailed description at a lower level, or in the case of some optimizing transformations, to an improved design at the same level. In short, selection consists of choosing a transformation, while elaboration consists of applying it.

The fact that such a selection is being made is obscured in a design system that knows only one elaboration for some construct. In such cases, the selection has effectively been made *a priori* by the system designer. (More on this in Section 3.)

Notice that this definition of design decision deliberately excludes *design process* decisions such as the choice of what graphics editor to use, except insofar as these constrain the resulting design to a particular style. Such decisions affect the route leading to the final design, while we are only interested here in decisions about the design itself. In the rest of this paper, the term "design decision" is used in the restricted sense of transforming a design description.

3. Division of Labor

A major reason for distinguishing between the selection and elaboration aspects of a decision is that in many systems they are separated. For example, in the transformational approach proposed in [2], an expert VLSI designer steers the design process by selecting a series of transformations, and the machine performs the tedious manipulation required to carry them out. This division of labor is based on the difference in skills needed for the two tasks. In VLSI, selecting the right transformation typically depends on understanding the eventual impact of alternative choices at much lower levels; a decision at the algorithm level may have major consequences on area and power costs at the layout level. In contrast, applying the transformation involves only adjacent levels but requires the sort of detailed manipulation vulnerable to error when performed by hand.

To understand what a hardware compiler does and does not do, we can ask two questions for each decision made in the design process:

- *Who* makes the decision -- the compiler (C) or the user (U)?

- *When* is the decision made -- before (<), during (=), or after (>) compile time?

Of course, the answers for the selection and elaboration aspects of a given decision need not be the same.

These questions provide a convenient framework for classifying the various ways a decision can be treated. One can summarize how some system treats a decision by specifying who performs the selection and who performs the elaboration, and when. For example, the combination U = ,C = characterizes the transformational paradigm: at runtime, the user selects a transformation and the compiler applies it. The combination C <,C = characterizes a system with a fixed implementation strategy: the transformation has effectively been selected *a priori* and is applied at runtime.

Not all combinations make sense. If one accepts the constraints that selection precedes elaboration, that C > is nonsensical (the compiler cannot decide anything after it's finished), and that C < makes sense for selection but not for elaboration (the compiler cannot do any actual processing before compile time), one obtains 13 possible combinations for selection and elaboration. Of these, several seem rather silly, e.g., C = ,U = -- at runtime, the compiler tells the user which transformation to use, and the user applies it by hand. The more common combinations are summarized in Table 3-1 and listed below:

1. *A priori* (C <,C =): The compiler may make the decision *a priori*, e.g., by using a fixed target architecture.

2. *Encode in input* (U <,U <): The user may be required to make and implement the decision in the input to the compiler.

3. *Annotate input* (U <,C =): The user includes advice in the input about which transformation to use, and the system implements it. For example, in the systolic design system described in [3], the user annotates each loop in an abstract algorithm with advice about whether to implement it in parallel, as a pipeline, or by sequentially reusing the same processor, and the system implements it accordingly. Similarly, [4] describes how a program in a high-level language can be refined into an efficient implementation by attaching to each abstract data object an annotation indicating the representation chosen to implement it (*selection*), and later replacing operations on the abstract object with their concrete implementations (*elaboration*). Thus not only can selection and elaboration be performed by two different agents (user and machine), but the mechanism of annotation allows the two processes to be separated in time as well.

4. *Automatic* (C = ,C =): The compiler may make the decision on its own at compile time.

5. *Manual* (U = ,U =): The user makes the decision at runtime and performs the manipulation (e.g., editing steps) required to carry it out; the system may provide support in the form of error-checking and other feedback.

6. *Interactive* (U = ,C =): The compiler may interact with the user at compile time to make the decision cooperatively. Such compile-time intervention may be needed if the decision is at too low a level to be stated in the input language. The interactive transformational paradigm is included in this category.

7. *Annotate output* (C = ,U >): The compiler may make a decision without actually carrying it out, but include an annotation in its output that records the decision. The user must either follow this advice manually or pass it to a lower-level translator. For example, [5] describes an expert system for data structure design that analyzes the abstract data structures used in a given task and outputs recommendations for how each one should be implemented, without actually doing it.

8. *Undecided* (U >,U >): A compiler that doesn't go all the way down to the layout level leaves certain decisions undecided in its output.

Table 3-1: Decision Modes: Who decides, and when?

Who selects: When:	Compiler	User
Before	*A priori* (C <,C =)	*Encode in input* (U <,U =) *Annotate input* (U <,C =)
During	*Automatic* (C = ,C =) *Annotate output* (C = ,U >)	*Interactive* (U = ,C =) *Manual* (U = ,U =)
After		*Undecided* (U >,U >)

The answer to the question "how is decision D treated in system S?" need not correspond to a single entry in the table. In a given system, a particular decision may be split between user and compiler, or spread out over time. For example, a compiler that narrows down the alternatives to a small set, lets the user select one, and then carries it out, is somewhere between "automatic" (C = ,C =) and "interactive" (U = ,C =). Similarly, a compiler that accepts advice and then automatically selects among several ways of implementing it would fall somewhere between "annotate input" (U <,C =) and "automatic" (C = ,C =).

Other attributes important for classifying hardware compilers include:

- *Domain*: What class of specifications can the compiler implement?

- *Range*: What kinds of designs does the compiler produce -- micro-processors, custom VLSI, processor arrays, communication protocols?

- *Performance*: How good are the designs?

These attributes can be related to the decision-based framework. Domain is determined by the set of constructs a compiler knows how to implement, and range by its repertoire of implementation methods: does it know only one valid implementation for each construct in its source language, or several? Thus range is related to the distinction between decisions made *a priori* and decisions made at runtime: if the compiler knows only one valid implementation for a construct, the choice of how to implement it is fixed *a priori*, while if it knows several, the choice is made by the compiler at runtime, or else by the user (either at runtime or in the form of advice). Of course, range is relative, depending on how many implementations the compiler can generate. For example, the systolic design system described in [6] only knows about certain scheduling schemes, and can be regarded as *a priori* restricting its designs to this set.

The performance of a compiler is affected both by the extent of its range of possible implementations, and by the amount of context it takes into account when selecting among them. Does it always choose the same default implementation for a given construct, or does it choose according to how the construct is used? For example, a hardware compiler that implements every multiplication as a full multiplier will produce a less efficient design than one that recognizes multiplication by two as a special case and implements it as a shift, which in turn is dominated by a compiler that performs global analysis to choose the best implementation for each multiplication.

Thus while Table 3-1 presents a simplified picture, it provides a useful conceptual framework for thinking about the sort of questions discussed above.

4. "Stylistic" versus "Specific" Decisions

It is useful to distinguish two classes of design decisions based on how early they can be made and how much they affect.

A "*global*" or "*stylistic*" decision can be made before the design is elaborated down to the level at which it takes effect, since it does not refer to details specific to the design being developed. Such decisions are often made quite early in the design process so as to constrain subsequent decisions, and can even determine what notation is used to describe the design. Examples of style decisions include the selection of a target architecture, the choice between synchronous and asynchronous control, and the decision to use Programmed Logic Arrays. In fact, all *a priori* decisions fall in this class, since a decision that is fixed in a compiler cannot refer to the details of a design.

In contrast, a "*local*" or "*individual*" or "*specific*" decision refers to particulars of the design description it transforms. For example, allocating logic terms to specific rows of a PLA is a set of local decisions, and cannot be described without referring to those terms. Thus while a designer may decide early in the design process to use PLAs, the rows and columns cannot be filled in until the design has been refined down to the logic level.

Of course, the distinction between the two types of decisions is somewhat relative, since one can make a stylistic decision confined to a portion of a design, such as deciding to use a PLA for a particular part of a chip. Thus they are ends of a spectrum rather than absolutes. Finally, it should be noted that although the Design Synthesis Working Group agreed on the distinction between the two types of decisions, it disagreed on what to call them. "Global" and "local" have unwanted spatial connotations -- a decision that is "local" in the sense intended here might have spatially widespread effects. On the other hand, the terms "stylistic" and "specific" are rather vague. The reader should feel free to substitute any preferred names for the intended concepts.

5. Exploration in Decision-Making

Design decisions are governed by various metrics and design criteria: how much area will this circuit require? will partitioning the algorithm in this way allow it to be implemented on replicated chips? A VLSI designer cannot always predict the low-level consequences of a high-level decision; it is often necessary to drive the design down to a detailed level and evaluate it there, revising high-level decisions according to the low-level concerns thereby revealed.

A nice example of the role of experimentation in hardware design is provided by the evolution of the Belle chess machine [7]. The initial "machine" was a program. Performance analysis led to implementing program bottlenecks in special-purpose hardware. Subsequent measurement led to a series of changes in both the program and the hardware, with an increasing amount of the program being converted into a hardware implementation. We can expect future complex special-purpose devices to follow similar evolutionary design paths. As the example suggests, a key problem will be what is known in Artificial Intelligence as credit/blame assessment: determining which of several related decisions is responsible for a good or bad implementation.

Like human designers, hardware compilers will need to evaluate design alternatives at various levels as they successively refine high-level specifications into detailed designs. They will use predictive models when possible, but this will not always be feasible. This is especially true in marginal cases where precise cost measurements are needed, such as deciding whether a complex design will fit on a single chip. When predictive models fail, experimentation will be required: intelligent selection among high-level design alternatives will require refining them down to a detailed level in order to evaluate their low-level consequences.

If one tries to draw a hardware-software analogy at this point, one is led to the question, "Where is the experimentation in programming language compilers?" In standard compilers, knowledge about efficient implementation has been factored into techniques like peephole optimization that produce efficient code without searching, i.e., explicitly enumerating and evaluating alternatives. A closer software analog seems to be provided by knowledge-based compilers that make high-level implementation decisions like data structure selection by explicitly evaluating alternatives [8]. One might also argue that program compilation is a relatively local mapping, in the sense that different parts of a program can be compiled independently. In contrast, problems like wire routing can cause complex interactions in laying out different parts of a circuit, typically resolved by experimenting with alternative layouts.

As VLSI design becomes better understood, hardware compilers may come to resemble current software compilers, with experimentation and measurement increasingly replaced by search-free analytic techniques.

6. Levels of Hardware Description

Another aspect of a VLSI design decision is the level(s) of description to which it applies. The following list of levels is sequential in that each level is an elaboration of the previous level:

1. *Requirements analysis*: An informal (natural language) description of what the device is supposed to accomplish.

2. *Specification of behavior and performance*: A formal description of the device's functionality and constraints on the resources for providing it.

3. *Abstract algorithm*: A data-flow-like description of the operations used to perform the computation, without specifying how they will be realized in hardware, which operations will share the same hardware, or the order in which they will be performed (except as implied by data dependencies).

4. *Computation structure*: A partitioning of the algorithm into abstract modules allocated to hardware, firmware, or software.

5. *Functional-level circuit*: A structure consisting of computational components and their interconnections.

6. *Elementary circuit*: A topological description at the logic, gate, or electrical level, depending on the design methodology.

7. *Layout*: A complete geometric chip description. Intermediate levels like flexible geometries are also used.

8. *Chip*: A physical piece of hardware, realized in a particular fabrication technology.

7. List of VLSI Design Decisions

Many design decisions are made in the course of developing a VLSI design. These decisions are listed below, ordered by the levels of description to which they apply. This is not necessarily the order in which they are made: low-level style decisions are often made very early (predictively) in the design process, and constrain subsequent higher-level decisions. For example, the choice of fabrication technology will among other things limit how complex a circuit can fit on one chip, which will in turn influence how an abstract computational structure is partitioned onto multiple chips. The Working Group did not always agree on a name for each decision, and the reader may prefer other names to those used below.

1. SPECIFY BEHAVIOR. Given a requirements analysis, develop a formal specification of functionality that satisfies the requirements.

2. DEVELOP ALGORITHM. Transform the specification into an executable algorithm by deciding how (by what operations) to realize the specified behavior.

3. PARTITION INTO ABSTRACT MODULES. Allocate operations to virtual components. Decide about sharing and multiplexing.

4. LEVEL OF INTERPRETATION. Allocate operations among hardware, firmware, and software.

5. SPLIT INTO CHIPS. Choose between bit-slice, multiple chip types, etc. Assign abstract ports to physical pins.

6. ALLOCATE TO FUNCTIONAL UNITS. Decide which hardware component will compute each operation.

7. TIMING. Decide when each operation will be performed.

8. COMMUNICATION PROTOCOLS. Decide what conventions will be used to pass data and control signals. This is a style decision.

9. CONTROL STYLE. Choose between central vs. distributed, synchronous vs. asynchronous control styles. If synchronous, choose 2-phase vs. n-phase clocking. Choose array style (PLA, Weinburger, etc.) vs. random logic.

10. CONTROL MECHANISMS. If n-phase clock, allocate operations to phases. If PLA, allocate logic terms to rows.

11. INTERCONNECTION STYLE. Select a bus discipline.

12. BUS STRUCTURE. Decide which data paths will be shared and which will be private.

13. LOGIC DESIGN. Translate functional-level circuit into logic equations.

14. CIRCUIT FAMILY. Choose register types (tri-state, master-slave, etc.). This is typically a global style decision.

15. LAYOUT STYLE. Choose planar vs. high-rise, grid (e.g., gate array) vs. free form.

16. SPECIFIC LAYOUT. Decide where to place components and where to route wires between them.

17. FABRICATION TECHNOLOGY. Choose among bipolar, CMOS, NMOS, etc.

8. Classification of Several Projects

This section attempts to classify several existing or proposed systems with respect to how they treat some of the decisions listed in Section 7. Although the list is by no means complete, and the characterization of the various systems doubtless suffers from incompleteness and inaccuracy, the main point of this section is to demonstrate the value of the decision-based framework for understanding how different efforts fit into the overall field, and clarifying the state and progress of the field. Capitalized keywords in parentheses, e.g. (SPECIFY), refer to the decisions listed in Section 7. The projects are roughly ordered by the levels of design they emphasize.

8.1. GIST

The GIST project at ISI is not hardware-specific, but is included here because it addresses the development of formal high-level behavioral specifications, i.e., in which the algorithm is not yet fixed (SPECIFY). It includes tools for paraphrasing a specification in English [9] and executing it symbolically [10]. This helps catch specification errors, i.e., discrepancies between the formal specification and the human specifier's actual intent. There are also algorithm development tools for transforming a specification into an efficient program [11] (ALGORITHM). The overall project is in the development stage.

8.2. King's transformations

Richard King, at Kestrel Institute, is developing general transformations for mapping high-level specifications into systolic designs.

The user provides an initial formal specification of the problem to be computed (SPECIFY).

Various rules are then used to map the specification into an algorithm (ALGORITHM), decompose it into communicating computations (PARTITION), assign processors to data elements (ALLOCATION), and determine the communication paths between them (BUS).

The timing of the processors is then determined based on data dependencies (TIMING).

Two of the key transformations are *virtualization*, which unrolls a processor array into a data flow graph of operations by adding a time dimension, and its inverse, *aggregation*, which collapses such a graph by combining operations performed at different times into a single processor. Interesting designs can be derived by unrolling along one axis and collapsing along another. For example, unrolling a 2-dimensional processor array into a cube and then collapsing it along a 45 degree axis produces the hexagonal configuration one sees when one looks at a cube from one of its vertices. This has been used to re-derive, interactively, the hexagonal-mesh matrix multiplier described in [13].

8.3. SYS

The SYS program [3] accepts an abstract algorithm expressed in terms of FOR loops and begin-end blocks, together with a bit of implementation advice, and produces a systolic functional-level circuit. (Systolic circuits are regular arrays of replicated, locally connected elements computing in parallel; for a good introduction to systolic design, see [14].)

The user is responsible for developing an algorithm (ALGORITHM) in the highly regular form suited to systolic implementation, i.e., nested loops without complex conditionality, whose primitive actions are executable in a single time step.

SYS assumes that the entire algorithm is to be implemented in hardware (HW/FW/SW).

SYS allocates operations to functional units and times at runtime (ALLOCATION, TIMING), guided by the advice, which specifies for each loop whether to implement it as a serially re-used single unit, an array of replicated units, or a pipeline.

SYS assumes a synchronous control scheme (CONTROL STYLE), but does not at present design control mechanisms capable of making a functional unit do different things at different time steps; in particular, it does not yet handle the problems of preloading data and unloading results.

SYS designs the communication scheme between functional units (BUS) and specifies what each unit does at each time step (TIMING), but leaves logic design and lower level issues (LOGIC, ...) undecided.

SYS produces efficient systolic designs at this level, and has been used to re-derive several published systolic designs, including polynomial evaluation, matrix multiplication and triangularization, and convolution.

8.4. TRANSFORM

The TRANSFORM project [2] is concerned with transforming an abstract algorithm into a functional-level circuit. Circuits are represented as programs adhering to a restricted form with a direct hardware analog, so the design process is modelled as a series of source-to-source transformations that map the algorithm, encoded as an ordinary program, into the restricted form. Consequently the resulting design could in principle be implemented in a combination of hardware, firmware, and software (HW/FW/SW), although the interpreter would have to be fast enough to avoid problems at the interface.

The algorithm is interactively partitioned into abstract modules (PARTITION) and allocated to functional units (ALLOCATION) and times (TIMING) by means of transformations selected by the user and applied by the program.

A 2-phase clocking scheme (CONTROL STYLE) is assumed *a priori*. The control mechanisms (CONTROL) are designed by transformation rules at runtime if the user is willing to accept a particular control style; otherwise they can be designed interactively by letting the user select which transformations are used.

The data paths between components are made explicit (BUS), but lower-level issues (LAYOUT, ...) are left undecided.

The transformation rules have been used to re-derive the Pixel Planes graphics display chip [15], and many of them have been implemented.

8.5. KBVLSI

The Knowledge-Based VLSI Design Project (KBVLSI) at Xerox PARC and Stanford University is concerned with defining the levels of description in a way that partitions the design concerns addressed at each level [16]. By choosing the levels carefully and defining composition rules at each level, certain classes of bugs can be avoided.

Of most interest here is the LMA ("Linked Module Abstraction") level, which addresses event sequencing concerns (TIMING). An LMA description consists of a hierarchy of abstract modules, composed according to a restricted set of composition operators; the user must partition any task into abstract modules in order to represent it (PARTITION). The composition rules prevent deadlock and data-not-ready errors.

The semantics of the language is defined in terms of a distributed, self-timed control style (CONTROL STYLE), and a specific communication protocol (PROTOCOL), but in fact there is a systematic mapping from an LMA description to a 2-phase clocked design, so the control style must be regarded as being left undecided.

Each abstract module maps into one physical module, so any decisions about sharing must be made by the user and encoded in the input (ALLOCATION).

A higher level called CBA ("Computational Blocks Abstraction") is currently being developed by Chris Tong in his Ph.D. thesis at Stanford. At the CBA level, a hardware device (e.g., a stack) is represented as an abstract data type: a set of operations and data structures, defined by axiomatic specifications. Thus a CBA description reflects a particular partitioning of the task (PARTITION), but can lead to different implementations (ALLOCATION). Tong is building transformations from CBA to LMA; a translator from LMA to lower levels has not yet been built.

8.6. The Utah project

The five-year Utah project has as its goal the transformation of Ada programs into silicon [17] [18]. The principal case study is the conversion of the DoD Internet Protocol, encoded in Ada, into NMOS circuitry.

The partitioning of the protocol into three modules (PARTITION) has been done by hand.

Thus some decisions about sharing (ALLOCATION) are incorporated in the input. In general, abstract modules are represented by Ada packages and tasks; globally accessible objects are disallowed, so the Ada program units map naturally into engines that communicate asynchronously through interfaces corresponding to Ada interfaces. Each program unit is then transformed into a ⟨state machine, environment⟩ pair; this process allocates operations onto primitive functional units (ALLOCATION), and has been applied to several examples using the POPART transformational development system [19].

A private bus structure (BUS STYLE) seems to be assumed, insofar as assignment statements correspond directly to busses [17].

An asynchronous communication protocol (PROTOCOL) is adopted a priori at the module interface level, so that a hardware implementation of a program unit is interchangeable with compiled machine code running on a general-purpose processor, and can be tested as a program unit since it has the same semantics (HW/FW/SW).

The data path for each program unit is derived from the declarations (ALLOCATION), which instantiate generic data abstractions for storage and functional units.

The internal control mechanism of each module is derived from the program unit's control flow (CONTROL), and could be either synchronous or asynchronous, centralized or distributed (CONTROL-STYLE).

The Speed-Independent Control-Unit Design System (SICU) being developed as part of the Utah project assumes a centralized, asynchronous PPL (Path Programmable Logic) array

as a target (CONTROL STYLE, LAYOUT STYLE). PPLs are a variant of Stored Logic Arrays [20]), which resemble PLAs (Programmed Logic Arrays) but fold the AND and OR planes and allow arbitrary memory cells to be placed anywhere within the array.

SICU automatically compiles state machine descriptions into integrated circuit composite layouts for control-units (CONTROL, LAYOUT).

8.7. MIT Data Path Generator

The MIT Data Path Generator [21] used in designing the Scheme-81 chip maps Scheme, a dialect of LISP, into a module layout.

A data path architecture with a centralized synchronous controller is assumed a priori as a target (CONTROL STYLE).

A succession of programs map the Scheme input through various levels down to the layout level; presumably some of these decide how to allocate the Scheme operations onto functional units (ALLOCATION) and decide when they will be performed (TIMING).

Some of the layout programs are chip-specific: rather than lay out a circuit by hand, the designer writes a program for laying out that particular circuit (LAYOUT). Layout decisions can then be revised by editing only the relevant parts of the program, rather than by tediously redrawing the layout itself.

8.8. MacPitts

The MacPitts project at Lincoln Labs [22] translates an ISP-like description into CIF code.

The user must partition the task (PARTITION) into parallel processes.

These processes communicate asynchronously (PROTOCOL) but are implemented synchronously and in fact share the same clock.

Each process has its own controller (CONTROL STYLE), implemented as a Weinberger array (LAYOUT STYLE).

The user must also decide what operations each process will perform at each clock cycle (TIMING).

MacPitts is biased towards parallelism, and shares functional units only when the same operator is used in different clock cycles by the same process (ALLOCATION).

A tri-state register discipline (CIRCUIT FAMILY) is assumed a priori.

The target layout is a 2-dimensional array of "organelles" (LAYOUT STYLE); each column is a bit-slice, and each row is a register or functional unit. The MacPitts compiler automatically translates the program into this kind of layout (LAYOUT) for NMOS or CMOS (FABRICATION TECHNOLOGY).

A 6500-transistor 16-bit simplified microprocessor has been compiled, but only small test circuits (4-bit counters and shift registers) have been fabricated [23].

8.9. C-MU Design Automation Project

The C-MU Design Automation project [24], one of the most ambitious design synthesis efforts to date, translates ISP descriptions [25] for processors into various fabrication technologies.

The ISP description is first "decompiled" into a data flow description, to which optimizations are applied (ALGORITHM).

The optimized description is then mapped into a register-transfer level data path (ALLOCATION) and a control engine (TIMING). Allocation is performed by a module binder that maps nodes in the abstract data path to physical modules described in the data base for the chosen fabrication technology. A unique aspect of the CMU-DA system is its ability to generate different design styles depending on general preferences expressed by the user:

- a *distributed* style with duplicated functional units and little sharing (ALLOCATION), and independent paths between registers and operators (BUS-STYLE), with multiplexors for sharing

- a *bus* style with a high degree of sharing (ALLOCATION) and a common bus (BUS STYLE)

- a *pipeline* style with high register and data path usage to sustain constant flow of data (TIMING, BUS STYLE)

Similarly, the controller can be implemented in a microcoded ROM or a PLA (HW/FW/SW, LAYOUT STYLE). For microcode-style control, the system packs micro-operations into microinstructions and designs the microinstruction format and control store.

Using TTL 7400 series SSI/MSI modules as a target (LAYOUT), the system designed a PC board for the PDP-8/E processor with about 30% more chips and gates than the commerical product. With Sandia CMOS Standard Cells as a target (LAYOUT), using the MP2D cell placement and channel router [26], the system designed a Voter chip for fault-tolerant systems that used only 20% more cell area than Sandia Laboratories' hand design. These and other results are described in [27].

8.10. Kelem's thesis

Kelem's system, currently in the design stage, will translate a subset of Algol68 into a layout described in CIF.

The user is responsible for designing the algorithm (ALGORITHM) and partitioning it into program modules (PARTITION).

The system assumes *a priori* that the entire program is to be implemented in hardware (HW/FW/SW).

All decisions about sharing components must be incorporated by the user in the input, since the system compiles all non-recursive procedure calls "in line," i.e., every operator in the input is allocated to a separate functional unit (ALLOCATION).

A distributed self-timed control scheme (CONTROL STYLE) is assumed *a priori*, and all buses are private (BUS STYLE).

8.11. CADOC

Saucier's CADOC system starts at the functional circuit level; the user must design the algorithm (ALGORITHM) and allocate it to functional units (ALLOCATION).

However, each unit can be implemented either in hardware, firmware, or software (HW/FW/SW).

CADOC assumes a target architecture consisting of a centralized controller (CONTROL STYLE) and a data path (BUS STYLE).

CADOC's input language consists of control graphs where a node is a controller state, annotated with the register transfers and control signals for that state, and an arc is a state transition, annotated with the condition under which that transition occurs. A centralized synchronous control scheme (CONTROL STYLE) is assumed *a priori*, but the detailed timing (TIMING) and a preliminary floorplan (LAYOUT) are designed at runtime.

The user can then use tools for data path and controller compilation, automatic placement and routing in NMOS, and automatic layout in ECL cell arrays (LAYOUT).

8.12. McBride's thesis

Dennis McBride's thesis project at Brooklyn Polytechnic Institute mapped ISP into a machine organization at the functional level (ALLOCATION).

The system *a priori* assumed a target consisting of an array of highly functional blocks and a fixed set of possible interconnections between them (LAYOUT STYLE). Each block could be instantiated by any of a fixed kernel set of functional nodes, all of the same data width.

The system allocated the ISP description into hardware (ALLOCATION, LAYOUT) by deciding the functionality of each block.

It solved the routing problem by choosing which interconnections to use (LAYOUT).

8.13. Joyner

Joyner's project at IBM translates register-transfer level descriptions into gate array layouts.

The logic design process (LOGIC) translates such descriptions into target boolean primitives (NANDs and NORs), with simplifying transformations applied at successive levels. The system enforces restrictions on fan-in, fan-out, and combinational path length.

The target is technology-specific (FABRICATION TECHNOLOGY): the 3081 gate array, with 700 NAND gates (LAYOUT STYLE).

The system places gates by allocating array elements, and routes connections along channels between them (LAYOUT). This produces layouts that are far from area-optimal, but are cheap to design and fabricate.

8.14. SLAP

The SLAP system at Brown [28] seeks to compile functional descriptions into layouts. The descriptions consist of boolean equations with feedback, so the user must perform the logic design (LOGIC) and higher-level decisions.

The system represents the equations in a graph, assigns levels to nodes, and inserts delay elements so that each node is one level above its sons; each level is then mapped into a row (LAYOUT). The system has heuristics for improving the layout by reordering row elements.

8.15. Other efforts

A recent survey of silicon compilers can be found in [23], which describes other efforts, including:

- Steve Johnson's project at Bell Labs compiles XI, a dialect of the C language, into chip layouts, and has been used to design a FIFO controller, a floating point adder, and a chess clock.
- Bristle Blocks [29] [30], which assumes a target floor-plan
- The SCULPTOR module (datapath and PLA) generators and interconnect programs, part of Caltech's Silicon Structures Project (SSP)
- Edinburgh University's FIRST (Fast Implementation of Real-time Signal Transforms) system
- Brookhaven National Labs' program for compiling a FORTRAN 77 behavioral specification into a low-level hardware description language [31]

9. Conclusion: A Snapshot of the Field

This paper is not intended as an exhaustive enumeration of silicon compiler projects, and does not present a complete up-to-date description of the projects it does mention. It aims to provide a rudimentary framework that classifies systems according to which decisions they address and which ones they leave to the user. If it leaves the reader with a clearer picture of the field, it has served its purpose.

In that spirit, Table 9-1 gives a simplified snapshot of the field by showing how the main decisions listed in Section 7 are treated in the projects described above. The (S,D) entry in the table tries to characterize how selection and elaboration are handled for decision D in system S, using the notation of Section 3. To avoid cluttering the table, decisions not handled by the system are left blank, whether they must be decided before (U <,U <) or after (U >,U >) compile time.

The table suggests some gaps in the field. For example, the blank entries for CHIP SPLIT indicate that none of the projects listed automates the task of splitting a design into multiple chips. Similarly, the dearth of C= entries under HW/FW/SW indicates that research is needed on machine techniques for choosing whether to implement a given operation in hardware, firmware, or software. The reader may find other such patterns in the table, but should be cautioned that its oracular potential is primarily in the eye of the beholder.

Table 9-1: How is decision D treated in system S?

Decision:	GIST	King	SYS	TRANSFORM	LMA	Utah	MIT	MacPitts	CMU DA	Kelem	CADOC	McBride	Joyner	SLAP
SPECIFY	U=,U=													
ALGORITHM	U=,C=	U=,C=							U<,C=					
PARTITION		U=,C=	U=,C=			C<,C=			C=,C=					
HW/FW/SW		HW	HW	U>,U>	HW	U>,U>	HW	HW	U<,C=	HW	U=,U=	HW		
CHIP SPLIT														
ALLOCATION		U=,C=	U<,C=	U=,C=		U<,C=	U<,C=	C<,C=	C=,C=	C<,C=		U<,C=		
TIMING		C=,C=	U<,C=	U=,C=	U<,C=	U=,C=	U<,C=	U<,C=	C=,C=	C<,C=	C=,C=	U<,C=		
PROTOCOL				C<	C<	C<	C<	C=	C<	C<	C<			
CONTROL				U=,C=	C<,C=	C=,C=	C<,C=	C<,C=	C=,C=	C<,C=	C<,C=	C<,C=		
BUS		U=,C=	C=,C=	U=,C=	U<,C=	C<,C=	C<,C=	C<,C=	U<,C=	C<,C=	C<,C=	C<,C=		
LOGIC					C=,C=	U<,C=	C<,C=	C=,C=	C=,C=	C=,C=		C<,C=	C=,C=	
LAYOUT					C<,C=	U<,C=	C<,C=	C=,C=	C=,C=	C=,C=	C=,C=	C<,C=	C<,C=	C=,C=

The CMU-DA system is a partial exception: it implements a controller either as a PLA (hardware) or in microcode (firmware), depending on user-specified general area-vs.-speed preferences.

References

1. Stefik, M., and Conway, L., "Towards the principled engineering of knowledge," *AI Magazine*, Vol. 3, No. 3, summer 1982, pp. 4-16.

2. Mostow, J., and Balzer, B., "A Program-Transformation Approach to VLSI design," *Proceedings of the 1982 Workshop on Software Engineering and VLSI*, IEEE, 1983.

3. Lam, M., and Mostow, J., "A transformational model of VLSI systolic design," *IFIP 6th International Symposium on Computer Hardware Description Languages and their Applications*, Carnegie-Mellon University, May 1983.

4. Dewar, R. B. K., Grand, A., Liu, S.-C., Schwartz, J. T., and Schonberg, E., "Programming by refinement, as exemplified by the SETL representation sublanguage," *ACM Transactions on Programming Languages and Systems*, Vol. 1, No. 1, July 1979, pp. 27-49.

5. R. Zimmerman, "An advisory system for developing data representations," *IJCAI-7*, Vancouver, BC, 1981, pp. 1030-1036.

6. Lam, M., "Extensions to Lisp for the specification of systolic algorithms", Unpublished working paper.

7. Thompson, K., and Condon, J., *BELLE*, Springer-Verlag, 1982, .

8. E. Kant, "A knowledge-based approach to using efficiency estimation in program synthesis," *IJCAI-6*, Tokyo, Japan, 1979, pp. 457-462.

9. Swartout, B., "GIST English generator," *AAAI82*, American Association for Artificial Intelligence, Pittsburgh, 1982, pp. 404-409.

10. Cohen, D., Swartout, W., and Balzer, R., "Using symbolic execution to characterize behavior," *Proceedings of the Second Software Engineering Symposium: Workshop on Rapid Prototyping*, ACM SIGSOFT, April 1982.

11. London, P. & Feather, M.S., "Implementing specification freedoms," Tech. report RR-81-100, ISI, 4676 Admiralty Way, Marina del Rey, CA 90291, 1981.

12. Mead, C. A., and Conway, L. A., *Introduction to VLSI Systems*, Addison-Wesley, 1980.

13. Kung, H. T., and Leiserson, C. E., "Systolic arrays (for VLSI)," *Sparse Matrix Proceedings 1978*, Duff, I.S., and Stewart, G. W., ed., Society for Industrial and Applied Mathematics, 1979, pp. 256-282, A slightly different version appears in[12], Section 8.3.

14. Kung, H.T., "Let's Design Algorithms for VLSI Systems," *Proc. Conference on Very Large Scale Integration: Architecture, Design, Fabrication*, California Institute of Technology, January 1979, pp. 65-90.

15. Fuchs, H., and Poulton, J., "Pixel-Planes: a VLSI-oriented design for a raster graphics engine," *VLSI Design*, No. Third Quarter, 1981, pp. 20-28.

16. Stefik, M., Bobrow, D., Bell, A., Brown, H., Conway, L., and Tong, C., "The partitioning of concerns in digital system design," Tech. report VLSI-81-3, Xerox Palo Alto Research Centers, December 1981, Presented at the MIT Conference on Advanced Research in VLSI, January 1982.

17. Organick, E., Lindstrom, G., Smith, D. K., Subrahmanyam, P. A., and Carter, T., "Transformation of Ada programs into silicon," Tech. report UTEC-82-020, University of Utah, March 1982.

18. Subrahmanyam, P.A., and Rajopadhye, S., "Automated design of VLSI architectures: some preliminary explorations," Tech. report, Department of Computer Science, University of Utah, 1982.

19. Wile, D. S., "Program developments: formal explanations of implementations," Tech. report RR-82-99, USC/Information Sciences Institute, August 1982.

20. Patil, S. S., and Welch, T., "A programmable logic approach for VLSI," *IEEE Transactions on Computers*, Vol. C-28, September 1979, pp. 594-601.

21. Shrobe, H. W., "The data path generator," *MIT Conference on Advanced Research in VLSI*, 1982.

22. Siskind, J. M., Southard, J. R., and Crouch, K. W., "Generating custom high performance VLSI designs from succinct algorithmic descriptions," *MIT Conference on Advanced Research in VLSI*, 1982.

23. Werner, J., "The silicon compiler: panacea, wishful thinking, or old hat?," *VLSI Design*, September/October 1982, pp. 46-52.

24. Hafer, L. J., and Parker, A. C., "Automated synthesis of digital hardware," *IEEE Transactions on Computers*, Vol. C-31, No. 2, February 1982, .

25. Barbacci, M. R., "Instruction set processor specifications (ISPS): the notation and its applications," *IEEE Transactions on Computers*, Vol. C-30, No. 1, January 1981, pp. 24-40.

26. Feller, A., "Automatic layout of low-cost, quick-turnaround, random-logic custom LSI devices," *Proceedings of the 13th Annual Design Automation Conference*, June 1976.

27. Director, S. W., Parker, A. C., Siewiorek, D. P., and Thomas, D. E., *A design methodology and computer aids for digital VLSI systems*, Department of Computer Science, Carnegie-Mellon University, 1982, .

28. Reiss, S., and Savage, J., "SLAP: a silicon layout program," *Proceedings of the International Circuits and Computers Conference*, New York, NY, 1982, To be presented.

29. Johannsen, D. L., "Bristle blocks: a silicon compiler," *Proceedings of the 16th Design Automation Conference*, 1979.

30. Johannsen, D. L., *Silicon compilation*, PhD dissertation, California Institute of Technology, 1981, Technical Report 4530.

31. Peskin, A. M., "Toward a silicon compiler," *Proceedings of the 1982 Custom Integrated Circuits Conference*, Rochester, NY, 1982.

A Program-Transformation Approach to VLSI Design

Jack Mostow and Bob Balzer

USC Information Sciences Institute
4676 Admiralty Way, Marina del Rey, CA. 90291*

Abstract

Recently we have been applying our experience with transformational software development to the domain of VLSI. For hardware as well as for software, the design process can be modelled as a series of transformations leading from a high-level formal specification to a concrete implementation. Automating such transformations offers a way to improve the correctness of the design process while reducing its cost.

This paper addresses the portion of the design process that converts abstract algorithms into functional-level circuits (i.e., topological descriptions rather than geometric). By defining an isomorphism between such circuits and a highly restricted subset of programs, we are able to apply source-to-source program transformation methodology to the problem of mapping algorithms into circuits. This methodology has been implemented in a system that has successfully rederived much of the design of a published VLSI graphics display processor.

1. Introduction

Continuing advances in VLSI fabrication technology are making the development of correct, efficient VLSI designs a crucial bottleneck in the same way that falling hardware costs have exposed a similar bottleneck in software development. Our research group at ISI has been attacking the latter problem for several years [1], and we believe that the similar character of VLSI design makes it amenable to the same transformational design paradigm we have been using for software. The design process code or layout; we propose to move much of this design process out of the designer's head into the machine where it can be assisted and recorded.

We have focussed on the early phases of the design process, where a formal specification is developed and an algorithm for achieving the specified behavior is developed and (in the case of VLSI) mapped into a functional level circuit. We envision that the design process can be carried the rest of the way to the mask level by "silicon compiler"-like systems being developed elsewhere.

*This research was supported by DARPA Contract MDA-903-81-C-0335. The views and conclusions contained in this document are those of the authors and should not be interpreted as representing the official policies, either expressed or implied, of the Defense Advanced Research Projects Agency or the US Government. We are grateful for intellectual contributions by Monica Lam, patient explanations by Vittal Kini of many hardware issues, and comments by David Wile and other ISI colleagues.

2. The Transformational Paradigm

To motivate our transformational approach to software development, we first present our view of the traditional programming process, in which the programmer starts with an informal specification, develops an implementation plan, and uses it to translate the informal specification into a program. The key point is that testing, tuning, and maintenance are applied directly to the program itself.

We see two fundamental problems in this picture. First, the programming process occurs outside the machine. Only the result of the process, the source code, is entered into the machine. This means that the design decisions incorporated in the program are unrecorded and therefore unavailable for machine analysis. Yet these decisions are precisely the information required to maintain the program.

A related problem has to do with an inherent conflict between optimization and maintenance. Optimizing a program tends to *spread information* throughout it in the form of implicit assumptions and interdependencies. But maintaining a program is easiest when such information is *localized*. As long as optimization and maintenance are carried out on the same physical program, optimizing a program with respect to performance will tend to pessimize it with respect to ease of maintenance.

2.1. Move Software Development into the Machine

These problems will not be resolved until the development process is moved inside the machine. This implies that the program specification must be formal. Unless it is, the decisions made in implementing it can only be passively recorded and must still be manually documented by the programmer. A decision-recording system has been implemented [2], but such a tool is inherently limited: it leaves the programmer with the burden of describing and implementing each decision, and provides only limited assistance in subsequent maintenance. Without formally representing design decisions, the machine cannot analyze their interactions and determine the effects of revising them. Thus further progress requires both formal specification and formal design decisions as basis for a machine-supported development paradigm.

Given a formal specification, one might attempt to translate it into a program purely automatically. This is automatic programming, and at present is still too hard for real-world programs. The alternative is to insert a human programmer in the stepwise refinement loop. One way to do this is to let the programmer select a transformation to apply at each point in the design process, and have the machine apply the transformation. This has the advantage of avoiding implementation errors, assuming that the transformation is performed by a correctness-preserving rewrite rule. In cases where the machine lacks a necessary problem-specific transformation, a second mode is possible: the user can manually transform the program, and the machine can attempt to verify that the transformation preserves correctness. This should be easier than verifying the final program against an initial specification from which it is far removed.

The resulting transformational paradigm factors the programming process into two phases: specification and implementation.* The first phase consists of developing a formal specification of the desired program behavior. Researchers at ISI have developed a high-level formal specification language called GIST [4]. GIST is abstract in that it specifies *what* behavior the program should exhibit, without describing *how* that behavior should be implemented. At the same time, GIST is operational in the sense of being executable without regard to efficiency. We recognize that the process of developing a formal specification for a real task is non-trivial, and are developing several tools to support this process [5] [6]. With the help of such tools, testing and maintenance can be applied directly to the GIST specification. Detecting bugs during the specification phase should reduce the cost of fixing them by an order of magnitude.

The implementation phase consists of applying a series of user-selected optimizing transformations to convert the specification (which can be executed, but only very inefficiently) into an efficient program. Producing complex programs involves long sequences of detailed transformations that would be onerous to select manually, but most of the steps can be generated automatically given some high-level user guidance [7].

The transformational approach offers a solution to the maintenance problem. If the specification is modified, the implementation process should be repeated rather than editing the program itself, just as today a modified high-level program is recompiled rather than trying to patch the compiled code. By "replaying" the development (sequence of transformations) used to implement the original specification [8], all the manual effort invested in that implementation need not be repeated. Some of these implementation decisions may need to be changed because of specification changes or performance considerations; this can be done by replacing them in the development and then replaying the altered development.

3. Application to VLSI

We believe that the VLSI design process can likewise be modelled as developing a behavioral specification and then transforming it stepwise into a circuit design. At each step in the implementation phase, the user makes a design decision, and the machine carries it out.

It is useful at this point to clarify the notion of "design decision." We view a design decision as selecting a particular transformation

---
*This is a simplified description; implementation choices can affect the specification [3].

from a set of alternatives [9]. The transformation *elaborates* a design description at some level of abstraction into a more detailed description at a lower level, or in the case of some optimizing transformations, to an improved design at the same level. In VLSI design, selecting the right transformation typically depends on understanding the eventual impact of alternative choices at much lower levels; a decision at the algorithm level may have major consequences on area and power costs at the layout level. Our approach makes a division of labor between selection and elaboration: an expert VLSI designer steers the design process by selecting transformations based on knowledge of their lower level consequences, and the machine performs the tedious manipulation required to carry them out.

A designer cannot always predict the low-level consequences of a high-level decision based only on general expertise; it is often necessary to drive the design down to a detailed level and evaluate it there, revising high-level decisions according to the low-level concerns thereby revealed. While the transformational approach does not eliminate the need for such backtracking, it should assist the decision process by making it easier to explore the effects of alternative decisions.

The rest of this paper starts at the point where a specification has been developed and mapped down to the algorithm level, and shows how transformations can be used to take it from there to the functional-circuit level.

4. A Program Transformation Model of Design

We have identified three classes of decisions made in mapping an algorithm into a functional-level circuit:

1. *Allocation*: Each execution instance of an operator used in the algorithm must be assigned both a component and a time. This may result in distribution of the operator in time and/or space. For example, a multiplication inside a loop may be implemented by re-using a single multiplier, or by replicating the multiplier and executing the loop body simultaneously for all values of the loop index in parallel.

2. *Data flow*: Communication paths between components must be made explicit. An algorithm can refer to the value of a variable simply by naming it, but in VLSI accessing a variable requires wiring a connection to the point of use from wherever the variable is stored.

3. *Control*: Mechanisms must be designed to implement high-level control constructs used in the algorithm, such as iteration and complex conditionals, in terms of hardware constructs, such as registers and combinational logic.

Now consider the requirements for a design language in which to represent these decisions transformationally. It must be able to:

- Represent the initial algorithm.

- Represent the intermediate states in the design process. In particular, the language should make it easy to write transformation rules to get from one state to the next.

- Represent the result of the design process, a functional-level circuit consisting of a collection of hardware cells and their interconnections.

To simplify the language problem, we have restricted ourselves to clocked (synchronous) circuits for now. Synchronous circuits can be represented in a specialized notation much more concisely than in a more general notation capable of describing asynchronous circuits, such as Hoare's communicating sequential processes [10]. Specifically, we assume a two-phase clocking scheme that reads registers and computes combinational functions in phase 1, and writes registers in phase 2. This scheme is sometimes called "register-transfer" clocking; lower-level 2-phase clocked logic uses alternating clock phases for successive combinational operations. Extending our approach to handle the latter scheme requires further work.

4.1. Represent Circuits as Programs

Our approach to the language problem represents algorithms, circuits, and intermediate design states uniformly as programs. Not all programs represent circuits, however -- only those that satisfy certain restrictions corresponding to constraints of the VLSI domain. We model the algorithm-to-circuit design process as a series of program transformations that maps an ordinary program into the restricted form conforming to the VLSI constraints.

The correspondence between programs and circuits is defined as follows:

1. Procedures represent hardware modules.

2. Procedure arguments represent module input and output ports.

3. "Own" variables (local variables that retain their value between successive calls to the procedure containing them) represent registers.

4. Procedure declaration nesting represents module nesting; subroutines correspond to submodules.

5. Calling a procedure with a list of actual input arguments corresponds to placing the values of those arguments at the input ports of the module and invoking the module. The symbol "--" is used to denote don't-care values.

6. Returning a list of values corresponds to placing them at the output ports.

7. Assignment statements denote register transfers.

8. References to variables correspond to reading registers or input ports.

In order to be interpreted directly as a circuit, a program must satisfy several restrictions imposed by hardware constraints:

Static allocation: Procedures and data must be mapped onto hardware before fabrication time. This rules out recursive procedures (a circuit cannot contain itself), procedural arguments (a circuit cannot be passed from one location to another), and dynamic array bounds (the amount of memory must be fixed before the chip is made).

No data collision: Parallelism is allowed, but simultaneous assignments to the same variable are prohibited, as they must be in any deterministic parallel algorithm.

Explicit scheduling: Concurrent calls to the same procedure are generally prohibited, since the same module cannot accept two different sets of inputs simultaneously. In such cases, the module must be replicated, with one copy for each caller. This is represented by an array of procedures -- an odd construct for a programming language, but a reasonable one for representing hardware.

This restriction is actually overly severe; multiple callers can call the same module simultaneously through different data ports. Thus an exception to the prohibition on concurrent calls is made in the case of arbitrator-like modules that are called simultaneously by several callers through distinct input ports. A special case is an output-only module such as a time-of-day server. Another exception is pipelining: a multi-stage module can process several overlapping calls, provided none of them tries to use the same data line at the same time.

Explicit data flow: No global variables are allowed, and a procedure body may refer only to its input arguments and its **own** variables. This is because in VLSI, accessing a variable requires a physically wired path to the place where it is stored. To model these paths, we require that non-local values be explicitly passed as arguments or returned as procedure results.

Explicit control: A procedure body must be a finite state machine that executes one transition per clock cycle and stores all its state in its local variables; all functions computed in a single cycle must be combinational. Functions that satisfy this restriction have a straightforward hardware analog. More complex functions must be implemented by breaking them down into a series of single-cycle computations.

4.2. A Simple Example: Accumulate a Sum

To illustrate how circuits can be represented as programs, consider the problem of summing a sequence of values $x_1, ..., x_n$ and putting the result in some variable, call it Total. This can be done by a simple program:

```
procedure Accumulate(S);
local Sum;
begin
Sum ← 0;
for each x∈S do Sum ← Sum + x;
return Sum;
end;
end Accumulate;

Total ← Accumulate(<x_1, ..., x_n>)
```

This program might be interpreted as an abstract description of a hardware module that sums its inputs, but it fails to make explicit such details as how the module implements the sequential control of the **begin...end** block and the **for** statement, and how the set S is input. One hardware implementation of Accumulate is depicted in Figure 4-1, and is represented by the following program:

```
procedure Accumulator(ctrl, x);
own Sum;
case ctrl of
        reset:  Sum ← 0;
        add:    Sum ← Sum + x;
        no-op:  ;
        report: return Sum;
end;
end Accumulator;

begin
Accumulator(reset, ··);
for each x∈<x₁, ..., xₙ>
    do Accumulator(add, x);
Total ← Accumulator(report, ··);
end
```

The body of the procedure describes what the Accumulator module does in a single clock cycle, and the driver code for calling it describes the calling sequence required to make the module compute the desired result, i.e., what inputs to give it in successive cycles and when to get the result from the output.

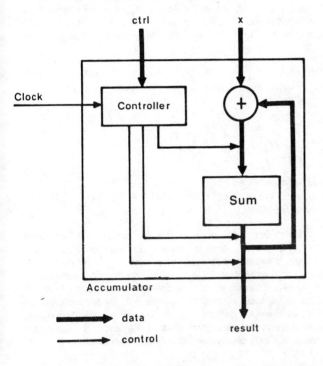

Figure 4-1: A hardware implementation of Accumulator

The module's basic action is to input the value x and add it to the running sum stored in the register Sum (case "add"). However, the module must also be able to reset Sum to zero (case "reset"), to leave it unchanged in cycles when no value is presented (case "no-op"), and to report its value on demand (case "report"). Thus the module has an output port, called result, and a second input, called ctrl, that tells the module which action to perform. This is represented in the procedure by a **case** statement that selects which action to perform based on the value of the ctrl input. In addition, the module has a controller that decodes the ctrl input and regulates the initialization and updating of the Sum register and the output of the result. This mechanism

is not explicitly modelled in the procedure, which represents the module at a level of abstraction in which switches and bus structure are left implicit.

Observe that the problematical control constructs in the first program (**begin...end** blocks and iteration) have been extracted into the driver in the second one. Unlike the Accumulate procedure, the Accumulator procedure has a straightforward hardware interpretation. We have developed a collection of transformations for mapping ordinary programs into the restricted form, and have implemented several of them in Interlisp, making use of its Pattern Match Compiler [11]. The transformations can be classified according to the type of decisions they make: allocation, data flow, or control. The next few sections present some example transformations and then show how they apply to the Pixel Planes [12] graphics display chip.

4.3. Allocation Transformations

Suppose we wish to implement in hardware a For loop in an algorithm:

```
for each x∈S do <body>;
```

One way is to build a module M that inputs x and performs the loop body, and then invoke this module for each x in sequence:

```
procedure M(x); <body>; end M;

for each x∈S in sequence do M(x);
```

This allocation scheme is called *sequential re-use* (of M), as indicated by the keyword **sequence**.

An alternative is to build one module for each element $x_1, ..., x_n$ of S, and invoke all the modules in parallel:

```
procedure M[i∈1..n](x); <body>; end M;

for i from 1 to n in parallel do M[i](xᵢ);
```

This allocation scheme is called *parallel replication*. It requires that executing <body> for one element x does not affect the result of executing it for another element. Note that in the expression $M[i](x_i)$, the index i distinguishes among modules in the array, while the argument x_i represents a value passed to an input port in module M[i]. One might choose to eliminate this port by hardwiring the value x_i into the module.

A third alternative, pipelining, is discussed elsewhere [13], but further work is required to fit it into the program representation used here. Also, the allocation transformations remain to be implemented.

4.4. Data Flow Transformations

The transformation program we have implemented contains one interactive procedure, called MAKEARGSEXPLICIT, for making data flow explicit. Suppose we have decided to implement in hardware an algorithm containing a nested function call f(g(x)), where the variable x is defined external to the function call. Some module F will compute the expression f(g(x)). The data flow question (in its simplest form) is, will module F input x and compute g(x) itself, or will the value of g(x) be computed externally and supplied as input? In general, the functions may take multiple arguments and the function calls in the algorithm may be more deeply nested, but this is the basic idea. MAKEARGSEXPLICIT systematically traverses an expression being implemented in a module, asking the user whether each sub-expression that uses data external to the module will be computed inside or outside the module. Based on this information, it determines the input ports for the module.

Such decisions may appear unimportant: after all, $g(x)$ must be computed somewhere, so what does it matter how the computation is partitioned into modules? The answer is that different decisions can in fact lead to very different designs. For example, if $f(g(x), y)$ is computed by many F-cells (one for each value of y), then computing $g(x)$ externally enables its value to be computed once and broadcast. Whether this is better than broadcasting x and computing $g(x)$ inside every cell can depend on such factors as the relative data widths of x and $g(x)$, and the relative area costs of computing g versus transferring data.

4.5. Control Transformations

In general, the purpose of control transformations is to translate software control constructs into forms that correspond directly to hardware constructs, or to move them out of module definitions into the enclosing driver. By doing this repeatedly, problematical constructs can be translated away or extracted into the driver for the whole chip. The chip driver is simply a description of how to use the chip, so it is allowed to contain such constructs. For illustration, we present two transformations used in the Pixel Planes example.

The first transformation implements complex conditional statements of the form

```
if forall x∈S P(x)
then <body>;
```

Note that the If-then construct represents conditional execution rather than a boolean expression: <body> is an action to be performed, not an expression to be evaluated. The transformation implements this conditional by introducing a one-bit Enable register, initialized to True, and using it to compute the condition incrementally. If afterwards the register is still enabled, the <body> is performed:

```
begin
own boolean Enable;
Enable ← T;
for each x∈S
        do Enable ← Enable ∧ P(x);
if Enable
then <body>;
end;
```

The transformed program is closer to the hardware level because the complex condition in the conditional has been replaced with a simple flag. This can be implemented by gating the Enable register with the evoke signal for <body>. For example, if <body> is a register assignment, Enable would be gated into the register's write-enable line.

One may object to this implementation on the grounds of inefficiency: although the Enable register may be disabled early

on, $P(x)$ will still be computed for every element of the set S. The answer to this objection in the Pixel Planes example is that the transformation is used to implement a conditional performed at every pixel in parallel. By iterating unconditionally, the pixels can share control signals broadcast from a common driver. This illustrates how a program ill-suited to execution on an ordinary sequential processor may represent a hardware-efficient implementation.

A second transformation helps implement **begin...end** blocks. Consider a call to a procedure whose body is a **begin...end** block:

```
procedure F(x);
begin <stmt₁>; ...; <stmtₙ>; end;
end F;

F(<expr>);
```

The transformation extracts the **begin...end** block into the driver for F by converting the body of F into a **case** statement and adding a control input to module F that tells it which action to select. Such a **case** statement can readily be implemented in hardware by combinational logic that decodes the control input and invokes the selected action. The driver is changed into a series of calls to F, one for each statement in the **begin...end** block:

```
procedure F(ctrl, x);
case ctrl of
        case₁: <stmt₁>;
        ...;
        caseₙ: <stmtₙ>;
end;
end F;

begin
F(case₁, <expr>); ...; F(caseₙ, <expr>);
end;
```

When this transformation and its analog for For loops, described earlier, are recursively applied to a procedure containing nested sequential control constructs, they transform its body into a finite state machine of the sort described earlier. The implemented transformation identifies which calls actually use the value of the input x. In those that do not, the pseudo-argument "--" is passed instead. This facilitates input-line-sharing optimizations (not yet implemented). For example, if F has several inputs, but only one is used at a time, they can share the same input line.

The above transformation implements *external control*: an external control input tells the module what to do for each call. An alternative is to introduce an internal state register and update it after each call, returning a control signal to notify the caller when the block is completed:

```
procedure F(ctrl, x);
own state;
case ctrl of
        reset:  state ← 1;
        normal: begin in parallel
                case state of
                        1: <stmt₁>;
                        ...;
                        n: <stmtₙ>;
                end;
                if state < n
                then return busy
                else return done;
                state ← state + 1;
                end;
        end;
end F;

begin
F(reset, ··);
do flag ← F(normal, <expr>) until flag = done;
end;
```

Two points should be noticed here. First, although the control state is now internal to module F, an input signal is still needed in order to reset to the initial state, and an output signal is used to notify the caller of completion.* This is still an improvement, since each signal is only one bit wide, whereas an input line for external control must be $\log_2(n)$ bits wide. Second, this transformation makes use of the two-phase clocking scheme mentioned earlier. Since all reads are done in phase 1 and all writes in phase 2, the old value of the state register will be used in phase 1 to select which statement is performed; it will not be updated to the incremented value until phase 2.

Several control transformations are implemented in programs called PRIMITIVIZE and CASIFY. PRIMITIVIZE maps high-level control constructs into lower-level constructs, and CASIFY transforms a PRIMITIVIZEd procedure into a **case** statement body and an external control driver. Both programs operate without user intervention, since they incorporate fixed control style decisions, e.g., use external rather than internal control.

4.6. The Pixel Planes Example

We now show how transformations like those described above can be used to re-derive the design of the Pixel Planes graphics display processor [12]. As Figure 4-2 shows, successive scenes consisting of polyhedral objects with colored faces are to be displayed, with hidden surfaces eliminated and the shading of each face interpolated from the colors of its vertices. A pre-processor segments the objects into triangular faces and transforms them into viewing coordinates. The position and color of every vertex are input to the Pixel Planes chip, which must compute what color to paint each pixel on the display screen.

A formal specification in the GIST specification language [4] has been developed for this task, but is outside the scope of this paper, since we are focussing here on the transformation from algorithm to circuit. The high-level specification can be expressed

---

*The output signal could be eliminated at the cost of having the caller keep track of the state separately. This might be worthwhile in cases where a single caller controlled many copies of F in lockstep.

informally as "for each scene, color each pixel the shaded color of the nearest face."

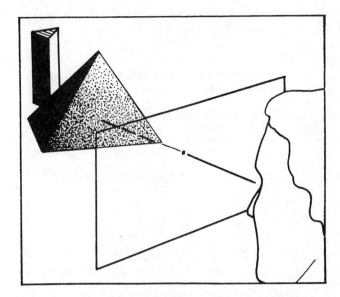

Figure 4-2: Pixel Planes chip does color shading and hidden surface elimination for scenes of polyhedral objects.

The algorithm can be expressed as:

```
for each s∈Scenes do
    for each p∈Pixels do
        begin
        minZ ← ∞;
        for each t∈Faces do
        if forall e∈Edges(t)
                Aₑxₚ + Bₑyₚ + Cₑ > 0
             ∧ Aₜxₚ + Bₜyₚ + Cₜ < minZ
        then begin
                minZ ← Aₜxₚ + Bₜyₚ + Cₜ;
                Display[p] ← Aₛxₚ + Bₛyₚ + Cₛ;
                end;
        end;
```

How this algorithm works is irrelevant here; we are interested only in its syntactic form. First, notice that it contains several planar expressions of the form $Ax_p + By_p + C$. Second, notice the presence of the **begin...end** blocks and the complex conditional statement "**if forall**... ∧... **then**...."

By applying transformations such as those described in the previous sections, we obtain the program shown in Figure 4-3. This program reflects the following design decisions (some of which are revised by subsequent optimizations):

1. *Allocation*:

    · Use a replicated PixCell[p] to compute pixel color in parallel for each pixel p.

    · Multiplex hardware for $Ax_p + By_p + C$.

2. *Data flow*:

- Compute $Ax_p + By_p + C$ inside PixCell[p].[*]

- Import planar coefficients A, B, C from outside PixCell[p].

3. *Control*:

- Implement the complex conditional using an Enable register.

- Use an external control line to select the action performed by PixCell[p].

```
procedure PixAry(ctrl, A, B, C);

procedure PixCell[p∈Pixels](ctrl,x,y,A,B,C);
own Enable, minZ, Z, display;
case ctrl of
        case1:  minZ ← ∞;
        case2:  Enable ← T;
        case3:  Z ← A*x + B*y + C;
        case4:  Enable ← Enable ∧ (Z > 0);
        case5:  if (Enable ←
                    (Enable ∧ (Z < minZ)))
                then minZ ← Z;
        case6:  if Enable
                then Display ← Z;
        no-op:  ;
end;
end PixCell;

for each p∈Pixels in parallel do
    PixCell[p](ctrl, x_p, y_p, A, B, C);
end PixAry;
Driver:

for each s∈Scenes in sequence do
        begin
        PixAry(case1, ··, ··, ··);
        for each t∈Faces do
                begin
                PixAry(case2, ··, ··, ··);
                for each e∈Edges(t) do
                        begin
                        PixAry(case3, A_e,B_e,C_e);
                        PixAry(case4, ··, ··, ··);
                        end;
                PixAry(case3, A_t,B_t,C_t);
                PixAry(case5, ··, ··, ··);
                PixAry(case3, A_s,B_s,C_s);
                PixAry(case6, ··, ··, ··);
                end;
        end;
```

Figure 4-3: Program corresponding to an intermediate stage in the design of Pixel Planes

At this stage in the design process, PixAry represents a pixel array that inputs a control code and the coefficients A, B, and C, and broadcasts them to all the PixCells, as well as sending each PixCell its x and y coordinates. The control code tells each PixCell

---

[*] This would be a poor decision if it were allowed to stand, since using two multipliers for every pixel would be very costly in area. It also pretends that the multiplication is performed in a single clock cycle. In the actual design, the products Ax_p (and By_p) are computed externally and broadcast bit-serially to all pixels with the same value of x_p (or y_p). These refinements are omitted above for simplicity.

what do to in a given clock cycle; note that case3 is the computation of a planar combination. The nested assignment in case5 specifies that the value of Enable ∧ (Z < minZ) is both stored into the Enable register and used as a condition for whether to update the minZ register. The driver tells what sequence of control signals and data to send to PixAry; note that case3, for computing planar combinations, is used several times.

A key point here is that the transformations used to model these decisions are general, even though the decision to select them instead of alternative transformations is based on low-level considerations specific to the problem at hand. This theme harks back to the distinction made earlier between elaboration and selection in design decisions. Each transformation automates a particular kind of elaboration, but the problem of selecting among alternative transformations requires predicting their low-level consequences and is left to a human expert.

5. Conclusion

We have modelled the design process as a series of transformations leading from a specification to a design. Letting the machine apply these transformations should decouple the human selection of design alternatives from the mechanical manipulations required to carry them out, reducing errors and freeing the designer to explore a wider range of design alternatives.

We have described a particular source-to-source program transformation model of functional-level VLSI design and showed how it was used to re-derive part of the Pixel Planes design. We have also developed a more specialized model that takes an algorithm containing **for** loops and **begin...end** blocks, plus a bit of implementation advice, and applies a series of transformations to produce a functional-level systolic circuit [13]. The two models use somewhat different representations. While the source-to-source transformation model represents both algorithms and circuits as programs, the systolic model represents circuits in terms of their interconnection structure and their input and output data streams. Incorporating the specialized systolic constructs (e.g., pipelining) into the more general model requires further research.

Modelling VLSI design as source-to-source program transformation offers several potential benefits [14]. First, it should be possible to use simulation techniques at any intermediate stage of design to provide both performance feedback on the design so far, and guidance for the decisions yet to be made. Such simulation should be possible because at all times the evolving design is an executable program. Actually, a special interpreter may be required for simulation in order to enforce the special hardware semantics. For example, all computation in a given clock cycle should be performed before any registers are written, and parallel constructs like the arbitrator mentioned earlier must be treated correctly. Otherwise, however, most of the language appears simulatable by simple sequential-processor execution. Such simulation may serve as a useful instrumentation tool in exploring the performance issues that guide selection among design alternatives.

The transformational model should clarify the design process by describing intermediate design states in the relatively well-understood language of programs, and by explaining circuits in terms of the decisions that produced them, rather than trying to describe the detailed results.

It should assist circuit design by automating such tedious and error-prone details as designing control logic.

Finally, the transformational approach should help to verify a circuit by treating successive decisions in the design process individually, rather than trying to match the complex circuit resulting from many decisions against the algorithm it is intended to implement. Even a simple circuit can be so complex that one cannot infer its function from its structure. Moreover, if design decisions are carried out by correctness-preserving transformations, the design process itself validates the circuit with respect to the initial algorithm.

VLSI design traverses many levels, going from specification to algorithm to functional-level circuit to layout. The problems of developing a formal specification and mapping it into a compilable algorithm are receiving attention at ISI [15] and elsewhere. We have focussed in this paper on a narrow slice of the design problem: getting from algorithm to functional-level circuit. Practical application of this work will require a "silicon compiler"-like mechanism for completing the design process that we have begun.

References

1. Balzer, R., N. Goldman, and D. Wile, "On the transformational implementation approach to programming," *Proceedings of the 2nd International Conference on Software Engineering*, IEEE, 1976, pp. 337-343.

2. Balzer, R., "DEVELOP system", Online documentation.

3. Swartout, W., and Balzer, R., "On the inevitable intertwining of specification and implementation," *CACM*, July 1982, pp. 438-440.

4. Balzer, R., Goldman, N. & Wile, D., "Operational specification as the basis for rapid prototyping," *Proceedings of the Second Software Engineering Symposium: Workshop on Rapid Prototyping*, ACM SIGSOFT, April 1982.

5. Cohen, D., Swartout, W., and Balzer, R., "Using symbolic execution to characterize behavior," *Proceedings of the Second Software Engineering Symposium: Workshop on Rapid Prototyping*, ACM SIGSOFT, April 1982.

6. Swartout, B., "GIST English generator," *AAAI82*, American Association for Artificial Intelligence, Pittsburgh, 1982, pp. 404-409.

7. Fickas, S., *The Use of Planning to Help Automate the Transformational Development of Software*, PhD dissertation, University of California at Irvine, 1982, To appear.

8. Wile, D. S., "Program developments: formal explanations of implementations," Tech. report RR-82-99, USC/Information Sciences Institute, August 1982.

9. Stefik, M., and Conway, L., "Towards the principled engineering of knowledge," *AI Magazine*, Vol. 3, No. 3, summer 1982, pp. 4-16.

10. Hoare, C.A.R., "Communicating Sequential Processes," *CACM*, August 1978, pp. 65-90.

11. Teitelman, W.Xerox Palo Alto Research Center, *Interlisp Reference Manual*, 1978.

12. Fuchs, H., and Poulton, J., "Pixel-Planes: a VLSI-oriented design for a raster graphics engine," *VLSI Design*, No. Third Quarter, 1981, pp. 20-28.

13. Lam, M., and Mostow, J., "A transformational model of VLSI systolic design," *IFIP 6th International Symposium on Computer Hardware Description Languages and their Applications*, Carnegie-Mellon University, May 1983.

14. Organick, E., Lindstrom, G., Smith, D. K., Subrahmanyam, P. A., and Carter, T., "Transformation of Ada programs into silicon," Tech. report UTEC-82-020, University of Utah, March 1982.

15. London, P. & Feather, M.S., "Implementing specification freedoms," Tech. report RR-81-100, ISI, 4676 Admiralty Way, Marina del Rey, CA 90291, 1981.

Compilation Techniques in Logic Synthesis

William H. Joyner, Jr.
IBM Thomas J. Watson Research Center
Yorktown Heights, New York 10598

Abstract

The logic synthesis system described in [1,2,3] attempts to generate technology-specific logic for gate-array implementations from functional specifications. The system uses a series of local transformations to improve a naive technology-independent implementation and make it realizable in a particular technology. The synthesis system is in many ways like a compiler for a high-level language. It uses standard parsing techniques to translate a register-transfer level description of logic to an intermediate realization in terms of generic NAND or NOR gates and generic registers, with unlimited fan-in, fan-out, and path lengths. Transformations, some similar to compiler optimizations, make local improvements to the NAND or NOR design. A back end of technology specific transformations converts this optimized intermediate design to a technology-specific design, with fan-in, fan-out, path length, and other restrictions enforced. This paper describes some of the similarities and differences in the techniques used in synthesis and compilation.

Common subexpression elimination in compilers is similar to common term elimination in logic synthesis. In synthesis, this means combining two gates which have the same function and the same inputs. For commutative gates, permutations of the inputs must be considered. Since the value computed by such a gate is used simultaneously (in parallel) as input to several other gates, rather than serially in compiled code, care must be taken to avoid introducing fan-out violations, or to correct such violations in the back end.

Constant propagation is used in the early stages of synthesis to move zeroes and ones through the generic boxes. Many constants arise because of the way in which the parsing and generation of the initial design is done. A cleanup transformation, the analog of dead code removal, is applied often in all parts of the synthesis process. Gates with no inputs or no outputs, and signals with no sources or no sinks, arise from the optimizing transformations, which are simplified by not having to remove the unreachable gates or signals themselves.

The synthesis system allows high-level functions to be specified in the register-transfer level description and to be preserved as single primitives until expanded at a desired point in the scenario. This allows hierarchical descriptions of parts of an implementation to be described and/or synthesized separately, and combined with other parts at either the intermediate or hardware-specific level. The technique is similar to procedure integration in compilers.

The process of mapping a generic description to a technology-specific description is similar to code selection in a compiler back end. When translating the NAND or NOR intermediate description to an interconnection of technology-specific primitives, more complicated functions may be available in the target technology. Transformations in the synthesis system search for patterns of NANDs or NORs which can be realized using these functions, and where possible replace these patterns with single boxes, usually saving area or path length.

References

[1] J. A. Darringer and W. H. Joyner, "A New Look at Logic Synthesis," *Proceedings of the Seventeenth Design Automation Conference,* Minneapolis, MN, 1980, pp. 543-549.

[2] J. A. Darringer, W. H. Joyner, C. L. Berman, and L. Trevillyan, "Experiments in Logic Synthesis," *Proceedings of the IEEE International Conference on Circuits and Computers,* Port Chester, NY, 1980, pp. 234-237A.

[3] J. A. Darringer, W. H. Joyner, C. L. Berman, and L. Trevillyan, "Logic Synthesis through Local Transformations," *IBM Journal of Research and Development 25,* 272-280 (1981).

Tools for System Level Design, Test, and Prototyping

Randy H. Katz
Computer Sciences Department
University of Wisconsin-Madison
Madison, WI 53706

1. Introduction

VLSI designs are rapidly approaching the levels of complexity that have faced software designers for some time. There is a general consensus that a structured approach to VLSI circuit design is essential, as it is for any large scale design task. Methodologies for *system* design, and the tools to support them, are beginning to emerge. Further, as more sophisticated tools for creating special purpose integrated circuits become available, the traditional hardware/software tradeoffs will be reevaluated. For example, in the 1950's it was thought that floating point hardware was too expensive, and the function was implemented by software packages. Few designers would build a mainframe computer today without some hardware support for floating point. Other functions, currently implemented in software, could be replaced by hardware implementations. If we are to fully exploit VLSI's capability to replace software functions with special purpose integrated circuits, then we need support for a flexible choice of implementation mediums. *System level* tools, encompassing both hardware and software design, can provide this support.

In this paper, we describe a system design tool, called a *chip assembler*, that manages the information about a VLSI chip design project. The tool can be used in any design activity, hardware or software, that is undertaken by teams of designers who need to (1) control the communication among themselves and (2) maintain the consistency of their design. We also describe how to rapidly breadboard VLSI prototype systems with a *design frame*, i.e., a hardware environment that provides system level capabilities to an interfaced prototype circuit. Special design frames oriented towards integrated circuit debugging are also described. We discuss how design frames and engineering workstations, supporting standard interfaces, can integrate the design, test, and prototyping environments.

2. Managing a Large Design Project

Large projects, such as software systems or VLSI chips, are undertaken by design teams. Such projects are too complicated for a single designer, who would be overwhelmed with the vast quantity of data describing a large design. Special facilities are needed to manage the information about the system being designed. We have called a tool that provides such facilities for VLSI designs a *chip assembler* [KATZ82], but many of the ideas apply equally well to software projects.

A chip assembler structures and controls the chip design database. The database contains the basic representational data about a design, such as its geometrical, transistor, and logical descriptions. It also incorporates information that enhances the chip assembler's ability to maintain the consistency of the design data. Critical design information, e.g., interface documentation and descriptions of how modules of the system are to be used, is usually found only in off-line design notebooks or in designers' heads. It must be made known to the system. Designers can browse it to obtain up to the minute documentation on the design. The information includes: interface specifications of a module, alternative implementations of its function, progressive versions reflecting corrections and enhancements to its implementation, and explicit descriptions of the hierarchical construction of a design across its many representations. The point of capturing this information within the design system is to insure that (1) the design and its documentation are completed simultaneously, and (2) the design is self-consistent: all of its representations describe the same object (i.e., equivalence checking) and implementations support their specified interfaces (i.e., conformability checking).

Modern programming language methodology advocates the separation of module interfaces from their implementations. The interface concept is important for VLSI design methods as well. An interface describes the behavior of a module and how it can be used, without giving its detailed implementation. Module inputs and outputs, as well as their types, are included in the interface specification. This facilitates compatibility checking when modules are composed by interconnection of outputs to inputs. For example, a restored logic level input is incompatible with an unrestored logic level output.

Interfaces furnish a mechanism by which a system can be decomposed into subsystems and allocated to members of the design team for implementation. A designer can implement his assigned subsystem in any desired way, as long as the interface is maintained. Designers who use the module need only know its interface. The detailed implementation does not concern them.

In addition to describing how an associated module behaves, interfaces are constraints on how it is implemented. An interface is defined before its implementation, and incorporates performance metrics such as area, power, and delay estimates. The information can be used for system level characterizations of performance while a design is still in progress, i.e., before the system has been completely implemented. Interfaces with delay estimates can be used for multi-level simulations of the design. Detailed timing information can be used where the design has been specified in detail, otherwise the estimates are used to obtain an approximate characterization.

An interface is a "promise" made about a module's behavior and performance. Designers who interface to the module expect the promise to be kept. Thus, the system must verify that the implementation is consistent with the behavioral and performance specifications of its interface. If an implementation and its interface do not agree, then one or the other must be changed. An interface can only be

CH1815-0/83/0000/0135$01.00 © 1983 IEEE

changed by negotiation with the other designers who use the module. Who is using which design modules is an important piece of information maintained by the chip assembler. It allows a designer to determine the consequences of a change to the interface, e.g., how many other modules are affected by the change.

The separation of interface from implementation is also a good way to structure a design library. There is one interface specification for each function found in the library, although there may be many different implementations of the function with different performance characteristics. An incremental approach for building a family of design implementations is easily supported. An initial hastily constructed implementation of a function can be replaced later by alternative implementations with better delay, power, or area characteristics. Once alternative implementations have been added to the library, the design team can put together a version of the design in which critical paths use high power, high speed implementations while the non-critical portions use low power, low speed alternatives. Alternative implementations across technologies are also possible. For low power applications, an NMOS design can be rapidly converted to a CMOS design if CMOS alternatives exist for all functions in the original NMOS design.

New design tools are needed to support the interface concept. An "interface extractor" examines the detailed implementation of a module to determine its interface. The extracted interface and the specified interface must be compared for equivalence. This is difficult to do automatically, and is analogous to verifying the correctness of a program. However, some interface constraints are easy to verify. The area ("bounding box") can be determined from the geometrical representation of the module. Directionality and types of a module's inputs or outputs can be determined from the transistor description. Detailed behavior, however, can only be determined by simulation. The chip assembler can at best serve as a bookkeeping tool, insuring that the simulations of the appropriate versions of the modules have been performed with the same excitation vectors. Since the system knows about the interconnection of modules, and designer responsibility for each module, it can support the negotiations needed to arrive at a new interface if its specification has changed.

The interface notion extends upwards from chip subsystems to chips, from chips to boards, and from boards to multiple board systems. At each level, an interface describes how the module is used. A module's interface must be compatible with the composed interfaces of its components.

The generic facilities provided by a chip assembler are useful whether the team is designing a chip or a software system. A more sophisticated system would support both hardware and software design within the same environment. Such a design tool should rightly be called a *system assembler*. Modules can be implemented either by hardware or software. One of the great challenges of the VLSI era is choosing where hardware ends and software begins. A system assembler allows the design team to better explore the space of alternative implementations, to make a rational choice for the final implementation.

3. System Test and Prototyping

Fast turnaround integrated circuit fabrication is a reality, making it possible to rapidly prototype VLSI circuits. However, a circuit is not a system, and it is not a simple task to surround a prototype with the facilities needed to make it into a system. This is equivalent to requiring every programmer to create an operating environment (i.e., file and system services) for his program when he wishes to have it run. Such a situation has not existed for software since the early days of computing, yet it is still the state for VLSI circuits. Rapid *system* prototyping is needed.

The next generation of VLSI systems designers are as likely to be computer systems architects as traditional circuit designers. These individuals will be responsible for partitioning a system into its hardware and software components, and for realizing the system's implementations in both mediums. Testing and debugging VLSI systems pose new problems for these designers (as it does even for test engineers familiar with conventional test equipment and techniques!). The current generation of test equipment is difficult to use and ill-suited for prototype testing. There is virtually no integration of the design and test environments.

We have designed, implemented, and tested a standard *design frame* for VLSI prototypes [KATZ83]. The design frame is a mass produced printed circuit board and a specially designed integrated circuit that interfaces to it. The board contains RAM, which is dual ported with a standard industry bus (MULTIBUS), interrupt handlers, I/O ports, timers, and ROM. A VLSI prototype circuit, which must be designed to interface to the special control circuitry included on-chip, becomes a system by inserting the package with the prototype and the interface circuitry into the board. Thus, the design frame is a breadboard for VLSI system prototyping. Note that the printed circuit board is based on a readily obtainable microcomputer board.

The design frame described above is directed towards rapid system prototyping; it does not yet help with system debugging. A frame for debugging should incorporate standard test features, such as on-board control circuitry for on-chip scan logic and built-in test. Debugging should occur within the same computing environment in which the system was designed, since both tasks will be performed by the same design team. Test vectors applied to the simulated design should be applied to its hardware prototype, to verify that the implemented system behaves as designed.

The dual-ported memory feature of our design frame forms the basis for a sophisticated development environment for VLSI systems. The bus used in our frame is the MULTIBUS, which is compatible with a number of VLSI design workstations appearing in the marketplace. The design frame can be incorporated into this design environment by inserting it into the backplane of one of these stations. The workstation's processor can download data into the frame's memory and examine data placed in the memory by the prototype circuit. This makes it possible to configure the prototype with parameters, input data, microcode, instructions, etc., and to examine the results and the diagnostic data it produces.

Interfaces and protocols at various system levels underlie design frames for large scale system prototyping [CONW83]. A simple handshake sequence, initiated by the prototype circuit, is converted by on-chip circuitry into a protocol understood by the design frame printed circuit board. One of the components of the board, the MULTIBUS interface logic, can translate this into a protocol for communication across a standard system bus. Another board, an Ethernet communications controller interfaced through the system bus, supports communication over a local network. Exploitation of standard interfaces, such as the MULTIBUS and the Ethernet, make it possible to quickly create large scale systems with relatively little effort.

4. Conclusions

We have described some approaches for system level design, test, and prototyping. A system assembler is a design tool, based on the separation of interfaces from implementations, that manages the documentation and self-consistency checking of design data. The key problems encountered by large design projects, whether software or hardware, are (1) maintaining up to date documentation about design assumptions, i.e., how to use a module implemented by someone else, and (2) keeping consistent the vast quantities of data that describe a design, i.e., insuring that interfaces and implementations are compatible.

Support for prototyping VLSI systems can benefit from software system ideas. The design frame is an "operating" environment that provides system capabilities in an easily interfaced package. By exploiting standard interfaces -- an approach that has been used in many kinds of systems, e.g., network protocols -- prototypes can be leveraged into large scale systems with relative ease.

Engineering workstations promise to provide an environment in which VLSI design, test, and prototyping activities can all be supported. They will provide the focus for the integration of hardware and software design as well. The decision of what parts of a system to commit to hardware implementation, and what parts to software, is becoming more difficult. The great promise of VLSI technology, i.e., the capability of replacing software with special function integrated circuits, can only be fully exploited in environments that support integrated hardware and software design.

5. References

[CONW83] Conway, L., A. Bell, "System Kits, Design Frames, and Network Services for the Rapid Prototyping of Advanced Computing Systems," Xerox PARC Working Paper, (January 1983).

[KATZ82a] Katz, R. H., S. Weiss, "Chip Assemblers: Concepts and Capabilities," University of Wisconsin-Madison Computer Sciences Technical Report #486, (November 1982).

[KATZ83] Katz, R. H., S. Weiss, "A Standard Design Frame for VLSI Circuit Prototyping," *Journal of VLSI and Computer Systems*, Computer Science Press, V 1, N 1, (March 1983).

AN INDUCTIVE ASSERTION METHOD FOR HARDWARE DESIGN VERIFICATION

Vijay Pitchumani
Edward P. Stabler

Electrical and Computer Engineering Department
Syracuse University
Syracuse, N Y 13210

ABSTRACT

This paper presents an overview of an inductive assertion method for formal verification of register transfer level synchronous designs described in a procedural language. A time variable t, representing elapsed time, is introduced. The axioms describe how machine variables and time change with machine activity. Verification of logic as well as realtime performance is possible with this approach.

This paper presents an inductive assertion method for register transfer level hardware design verification. It is suited for a design methodology in which the logic is designed at the register transfer level, verified (by simulation or a formal method such as the following) and then the gate level logic mechanically synthesized by a reliable synthesizer[1], or manually synthesized but its equivalence with a mechanically synthesized logic verified completely by analytical means[2]. This will avoid the need for further gate level verification.

We restrict our attention to synchronous logic. Use of asynchronous preset and clear inputs of SEs (storage elements) during normal operation, or clocking SEs with the data outputs of other SEs creates asynchronous designs. Such designs are hard to verify, formally or otherwise. Fortunately, design for testability rules (such as LSSD[3]) usually result in synchronous designs.

Hardware designs may have to meet realtime requirements. Peripheral controllers, such as Universal Asynchronous Receiver Transmitters (UARTs), are an example. For instance, the receiver of a UART should not sample the same bit twice, or miss a bit for the assumed relative drifts between the transmitter and receiver clocks. The formal verification method we present below will help verify such realtime characteristics too[8].

We require an assertion at the top of the RTL description and at least one in each loop. The assertions specify relationships between current values of machine variables. An additional variable "t" representing elapsed time measured in number of clock cycles may appear in assertions too.

Assertions containing t may help verify realtime characteristics, and may also help prove termination. From a given RTL description, we derive some predicates known as "Verification Conditions" or VCs. The correctness of the design with respect to the assertions depends on these VCs being true. If all these VCs are proved true (by a theorem prover), the verification is complete. Each VC is derived by working backward on a path from an assertion (the "tail assertion" of the path) and deriving the "weakest preconditions" until an assertion (the "head assertion" of the path) is reached. The predicate "the head assertion of this path implies the weakest precondition derived for the head of the path" is the VC for the path. We now give rules for the backward propagation of assertions. If S is a statement, we use "pre(S)" to refer to the control point immediately preceding S. A similar remark applies to "post(S)".

The statement "NULL" means "do nothing but use up one clock cycle". It may be used to wait for an event to happen or for slower combinational logic units to settle. When an assertion (or derived condition) R is propagated backward through NULL, it becomes R_{t+1}^{t}. This notation means "R with t replaced by (t+1)". This captures the time change with no change in other variables. The Single Cycle Transfer Statement (SCTS)

$$x1 <- e1$$
$$\cdot$$
$$\cdot$$
$$xm <- em$$

represents several simultaneous register transfers in the same clock cycle. Reverse propagation of R will yield $R_{e1,\ldots,em,t+1}^{x1,\ldots,xm,t}$ where the substitutions are simultaneous. This models the simultaneous assignments and the passage of one clock cycle. If S1 and S2 are statements, "S1;S2" represents the execution of S2 after S1. Reverse propagation is done by successive reverse propagations through S2 and then S1. "if c then S1 else S2 fi" is a statement too. Its meaning is: Test c at the beginning of the clock cycle. If true, transfer control to S1 in the same clock cycle (so the first transfer or NULL executed in S1 happens in the same clock cycle in which c was tested). If false, transfer control to S2 in the same clock cycle. If we indicate the above if then else fi statement by S, then the following are the reverse propagation

138

rules: Reverse propagations from post(S) to both post(S1) and post(S2) are identity operations. Reverse propagation through S1 and S2 will depend on the exact nature of S1 and S2. When an R is reverse propagated from pre(S1) to pre(S), it becomes "c implies R". When an R is reverse propagated from pre(S2) to pre(S), it becomes "(not c) implies R". It must be noted that even though these rules are similar to the ones given for flow-chart programs by Floyd[4], they capture the additional semantics about time explained informally above. The statement "if c then S1 fi" is not the same as "if c then S1 else NULL fi". In the former case, no time, measured in full clock cycles, is lost when c is found to be false. In the latter case, one clock cycle is used up by NULL when c is false. Usually when an RTL description is written, the designer already has a particular clock frequency in mind. RTL verification will not prove that setup and hold time requirements can be met by the synthesized logic for the chosen clock frequency. Such timing verification must be done as a separate step later, after the physical design is complete.

The language has iterative constructs and their semantics are given in ref.[5,6,7]. Examples of proofs are given there too. Parallel control sequences and their proofs are discussed also[5].

We forbid loops containing potentially zero delay bodies. For instance,

    while a do
         if (not a) then NULL fi
    od

is a loop, whose body, the if then fi statement, consumes no time (measured in full clock cycles) when "a" is true. Such zero delay loops create asynchronous logic in the control section when logic is synthesized. We will outlaw it for that reason.

In software, the "well founded set method" is normally used for proving termination. We invent a non-negative integer function of program variables, and prove that each pass through the loop decreases the function. Because the function is non-negative, looping can not be infinite. In our RTL description, t can serve the role of such a function. By the restriction on zero delay loops placed above, t is guaranteed to increase by at least 1. So there is no need for proof of monotonically increasing (or decreasing) behavior. If we can prove that the value of t is bounded in either the loop invariant or the postcondition for the loop, then termination is guaranteed. Of course we can invent another function and carry out a proof as in software termination proofs, if we do not wish to use t.

In summary, we have presented an inductive assertion method for RTL verification. It extends software verification techniques to hardware. Complete verification through formal techniques such as this, needs to be investigated thoroughly for verification of VLSI designs.

REFERENCES

1. J.A. Darringer, W.H. Joyner, Jr., C.L. Berman and L. Trevillyan, "Logic Synthesis Through Logic Transformations", IBM Journal of Research and Development, Vol. 25, No. 4, pp. 272-289, July 1981.

2. G.L. Smith, R.J. Bahnsen and H. Halliwell, "Boolean Comparison of Hardware and Flowcharts", IBM Journal of Research and Development, Vol. 26, No. 1, pp. 106-116, Jan. 1982.

3. E.B. Eichelberger and T.W. Williams, "A Logic Design Structure for LSI Testability", 14th Design Automation Conference, New Orleans, pp. 462-468, June 1977.

4. R.W. Floyd, "Assigning Meanings to Programs", Proceedings of the Symposium on Applied Mathematics, American Mathematical Society, Vol. 19, pp. 19-32, 1967.

5. V. Pitchumani, "Methods of Verification of Digital Logic", Ph.D. Dissertation, Syracuse University, 1981.

6. V. Pitchumani and E.P. Stabler, "A Formal Method for Computer Design Verification", 19th Design Automation Conference, Las Vegas, pp. 809-814, June 1982.

7. V. Pitchumani and E.P. Stabler, "An Inductive Assertion Method for Register Transfer Level Design Verification", accepted for publication in IEEE Transactions on Computers.

8. Z.D. Umrigar and V. Pitchumani, "Formal Verification of a Realtime Hardware Design", to be presented at the 20th Design Automation Conference, Miami Beach, June 1983.

SYMBOLIC EXECUTION FOR VLSI DESIGN VERIFICATION

Zen Kishimoto and Kyushik Son

GTE Laboratories Incorporated
40 Sylvan Road
Waltham, Massachusetts 02254

ABSTRACT

This paper discusses a high level design verification of VLSI circuits that are described in a Hardware Description Language (HDL). Since a hardware chip cannot be physically modified, it is very important to assure that the functional specification be complete and correct, and that the transformation from the specification to the design be performed accordingly. The functional specification and the design both describe the particular function that the manufactured chip is expected to perform in two different forms. A symbolic execution technique is used to derive the functional information from the design written in an HDL. The comparison of these two forms of the function, the functional specification and the design described in an HDL can reveal any discrepancies in them.

1. INTRODUCTION

With the advent of VLSI technology, digital circuits are more frequently described in a hardware description language (HDL), and then simulated directly by a functional-level simulator. This trend has increased the difficulty of design verification for VLSI circuits.

The conventional gate-level model cannot be used for such a high level description of VLSI circuits. The problem with the gate-level modeling of a digital circuit lies in deriving the functionality of the entire circuit so that the implementation can be verified functionally and the manufactured product tested accordingly. The gate-level simulators are mainly concerned with the interconnections of physical gates, and current functional-level simulators do not deal with the high-level description of the entire circuit.

At present, the functional verification of gate-level modeling is performed solely by a designer of the circuit at an early stage. It is possible, however, to derive a high level architectural description based on this functionality and to use this description as a tool for design verification and/or test generation. This high level description can be derived from documentation and the functional specification.

When a digital circuit is designed on the basis of a program in an HDL, the correctness of the design needs to be verified against the circuit's high level description. The verification should be done in terms of the function that the manufactured chip is to perform. The design and the functional specification both describe this function. This function can be further decomposed into a finite number of subfunctions. A subfunction is represented by each path of the program in an HDL. The application of symbolic execution[1-4] on the path produces the subfunction information: a path constraint and symbolic algebraic expressions. A path constraint is conditions that must be satisfied to follow a given path and correspond to the domain of a subfunction. The symbolic algebraic expressions correspond to the computations of each subfunction. The functional specification can be specified in terms of the domain and the computation for each subfunction. If the functional specification is given in a program similar to the one in an HDL, the subfunction information can be obtained from that program by using symbolic execution, too. The comparison of two functional representations, the design and the functional specification can reveal the discrepancies in either the functional specification or the design.

In the next section, we will introduce the symbolic execution technique and symbolic execution tree. In Section 3, we will discuss the design verification technique for VLSI circuits which are described in an HDL.

2. SYMBOLIC EXECUTION AND SYMBOLIC EXECUTION TREE

During a symbolic execution, a symbol rather than an actual value is assigned to each input variable, and the execution is performed with respect to these symbols. The outcome of a predicate can be automatically determined if the symbolic expression, representing that predicate, consists only of a constant. Otherwise, an outcome of the predicate cannot be determined because it is impossible to evaluate a symbolic expression. In order to continue the execution, a particular outcome must be specified. This selection leads to a condition for selecting the outcome, which can be represented by a path constraint. Let this symbolic constraint be the path constraint (PC), which is considered to have an initial value of "TRUE." As the symbolic execution proceeds, more decision points are encountered and their outcomes are selected.

140

CH1815-0/83/0000/0140$01.00© 1983 IEEE

Each time an outcome is selected, PC is updated by taking an intersection of the previous PC and the symbolic constraint corresponding to the condition necessary to take the selected outcome. When the execution is terminated at the exit of the program, PC contains conditions necessary to execute the path during the symbolic execution.

The symbolic execution tree[1] is used to store the results of symbolic execution. More than one execution of paths are stored in this tree. As each statement is executed, a node representing the execution of the statement is attached to an existing leaf node of the tree. A new node B can be attached to an existing node A if and only if the execution of a statement in B can immediately follow the execution of a statement in node A. Furthermore, each node of the tree contains certain execution information, denoted as STATE={V,PC,LC}, where V is a vector containing all the symbolic values in the program, LC points to the statement number, and PC stores the path constraint for the path between the entry point and the current node in the tree.

A given program is considered to perform function F with a domain D and a computation Z. F can be further decomposed to a set of subfunctions f_i, where $1 \leq i \leq m$. Then, d_i is a domain of

$$f_i \left(\bigcup_{i=1}^{m} d_i = D \right),$$

and z_i is a computation of f_i. Each subfunction is considered to be implemented by each executable path in the program. When the program contains loops, the number of the paths may be infinite. Hence, it is necessary to derive a closed form[5] for each loop so that any two paths that differ only in their iteration number of the same loop can be considered to be one path. Each path in the symbolic execution tree corresponds to a subfunction and the functional information is stored at each terminal leaf. PC and V stored at each terminal leaf represent d_i and z_i for each subfunction, respectively. Hence, a symbolic execution tree is defined as a two-tuple of the path constraints and symbolic algebraic expressions.

Let T be a symbolic execution tree, and let P and E be sets of path constraints and symbolic algebraic expressions, respectively. Then,

$$P = \{ p_j \mid 1 \leq j \leq m \}$$

$$E = \{ e_j \mid 1 \leq j \leq m \}.$$

Example 1: Consider a program given in Figure 1. This example program accepts three inputs X1, X2 and N and returns output Z. Three symbols #x1, #x2, and #n are produced and assigned to X1, X2, and N, respectively. The symbolic execution tree containing the information for two subfunctions is given in Figure 2. The first statement Y2 := X1 is executed, changing the value of Y2 from undefined to #x1. The execution of this statement changes both V and

LC. Y2 is now assigned to #x1. The second statement Y1 = X1 + Y2 is executed. This changes the value of Y1 from undefined to #x1+#x2. Again only V and LC are changed. The third statement, which is a decision statement, needs special attention. Since the value of Y1 is #x1+#x2, the outcome is not automatically determined. The selection of the TRUE path leads us to statement 4 by computing a new PC: PC = TRUE and (#x1+#x2)<10. The execution continues in this way until the exit statement is executed. The first execution ends at tree node 4 and corresponds to subfunction 1. The next execution will be started from node 3. The selection of the FALSE path will lead to a loop. The closed form for this loop is represented as Y2 = X2 + N(N+1)/2. Therefore, we replace statement 5 with this statement. Only the variables changed due to the loop execution are shown in the symbolic execution tree. The STATE information stored at node 4 and 6 contains the path constraints and symbolic algebraic expressions for subfunctions 1 and 2.

```
Input(X1, X2, N)
Output( Z )


  BEGIN
1    Y2 = X2;
2    Y1 = X1 + Y2;
3    IF Y1 < 10 THEN
4       Z = Y1 + 10
     ELSE
5       FOR I = 1 to N
            Y2 = Y2 + 1;
6       Z = Y2;
  END
```

Figure 1. Example Program to Illustrate Symbolic Execution

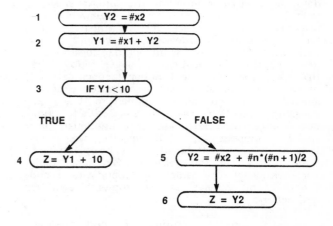

Figure 2. Symbolic Execution Tree for Example 1

3. VERIFICATION FOR VLSI CIRCUITS DESIGN

It is well known that the functional specification for a software system is very important. Without a complete and correct functional specification, a programmer cannot determine what should be developed and cannot verify that the implemented software is correct. In addition, errors caused by a faulty functional specification are generally the most expensive to fix.

Based on this experience with software, we believe that it is very important to have a complete and correct functional specification for VLSI circuits before the next level design is developed. Since a manufactured circuit, unlike a software system, cannot be physically altered to fix errors, it is especially important that this hardware functional specification be error-free and that the transformation from specification to design be done correctly.

The functional specification and design both describe the particular function that the manufactured chip is to perform in different forms. This function may be decomposed into a finite number of subfunctions. In this section, we show a procedure for comparing corresponding subfunctions specified in the specification and existing in the design. The discrepancies detected as the results of this comparison can reveal the existence of errors in either the specification or the design. Such a discrepancy makes it vital to examine the functional specification and the design to find the source of the problem. This comparison of two different forms that represent the same function is similar to the dual programming technique used in software development. Two teams develop two distinct programs based on the same specification and compare their results during the development. (It is assumed that the probability of two teams having the same kind of errors is very low.) Any discrepancies between the two programs indicate that errors may exist in either of them.

Now consider the two forms of the function: the functional specification and the design. To date, no particular form for the functional specification for VLSI circuits exists. However, the possible forms for it are: 1) in English, 2) in a table specifying the domain and computation of each subfunction, and 3) in another form of program possibly in abstraction level higher than HDL programs. If the functional specification is given something similar to a computer program, symbolic execution can be applied to it and the symbolic execution tree can be derived. However, since there exists no such functional specification language for VLSI circuits, we assume that the functional specification be given in a table form. Let this table be functional table. Each entry of the table corresponds to a subfunction and consists of two tuples: condition and action.

Let S be two tuples of conditions and actions, denoted by

$$C = \{ c_i \mid 1 \leq i \leq n \}$$

$$A = \{ a_i \mid 1 \leq i \leq n \}.$$

When the functional specification is given only in English, the functional table can be constructed by extracting the conditions described, considering the combinations of conditions, and associating them with the corresponding actions. Such a method has been successfully used in software testing.[6]

The functional table partitions the input space into n disjoint subspaces. Another partition was done by applying symbolic execution on the program written in an HDL and constructing symbolic execution tree. Note that a symbolic execution tree is represented by two tuples: P and E.

In order to verify the correctness of the design, it is necessary to associate each c_i with its corresponding p_j. After the relationships are established, corresponding computations can be examined and compared.

To find the relationship between two descriptions, we need to establish the mapping functions, starting from either the conditions in C or path constraints in P.

Let the mapping from c_i to p_j be denoted by

$$c_i(t) \rightarrow p_j(t),$$

such that c_i corresponds to p_j for some t in c_i.

Let the mapping from p_j to c_i be denoted by

$$p_j(t') \rightarrow c_i(t'),$$

such that p_j corresponds to c_i for some t' in p_j. Note that if there exists no such a mapping between them, then the domain of this mapping is null. If the mappings between c_i and p_j are bijective, then the relationship between them is represented by

$$c_i \Leftrightarrow p_j$$

The main steps of the verification method are as follows:

1. For each c_i, find t that satisfies the condition in c_i. Then, search the corresponding p_j that is also satisfied by t. Hence, $c_i(t) \rightarrow p_j(t)$.

2. For each p_j, find t' that satisfies the condition in p_j. Then, search the corresponding c_i that is also satisfied by t'. Thus, $p_j(t') \rightarrow c_i(t')$.

3. If $c_i(t) \rightarrow p_j(t)$ and $p_j(t') \rightarrow c_i(t')$, then $c_i \Leftrightarrow p_j$.

The procedure explained above can result in the following four categories of errors:

1. Any domain of the mapping is null. This means that some subfunction in one description is not specified in the other description.

2. For $c_i <\!=\!> p_j$, the evaluation of expressions with t and t' can result in either $a_i(t) \neq e_j(t)$ or $e_j(t') \neq a_i(t')$.

3. In the case that $c_i(t) \rightarrow p_j(t)$ and $p_j(t') \rightarrow c_k(t')$ for $i \neq j \neq k$, the evaluation of expressions with t and t' can result in either $a_i(t) \neq e_j(t)$ or $e_j(t') \neq a_k(t')$.

4. In case that $p_j(t') \rightarrow c_i(t')$ and $c_i(t) \rightarrow p_\ell(t)$ for $i \neq j \neq \ell$, the evaluation of expressions with t and t' can result in either $a_i(t') \neq e_j(t')$ or $e_j(t) \neq a_\ell(t)$.

Example 2: To illustrate the algorithm, consider a hypothetical machine that adopts register-storage instruction sets. The functional specification and design compute an effective address and return the contents stored at the effective address. The format of the instruction is given in Figure 3. This machine takes three different addressing modes: the first computes the address by summing the displacement, the contents of the base register, and the contents of the index register; the second is an immediate addressing; the third is an indirect addressing. The addressing modes are supposed to be specified by the values of bit positions 2 and 3 in the instruction. The functional specification is given in Figure 4 and the design is given in Figure 5. In both specification and design written in an HDL, we use a notation INST(n:m) for the binary value of bits from n to m in INST. For the design, this notation can be considered to be a subroutine which does a computation and returns the result. Symbolic execution can be extended to call such a subroutine. We deliberately seeded three errors to demonstrate the procedure: two into the design and one to the specification. The first error seeded in the design is a failure to specify the correct bit positions to specify the base register. Instead of correct bit positions 8 and 9, bit positions 9 and 10 are specified. This error may not be detected as long as bit positions 8, 9 and 10 contain the same number. The second error seeded in the design is an incorrect use of an address and a memory contents for the indirect addressing. The address and the contents are reversed in their specifications. This error may not be detected if the number of instructions adopting the indirect addressing is very small and seldom used. However, the error manifests when such an instruction is encountered. The error seeded into the specification is a failure to specify the handling of incorrect instructions whose operation codes end with 11.

From the symbolic execution we obtained the subfunctions' information, which is given in Figure 6. Although we need to generate symbolic values for all the inputs, we only showed symbolic values for INST and PC because the rest of the inputs are not used to express either the

path constraint or computation. Let #ij denote the symbolic values of INST(j) for $0 \leq j \leq 15$. For example, INST(6) is assigned to a symbolic value #i6. PC is assigned to a symbolic value #pc. Because of the ambiguous array reference, we cannot resolve array indexes. For such cases, we expressed outputs by using the arrays. Since no path constraint involves these arrays, the ambiguous array problem does not impose troubles.

REGISTER-STORAGE INSTRUCTION SET

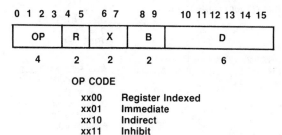

0 1 2 3 4 5	6 7	8 9	10 11 12 13 14 15		
OP	R	X	B	D	
4	2	2	2	6	

OP CODE

xx00	Register Indexed
xx01	Immediate
xx10	Indirect
xx11	Inhibit

Figure 3. Instruction Format of a Hypothetical Machine

For the first step of the algorithm, consider the following test data for each subfunction:

t_1 for c_1 xx01xx11xxxxxxxx
t_2 for c_2 xx00xx0110010111
t_3 for c_3 xx00xx0011000110
t_4 for c_4 xx00xx1000110000
t_5 for c_5 xx00xx0000100000
t_6 for c_6 xx10xx1010xxxxxx

By using these test cases, we obtain the following mappings:

$$c_1(t_1) \rightarrow p_7(t_1)$$
$$c_2(t_2) \rightarrow p_6(t_2)$$
$$c_3(t_3) \rightarrow p_5(t_3)$$
$$c_4(t_4) \rightarrow p_3(t_4)$$
$$c_5(t_5) \rightarrow p_5(t_5)$$
$$c_6(t_6) \rightarrow p_1(t_6)$$

For the second step of the algorithm, consider the following test case for each subfunction:

t'_1 for p_1 xx10xx1010xxxxxx
t'_2 for p_2 xx11xxxxxxxxxxxx
t'_3 for p_3 xx00xx1100100001
t'_4 for p_4 xx00xx0000010001
t'_5 for p_5 xx00xx0011011111
t'_6 for p_6 xx00xx1110010101
t'_7 for p_7 xx01xx11xxxxxxxx

By using these test cases, we derive the following mappings:

$$p_1(t'_1) \rightarrow c_6(t'_1)$$
$$p_2(t'_2) \rightarrow \phi$$
$$p_3(t'_3) \rightarrow c_4(t'_3)$$
$$p_4(t'_4) \rightarrow c_5(t'_4)$$
$$p_5(t'_5) \rightarrow c_3(t'_5)$$
$$p_6(t'_6) \rightarrow c_2(t'_6)$$
$$p_7(t'_7) \rightarrow c_1(t'_7)$$

CONDITIONS	ACTIONS
1 $(INST(2) = 0) \& (INST(3) = 1)$	EA = 0; CONT = INST(6:7); PC = PC + 1; ERROR = 0;

2 $(INST(2) = 0) \& (INST(3) = 0) \&$
$(INST(8:9) \neq 0) \& (INST(6:7) \neq 0)$
	EA = REG[INST(8:9)]
	    + REG[INST(6:7)]
	    + INST(10:15);
	CONT = MEM[EA];
	PC = PC + 2;
	ERROR = 0;

3 $(INST(2) = 0) \& (INST(3) = 0) \&$ $(INST(8:9) \neq 0) \& (INST(6:7) = 0)$	EA = REG[INST(8:9)] + INST(10:15); CONT = MEM[EA]; PC = PC + 2; ERROR = 0;
4 $(INST(2) = 0) \& (INST(3) = 0) \&$ $(INST(8:9) = 0) \& (INST(6:7) \neq 0)$	EA = REG[INST(6:7)] + INST(10:15); CONT = MEM[EA]; PC = PC + 2; ERROR = 0;
5 $(INST(2) = 0) \& (INST(3) = 0) \&$ $(INST(8:9) = 0) \& (INST(6:7) = 0)$	EA = INST(10:15); CONT = MEM[EA]; PC = PC + 2; ERROR = 0;
6 $(INST(2) = 1) \& (INST(3) = 0)$	EA = MEM[INST(6:9)] CONT = MEM[EA] PC = PC + 2; ERROR = 0;

Figure 4. Functional Specification for Example 2

From the third step, we obtain the following relationships:

$$c_1 <=> p_7$$
$$c_2 <=> p_6$$
$$c_3 <=> p_5$$
$$c_4 <=> p_3$$
$$c_6 <=> p_1$$

Since the relationships between c_i and p_j are established, the error detection procedure is continued, according to the error categories already explained.

1. Category One Error

$p_2 \rightarrow \phi$ indicates that a subfunction whose domain is p_2 in the design does not exist in the functional specification. The examination of both specification and design reveals that the functional specification failed to specify the case where an instruction contains an "inhibit" operation code.

2. Category Two Error

No errors can be detected in $c_1 <=> p_7$ relation. It turned out that these two subfunctions have a one to one correspondence and both are correct.

For $c_4 <=> p_3$, $c_3 <=> p_5$, and $c_2 <=> p_6$, errors can be detected unless outputs are coincidentally correct. These errors are due to the failure in the specification of the base register. The error affected both domains and computations. For example, consider the first relationship. The error is not detected if the contents of REG(1) is 0. Therefore, a test case to specify the non-zero contents of REG(1) can reveal the existence of the error. Although we cannot deny the existence of such coincidental correctness of the outputs, such a case is caused by double errors that are less probable.

For the relation $c_6 <=> p_1$, there is no domain error but the computation is wrong. Again unless the outputs are coincidentally correct, the error is detected.

3. Category Three Error.

For $c_5 \rightarrow p_5$ and $p_5 \rightarrow c_3$, errors are caused by the failure to specify the correct bit positions of the base register. Again unless outputs are coincidentally correct, the error is detected.

4. Category Four Error.

For $p_4 \rightarrow c_5$ and $c_5 \rightarrow p_5$, errors are caused by the failure to specify the correct bit positions of the base register. Again unless outputs are coincidentally correct, the error is detected.

Test cases generated to associate corresponding c_i and p_j can be used to test the manufactured chip. It is known from software testing that the general problem of deriving a set of values to satisfy an arbitrary path constraint is an unsolvable problem. Because of the theoretical limitation, two approaches are often taken in software testing. The first approach imposes an extra condition which requires that the path constraint should consist of solely linear constraints. The linear programming can be used for such constraints. The second approach searches a set of values which satisfies the path constraint by generating a set of values systematically.

```
INPUT(INST(0:15), PC, MEM(0:1023), REG(0:3))
OUTPUT(EA, PC, CONT, ERROR)

BEGIN
   BASE = 0; CONT = 0; EA = 0; INDEX = 0;

IF(INST(2) = 1) & (INST(3) = 0) THEN
   BEGIN
      IND = IND + INST(6:9);
      CONT = MEM(IND);
      EA = MEM(CONT);
      PC = PC + 2;
      ERROR = 0;
   END

IF(INST(2) = 1) & (INST(3) = 1) THEN
      ERROR = 1;

IF(INST(2) = 0) & (INST(3) = 0) THEN
   BEGIN
      BASE = BASE + INST(9:10);
      IF BASE ≠ 0 THEN
         BASE = REG(BASE);
      INDEX = INDEX + INST(6:7);
      IF INDEX ≠ 0 THEN
         INDEX = REG(INDEX)
      EA = EA + INST(10:15)
      EA = EA + BASE + INDEX
      CONT = MEM(EA);
      PC = PC + 2;
      ERROR = 0;
   END

IF(INST(2) = 0) & (INST(3) = 1) THEN
   BEGIN
      CONT = CONT + INST(6:7);
      PC = PC + 1;
      ERROR = 0;
   END

END.
```

Figure 5. Design Description in an HDL

One symbolic executor[2] for software testing uses the first approach and can be used to generate test cases for those programs whose path constraints consist of only the linear constraints. One study[7] on computer program characteristics indicates that many, if not all, programs possesses only linear constraints and that this assumption is practical. One symbolic executor[3] and its successor[4] employ the second approach. The successor version was successfully used to generate tests of a control program for a nuclear power plant.

Our example given here involves only linear constraints and hence, linear programming can be applied to generate a test case, although we manually generated the test for this example. Since each variable in the program in an HDL has only a discrete value, it is much easier to derive a set of values to satisfy the path constraint compared with that of software programs, even if the path constraint consists of nonlinear constraints.

CONCLUDING REMARKS

The function that a manufactured chip is intended to have is specified in two distinct forms: a functional specification and a program written in an HDL. The application of symbolic execution to the HDL program produces function information compatible with that of functional specification. The comparison of corresponding subdomains and computations in the two different representations can reveal possible errors in either the functional specification or the design.

SUBFUNCTION 1

$(\#i2 = 1) \& (\#i3 = 0)$

EA = MEM[MEM[8*#i6 + 4*#i7 + 2*#i8 + #i9)]]
CONT = MEM[8*#i6 + 4*#i7 + 2*#i8 + #i9]
PC = #pc + 2;
ERROR = 0

SUBFUNCTION 2

$(\#i2 = 1) \& (\#i3 = 1)$

EA = 0;
CONT = 0;
PC = #pc;
ERROR = 1;

SUBFUNCTION 3

$(\#i2 = 0) \& (\#i3 = 0) \& (2*\#i9 + \#i10 \neq 0) \& (2*\#i6 + \#i7 \neq 0)$

EA = REG[2*#i9 + #i10] + REG [2*#i6 + #i7]
    +32*#i10 + 16*#i11 + 8*#i12 + 4*#i13 + 2*#i14 +#i15;

CONT = MEM[REG[2*#i9 +#i10] + REG[2*#i6 + #i7]
          +32*#i10 + 16*#i11 + 8*#i12 + 4*#i13 + 2*#i14 +#i15]
PC = #pc +2;
ERROR = 0;

SUBFUNCTION 4

$(\#i2 = 0) \& (\#i3 = 0) \& (2*\#i9 + \#i10 = 0) \& (2*\#i6 + \#i7 = 0)$

EA = 32*#i10 + 16*#i11 + 8*#i12 + 4*#i13 + 2*#i14 + #i15;
CONT = MEM[32*#i10 + 16*#i11 + 8*#i12 + 4*#i13 + 2*#i14 + #i15
PC = #pc +2;
ERROR = 0;

SUBFUNCTION 5

$(\#i2 = 0) \& (\#i3 = 0) \& (2*\#i9 + \#i10 \neq 0) \& (2*\#i6 + \#i7 = 0)$

EA = REG[2*#i9 + #i10]
    +32*#i10 + 16*#i11 + 8*#i12 + 4*#i13 +2*#i14 +*#i15;
CONT = MEM[REG[2*#i9 + #i10]
          +32*#i10 + 16*#i11 + 8*#i12 + 4*#i13 + 2*#i14 + #i15]
PC = #pc +2;
ERROR = 0;

SUBFUNCTION 6

$(\#i2 = 0) \& (\#i3 = 0) \& (2*\#i9 + \#i10 = 0) \& (2*\#i6 + \#i7 \neq 0)$

EA = REG[2*#i6 + #i7]
    +32*#i10 + 16*#i11 + 8*#i12 + 4*#i13 + 2*#i14 + #i15;
CONT = MEM[REG[2*#i6 + i7]
          +32*# i10 + 16*#i11 + 8*#i12 + 4*#i13 + 2*#i14 + #i15]
PC = #pc +2;
ERROR = 0;

SUBFUNCTION 7

$(\#i2 = 0) \& (\#i3 = 1)$

EA = 0
CONT = 2*#i6 + #i7;
PC = #pc +1;
ERROR = 0;

Figure 6. Subfunctions from Symbolic Execution

Future work needed for this technique involves a development of a representation describing the functional specification on which symbolic execution can be applied. Such a representation expands the application area of this technique and makes the comparison of symbolically represented domains and computations possible. Also needed is a study collecting the characteristics for the programs in the HDL describing the VLSI circuits design. The result of such a study may suggest that it is practical to consider only the linear constraints.

145

REFERENCES

1. J. Darringer and J. King, "Applications of Symbolic Executions to Program Testing," IEEE Computer (April 1978).

2. L.A. Clarke, "A System to Generate Test Data and Symbolically Execute Programs," IEEE Trans. on Software Engineering, Vol. SE-2, No. 3, pp. 215-222 (September 1976).

3. C. Ramamoorthy, F. Ho, and W. Chen, "On the Automated Generation of Program Test Data," IEEE Trans. on Software Engineering, Vol. SE-2, No. 4, pp.293-300 (December 1976).

4. C. Ramamoorthy, Y. Mok, F. Bastani, G. Chin, and K. Suzuki, "Application of a Methodology for the Development and Validation of Reliable Process Control Software," IEEE Trans. on Software Engineering, Vol. SE-7, No. 6, pp. 537-555 (November 1981).

5. T. Cheatham, G. Holloway, and J. Townley, "Symbolic Evaluation and the Analysis of Programs," IEEE Trans. on Software Engineering, Vol. SE-5, No. 4, pp. 402-417 (July 1979).

6. G. Myers, Software Reliability: Principles and Practices, John Wiley and Sons, Inc, pp. 218-227 (1976).

7. L. White, "A Domain Strategy for Computer Program Testing," IEEE Trans. on Software Engineering, Vol SE-6, No. 3, pp. 247-257 (May 1980).

8. S. Su and Y. Hsieh, "Testing Functional Faults in Digital Systems Described by Register Transfer Language," 1981 International Test Conference, pp. 447-457 (October 1981).

9. W. Cory, "Symbolic Simulation for Functional Verification with ADLIB and SDL," 18th Design Automation Conference, pp. 213-219 (June 1981).

VLSI Computer Aided Design

INTEGRATION OF DESIGN AUTOMATION TOOLS
FOR THE CUSTOM VLSI CAPABILITY OF A SYSTEMS FIRM

by Jack S. Thomas

Design Automation Engineering Department
Aerojet ElectroSystems Corporation, Azusa, California

Abstract

The VLSI DA requirements of a systems firm are driven by the need to accomodate diversity in design approach and application. Support of a diversity of design approach for both linear and digital devices is necessary to enable new circuit concepts and to support the solving of unique system problems.

Various DA software components are available but no integrated system is yet available. Some companies are strong on analysis, others on graphics and other on verification systems. Engineering work stations have not yet reached an acceptable level of maturity.

This article will show a modular, upward expandable system of DA components offering a practical solution to these problems. Software engineering principles are applied to planning, organizing, staffing, directing and control of the system development. Individual DA components are acquired and integrated together with other existing components from past investment to meet near and far term needs of a systems firm.

Problem

There are significant problems dealing with the complexity and size of microelectronics and in the process of prototyping, validating and testing of microelectronics. The problems present in the development of microelectronics and card level electronic circuits though apparently similar, are sufficiently divergent such that different development processes are required. Design Automation (DA) techniques serve to reduce development time and cost and improve the integrity of card level circuits. However, the size and complexity of the design steps and the level of physical phenomenology required for LSI microcircuit development demand extensive DA capabilities.

The diversity of types of computer files representing the microcircuit design and their physical locations and size impose severe database managment problems. Typically, four different computer systems will be involved in the DA process of a single device with geometric files on two of the systems in excess of 10 megabytes. Intermediate files of approximately 100-200 megabytes will be generated by the verification software for each digital device. In addition, libraries of subcircuit cells for multiple fabrication processes must be managed and maintained on multiple physical computer systems. An integrated DA system that maintains data integrity in the translation of files from one form to another and between systems is required.

Trade secrecy among the successful microelectronics producers impedes the progress of setting up a new microelectronics design and manufacturing capability. Practically all aspects of the development process and methodologies are protected, including the DA software systems support. There is an unwillingness among producers to share DA software performance results for the same DA software purchased from a common vendor. When visibility is made available, usually due to the desire of a producer to market their DA software, a large discrepancy is often observed upon further investigation. This descrepancy is the difference between the methodology being promoted by the DA group and the actual methodology being followed by the device engineering close to the design fabrication and testing. Enrolled support and good working relationships are necessary with the producers and users of DA software to obtain clear visibility into performance of functional DA software systems.

The size, complexity, and cost of each individual DA program of an integrated CAD system and the amount of effort it takes to quantitize an evaluation of each program is staggering. Typically, vendor maintained logic and circuit simulators are implemented with 20K-400K lines of high order language code, usually FORTRAN and cost from $50K-$300K. Geometric analysis programs are of the same magnitude. Typically a dozen such programs will be involved in a microcircuit development cycle. A combination of techniques is required to accurately evaluate software programs for purchase as components in an integrated DA system.

There is a great deal of diversity in microelectronics design approaches, verification techniques, fabrication processes, and applications. The diversity problem has contributed to the lack of a commercially available integrated microelectronics DA system. Microelectronics producers typically operate with a fragmented set of DA tools from a multiplicity of vendors, requiring hand conversion of data from the output of one analysis tool to the next. Some microelectronics producers are in the process of integrating their tools, however, many of the individual tools were developed in-house and are not offered for sale as part of an integrated system. Other microelectronics producers have partial integrated systems in place with plans for full integration, but achieve integrated support by offering a narrow design approach. Support of a diversity of design approaches for both linear and digital devices is necessary to enable new circuit design concepts and to support the solving of unique system problems. The acquisition of a verification system independent from the design approach is necessary to support the diversity of design approach and to enable flexibility in the selection of fabrication vendors. This flexibility includes maintaining compatibility with in-house facilities.

In addition to the problem of satisfying the driving requirements of accommodation of diversity, there are other problems. The rapid evolution of host hardware and its support; the size, complexity and cost of each individual design automation tool; and the system's integration problem limits an individual vendor's ability to offer the turnkey system prior to its obsolescence. There may never be a commercially available turnkey system that satisfies the requirements for custom linear and digital VLSI design.

Objective

The objective is to set up an integrated microelectronics DA system commensurate with microcircuit development needs. One emphasis is to provide the kind of support that enables upward expandability of microcircuit development capabilities, while taking advantage of existent capital equipment from past investment. The major emphasis is for automatic check, analysis, and maintenance of data integrity for developing complex devices for production at different foundries and with differing technologies. Emphasis is also to be placed on an automatic checking, error detection and process oriented analysis. The following list of requirements are fundamental to stated objectives and were useful as criteria in the evulation of capability acquisitions:

General Requirements

1. In-house Microelectronics DA Capability--A microelectronics DA system shall be provided for in-house development and qualification of custom integrated circuits. The capability shall be complete to the geometric level such that proprietary symbolic circuit designs need not be exposed to outside supporting service vendors such as silicon foundry and test facilities.

2. Device Development Cost and Schedule Control--The system shall provide improved cost and schedule control over outside custom IC design services, while increasing its throughput capability.

3. Broad Based Support of Multiple Fabrication Processes--The system shall be broad based enough to accommodate a variety of IC fabrication processes and vendors. The bulk CMOS process for fabrication at five different silicon foundries shall be supportable.

4. Multiple Device Technologies--Diverse technologies such as bipolar, CMOS, NMOS, and GaAs shall be supportable through database expansion without replication of independent software systems.

5. Analog and Digital Device Support--The system shall support the development of analog (linear) devices as well as digital devices. For linear devices, specific capabilities shall be provided for switched capacitor filter development. For digital devices, extensibility to gate array and macrocell design capability shall be provided. For both digital and analog devices, a structured standard cell library DA architecture shall be developed.

6. Support of Multiple Design Approach--The system shall provide capability to the designer to take advantage of aggressive design automation processes, such as standard cell autorouting, even at the expense of reduced fabrication yield for low production volume devices. Capability shall also be provided for the designer to produce full custom optimized layouts for the high volume devices. The selection or intermixing of these two design approaches and use of tools within the system shall be at the discretion of the designer.

7. Common Database and Device Master Representation--The system shall be implemented with the concept of making all stages of the design cycle reference and use a common database to prevent hand translation of data from one form in one design step to the next step. The master representation, except for back-up copies, of each design shall be stored in only one designated location. This system shall be implemented without introducing compromising complexity to the user.

8. Common User Interface--The system shall provide a common software interface and operating procedure for design engineers to use for access to the wide variety of microelectronics DA software support tools.

9. Software Acquisition Through Purchase Rather Than Development--Software components shall be purchased with warantee, maintenance and training agreements where possible. Software shall only be developed where necessary in order to accommodate an interface or to perform some special application. Software development interface modules between two vendor supplied packages shall be pursued with each of the vendors prior to company internal development planning and committment.

10. Phased Delivery of Software--DA system implementation and integration planning shall provide for software receipt, installation, configuration control, acceptance testing, in-house training, and production operational readiness in a sequential/phased schedule. This is to allow computer system managers and DA engineers the ability to concentrate their efforts with maximum vendor feedback early after software receipt.

11. DA Toolsmith Specialists--Each particular software package such as the logic simulator, the circuit simulator, electrical parameter checker, etc., shall have two specialists assigned. They shall have responsibility for intimately knowing

the details of the program's applications language, operational procedures, documentation, failure report log, and general quirks. This cognizance shall be maintained such that other more casual users may depend upon the specialist for minor instruction and problem solving from time to time.

The specialists need not be members of the DA engineering or support staffs. It is preferable that the specialists be selected from the microelectronics or circuit engineering staffs who are the most frequent users of the programs.

12. New Software Evaluation Accommodation--The system shall be capable of accepting new DA software for both evaluation and mainstream use as new packages become available that are advertised to increase design integrity and/or productivity.

13. Upward Expandability--The system shall provide for the upward expandability into other front end DA tools outside the microelectronics domain, such as behavioral language analyzers, logic compilers, and symbolic schematic entry packages. Card level front end DA commonality and compatibility in the areas of schematic entry, and logic and circuit simulation shall be accommodated.

14. Software Library Support--The system shall encompass a library support facility for the control and maintenance of the operating system components, applications software, and standard cell libraries for each silicon foundry vendor and process that has been acquired. The system shall provide a method by which infrequently used libraries and sub-libraries can be conveniently maintained on tape and recalled when needed rather than on disc in order to effectively use computer resources. The capability to add new common and unique standard cells to the libraries shall be provided.

15. Intercomputer File Transfer Integrity--All mass file data that is transferred from one computer to another shall be accomplished with an error protection strategy capable of detecting bit dropout/dropin of single and multiple occurrences within the file. Transfers that are accomplished over phone line connections shall have the capability to retransmit erroneous messages automatically without re-transmitting the entire file.

16. Initial Work - 10 Devices--The system shall be capable of providing microelectronics DA support for the design, fabrication, and qualification of ten devices per year for the first two years. Add-on expandability shall accommodate a growth of 50%/year for the following 5 years.

17. Level of Device Complexity--The system shall provide computer resource capacity sufficient to handle the devices specified in requirement 16 with an average complexity of 12,000 transistors per device for the first two years. Thereafter, resources shall be allocated to handle a complexity of approximately double each year for the following three years.

18. System Usage Accountability--Capability shall be provided to obtain a centralized report on the usage of computer resources such as CPU time, terminal time, disc storage, tape inventory, etc.

for all physical machines. The report shall include accumulated charges from each timesharing bureau account.

Key Constraints

19. Use of Current In-house Facilities--The system shall take advantage of current in-house shared resource capabilities where possible. For example, graphics editing shall be accomplished with the Calma GDS II capabilities, and simulation and analysis shall be accomplished on the VAX 11/780.

20. Initial Use of High Cost Software Via Timesharing--System software that fits into the category of high cost software (>$40K) shall initially be acquired for use through a service bureau.

21. Compatibility of Timesharing Software To VAX--Consistent with requirements 19 and 20 above, system software that is acquired for bureau use shall be selected on the basis of its VAX compatibility. This is to allow the purchase of VAX compatable software when it becomes cost effective in conjunction with in-house VAX facility. It is desirable that the software be initially developed on a VAX 11/780 system for higher assurance of compatibility.

22. Compatibility of System to Silicon Foundry Vendor System--System software that is currently being used by the silicon foundry vendors in their design process shall be acquired as favored tools due to their compatibility with the vendors geometric and process parameter specification.

Approach

As a result of the approach to buy rather than develop capability, there are few in-house software development tasks to perform. This allows a rather small DA staff to concentrate on streamlining the system operation, keeping the system organized, planning improvements, formulating benchmarks, etc.

Using the objectives stated, a survey was conducted to purchase components to build the DA system.

Five major system components were selected to meet the objectives:

1. A Logic simulator was selected that is particularly well suited to simulate dynamic MOS device circuitry. It also feeds the heirarchical form of the logic network to the mask verification system, and performs fault simulation. Support of board level simulation with a library of logic models is one of the capabilities that a systems firm will generally have as a requirement that a semiconductor producer may not.

2. The circuit simulator SPICE was selected for in-house fabrication and for preliminary circuit studies prior to simulation runs by the simulator used by silicon vendors. Some silicon vendors use a different similator which requires operation of it remotely at the vendor facility or at timesharing bureaus. They are set up by the silicon vendor to accurately model transistors and other elements according to their specific fabrication process. The process parameters specified and controlled by process engineers in the vendors MOS

lab/fab facility are specified in the same format as the circuit simulator syntax. Using SPICE in this case requires a one time translation and verification of the parameters between the two forms. Using the vendor's circuit simulator is an alternate to the cost and risk of conversion.

3. A hierarchical symbolic layout system was selected, allowing the custom layout of devices in on symbolic layer rather than in several layers.

4. A mask verification system was selected that check electrical rules, design rules, consistency of the layout with schematic, feeds the circuit simulator with accuracy updates, and prepares the graphics data for mask making.

5. A local area network (LAN) was selected that links together the whole facility and allows each device engineer to access any of the data processing equipment including analysis and simulation software at timesharing bureaus from a single terminal at his desk. It also allows the transfer of files between different physical computers controlled from the terminal.

Future Enhancements

The DA system is structured to accommodate advances in capability from industry technology that is currently not sufficiently mature. These areas which are considered important potential cost and schedule savers are:

Automated Device Architecture Design--Current university work in this area, if fruitful, could save considerable engineering time in front-end analysis and layout. This research includes system and hardware description languages and compilers to convert system descriptions directly to hardware. Also in this area is silicon compiler research, which compiles high level descriptions all the way to VLSI layouts. These efforts are being monitored via journals and conference proceedings.

Automatic Test Pattern Generation--There are two bases for test vector adequacy determination for digital devices: (1) logic network analysis and, (2) topological analysis. Logic network analysis is supported by the logic simulator by providing gate activity reports, fault simulation, node controlability and observability analyses, and the generation of expect data test vectors. It ignores the device layout, concentrating only on detection of electrical node short faults. Topological analysis takes the device layout into account, is more subtle and is supported by DA software only in the area of expect data test vector generation. For proposed device stimulus test vectors it concentrates on soft error modeling and special process fault modeling.

The formulation of device stimulus test vectors is planned to be done manually during the initial logic simulation phase. Manual augmentation of the vectors will occur in the accuracy update logic simulation phase after layout when the topological fault sensitivities are better understood. There may also be more manipulation and optimization of the test vectors during the test program

development phase that takes place concurrently with fabrication.

Research and development into automatic test pattern generation is underway by various DA groups in academic institutions and in the industry. Most of the development is oriented toward automatically generating statistically cost effective test vectors based on the logic network. These test vectors are intended to detect a statistically acceptable number of possible electrical node shorts. Automatic test vector generation oriented toward detecting faults caused by topological effects is a far less mature DA science. It requires the analysis of sequential signal propagation, crosstalk effects, and estimated node sensitivities to data patterns.

It is expected that network based software will be available in the next one to two years. It's acquisition and use may prove to provide long range savings in engineer's time, computer resources, and schedule deviation. This would be possible because of the elimination of the manual creation of the test vector stimulus file and the exhaustive fault simulation and test vector refinement.

Full network and topology based software is of the complexity of silicon compiler systems and will probably not be available for several years.

Differential Distributed Data Base Management--This enhancement to the network system will be offered by the local area network vendor. It provides time saving and increased data integrity in the centralized management of change to device representation data bases stored on separate physical machines.

Path Extraction and Analysis--This add-on enhancement to the mask verification system will be developed by the mask analysis software vendor. It raises the confidence of successful first time device fabrication runs to excess of 90 percent. It will also save computer time on very large logic devices by separating logic simulation and timing analysis.

Automatic Placement and Routing Software--Another area where a substantial amount of computer science research is being devoted by the industry is in the development of these algorithms. At the 19th annual DA Conference approximately 122 papers were presented with about 25% of them on this topic; mostly for gate array applications. This area is something that computers do not do very well for custom or standard cell design, which is why it has not progressed as rapidly as almost all other areas of DA in the last ten years. Development in this area will be monitored for progress and applicability.

Add-on Engineering Workstations (EWS)--There are several EWS's on the market currently, that when connected to the the local area network, would improve the interactiveness and streamline the development process, expecially in the growth of documents and schematic entry. An EWS configuration, although easier to use, was not made part of the basic plan because it's capabilities are redundant to the existing Calma graphics system, although easier to use. However, if the volume of device design tasks increases, the additional capability required would be most cost effectively obtained via an EWS than by adding on Calma hardware. Another consideration is that the EWS market is moving very fast and is very competitive. In one to two year's time, EWS's will have an order of magnitude increase in capabilities with half the cost.

Facility Operation

A block diagram of the facility is shown in Figure 1. Almost all the work of the device engineer will be accomplished from the terminal on each desk, shown on the upper right hand side of Figure 1. Each device engineer has one of these VT/100 compatible terminals. It is connected via the local area network (LAN) to all the facilities shown in Figure 1. Using a single command, a "virtual circuit" through the LAN to the host computer is established. Without moving from his desk, the device engineer will do the following:

1. Fetch logic and circuit network files from the Calma that has been extracted from schematic diagrams at that facility.

2. Using the logic network and a separate stimulus/probe file, operate the VAX based logic simulator (digital devices only).

3. Store the circuit network file and a separate stimulus/probe file to a timeshare bureau and operate the bureau based circuit simulator. Alternately, operate the VAX based circuit simulator directly.

4. Fetch a device geometry file from the Calma based graphics facility to the VAX and operate geometric analysis programs. Store the geometric outputs back to Calma for display and plot the outputs on the electrostatic plotter over the LAN.

5. Store test vector sets from the logic simulator to the tester at the test facility, and operate tester based test program development software.

6. Set up process variations for individual device lots on the MOS lab/fab facility and monitor the progress of wafer fabrication runs.

7. Monitor the overall use of these resources and generate centralized reports on the usage and cost for management.

Other operations are required to be done at the individual facilities. For example, schematic entry and geometric layout require direct access to graphics workstations at the Calma facility. Wafer probing, packaged device handling, and production tester operation require direct test facility access. The MOS lab/fab facility similarly requires direct access due to physical handling of wafer lots. At each of these separate facilities there is an identical terminal to the desk terminals providing identical operations and access to the whole system. This is an important time savings feature of the system. For example, in standard cell development at the Calma facility the device engineer or layout specialist may perform graphics work and then use his Calma workstation as

a VAX "virtual terminal". In this mode he will transfer the circuit to the VAX and submit a geometric analysis job. Returning to normal graphics operation, another circuit (or portion of the same circuit) will be developed concurrently with the analysis run. It is not intended that the Calma workstations be used extensively in virtual terminal mode since the graphics workstations are a much more valuable resource than desktop terminals.

The two portable alpha-numeric terminals will allow up to two device engineers to have access to the system from remote locations such as at a vendor fab facility. They may also be used to access the system from residence during off hours, weekends, holidays or special circumstances.

Conclusion

There may never be a commercially available integrated DA system that can satisfy the custom microelectronics requirements of systems companies due to the diversity of applications and design approach. However, there are good commercial DA components available from individual vendors that when acquired and integrated meet the requirements of custom VLSI device design and test.

It is important for commercial DA software and turnkey DA systems companies to recognize where the greatest potential for success for their companies and industry lies. It is with the concentration of quality and comprehensiveness of one or two of the phases of VLSI design and the mutual cooperation with machine interface formats and languages. The IEEE should join the customer base of these companies in discouraging them from the practice of scrambling or untoward licensing of program interface formats.

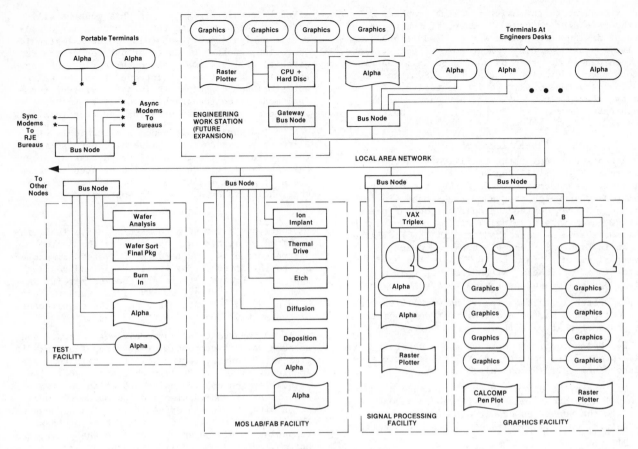

Figure 1 Integrated DA Facility

Part III: Reprints from COMPCON Spring 83

AN OVERVIEW OF VLSI INTERSECTED WITH SOFTWARE ENGINEERING

Mel Cutler

Office of Information Sciences Research
The Aerospace Corporation
P. O. Box 92957, Los Angeles, CA 90009
(213) 615-4524

ABSTRACT

The areas in which the disciplines of VLSI engineering and software engineering might interchange ideas are discussed. The presentation is organized around five working group topics devised in a recent workshop. Some of the areas of basic differences are also noted as a limiting boundary for the interchange.

INTRODUCTION

A Workshop on VLSI and Software Engineering was held from October 4-6, 1982, cosponsored by the IEEE Technical Committee on VLSI and the IEEE Technical Committee on Software Engineering. The goal was an interchange of ideas among researchers and practitioners in the two disciplines, hoping to discover areas for technology transfer between the two groups.

In order to provide more intensive interaction, the Workshop separated into five working groups.

1. Design Methodology

2. Design Synthesis and Measurement

3. Verification and Testing

4. Design Environment

5. Hardware Description Languages

The remainder of this paper is a personal view of the significant findings of the Workshop, allocated to the subject areas of those groups.

One major, but general, point is that there is a great deal of similarity in the design characteristics for real-time software and for custom VLSI. The case for an analogy between gate arrays/semi-custom and applications programming is weaker, as performance disappears as the major driver.

DESIGN METHODOLOGY

A significant area of agreement is that there is a common, cost-focusing life cycle in the two disciplines, sharing levels of development ranging from requirements analysis through evaluation.

Much of the thrust of the topic was also adopted by the Design Synthesis and Measurement group.

DESIGN SYNTHESIS AND MEASUREMENT

The goal of this group was to explore the **decision points** in existing processes of designing hardware/software systems.

The areas in which automation could be applied are where design decisions are currently made manually. Decisions are made among alternatives at different levels of abstraction because of the exponential complexity of the design and evaluation effort if the entire design space is explored only at the lowest level.

The impact of silicon compiler technology has yet to be felt because of the primitive nature and limited scope of the existing examples. Mature compilers do not allow the designer to make **any** decisions, but rather provide a default implementation structure. High level langage compilers generally share this characteristic, although various degrees of object code optimization can be selected for some compilers.

Another problem is the current state of hardware description language development (see that section). If a description language cannot specify, explicitly or implicitly, the intent of the designer, the tools must supply a default or set of default intents. Also, it is important to describe the environment as well as the device being modelled.

Thus, the group's view of the role of the synthesis language is to document the **decisions** made by the user/programmer to define the hardware/software system at the system requirements, specification of behavior and performance, abstract algorithm, computational structure (hardware/software), functional, Boolean equation, circuit families, elementary circuit, layout, and device physics levels.

In addition to functional behavior, the design must include other attributes. Performance, resource allocation, machine utilization reusability, reliability, testability, chip area and power budgets, timing strategy (asynchronous or synchronous or hybrid), control strategy (central or distributed or hybrid), are examples of areas in which the intent of the designer must be accommodated.

The group did not deal with the design and implementation of the synthesis tools themselves. The type and quality of interactive feedback, however, was deemed to be crucial to the success of the tools.

VERIFICATION AND TESTING

The generation and application of VLSI test patterns used to detect and diagnose manufacturing errors or hardware failures is a different process that has no analogue (no pun intended) in software engineering. Design verification, however, is an analogous problem in the two disciplines that is usually partially accomplished by testing the circuit or its representation (via simulation, for example) with representative inputs. However, the use of more advanced techniques has been under consideration for some time.

Application of formal software verification techniques to hardware is probable in the long term. The use of strategic software testing techniques in the VLSI design verification arena is more likely. These can provide acceptable probability of design correctness by exercising the different control paths and critical data values in a program.

Timing verification, currently under extensive development in the VLSI domain, could be applied readily to real-time software. The process is similar to functional verification in that assertions about the timing characteristics of a circuit might be attached to points in that circuit and internal timing characteristics (set-up times, hold times) be checked for consistency against these interface signal characteristics.

DESIGN ENVIRONMENT

In the tool system and user interface required for design, the needs of the two disciplines were found to be strikingly similar. The achievements in these areas are less similar, with VLSI ahead in capability and vision, but with standardization favoring Software Engineering.

The feeling was that neither discipline has developed the ideal design environment. Hence, the group concentrated on specifying the directions that such development should take. Summarizing some of these ideas:

- The environment should not restrict the methodology (n.b., the "design decisions" thrust of the Design Synthesis and Measurement group).

- The environment should include integrated support for the entire life cycle.

- The environment should support its **own** evolution, utilizing such techniques as metrics and adaptation.

- The environment should mechanize the reuse of components at various levels of design detail and life cycle, and the portability of proven concepts across different technologies/languages.

The challenge will be to make the environment usable, yet with adequate performance for production use.

There are a few differences between the two design disciplines that will countermand a parallel environment development. The major issue is that multiple domains exist in the VLSI arena, as design abstractions exist at multiple levels from system to circuit and process level. Also significant is that VLSI technology is determined very early in the life cycle, and this affects many aspects of the environment, such as libraries, test environment, and languages.

The group also addressed a variant of the theme of the Workshop -- that the issue was the **union** of VLSI and Software Engineering in order for the design environment to support **system** design.

HARDWARE DESCRIPTION LANGUAGES

Several areas for hardware description language development were identified. Most emphasized were the application of language features and orientations such as strong typing, abstract data types, generic objects, and functional programming. Monitors provide a language and system base for time-shared objects, and combine well with the abstract data type concepts. Another area that might adapt programming languages and techniques to the generally local control structure of digital hardware is event-oriented programming. Certain applications would benefit greatly from such approaches.

Encapsulation and structuring techniques are useful aspects of software design that can be adapted to hardware design, and that can be supported by language features. Exception handling is not well supported by hardware descrption languages, and a transfer of ideas from programming languages is indicated. Formal semantic specification and verification techniques require language extensions, and these could be provided from the programming languages experience. Non-deterministic programming might be applied to so-called "intelligent" VLSI circuits. The use of pedagogical languages has been useful in the teaching of and experimentation with programming language features and design techniques. This would be a novel area for application to hardware languages and design.

Although the research and experience are much richer in the field of programming languages, there are three areas in which the programming language designers and users might benefit from the languages used to describe hardware.

1. Refinement of a design from structure to behavior is possible within one language.

2. The use of graphics is considered to be necessary in order to visualize the design, often at multiple levels of abstraction.

158

3. Time is an explicit or implicit method of aggregating concurrent processing from independently-specified "processing elements" or processes.

The first two characteristics grew out of the engineering technique of drawing-based documentation. When automation began to be introduced to that methodology, the structural nature of the documentation evolved into a more formal hardware description language.

The graphics attributes could readily be applied to software, as the software design methodologies often include the structural visualization of the software system at different levels of abstraction. While some methodologies have recognized graphics as a tool, none has been utilized graphics as a design **capture** mechanism as formally as has been done in hardware design.

The third area of technology transfer is in the area of timing. Real-time program development, with much the same characteristics as hardware development, still utilizes traditional programming language constructs that say nothing about timing requirements or characteristics. In HDLs, time is an **ordering** concept for concurrent computations and helps to specify the semantics of timing-dependent functions.

The use of this characteristic in programming languages is predicated on the desire to write algorithm descriptions which transcend the von Neumann model of implementation. The maximum utilization of VLSI technology requires that a centralized locus of algorithm control be employed only at a local level (say, a chip), while distributed, concurrent, time-ordering-based control of large scale computations provides high effective throughput. The algorithm description language is the key to this capability, and transfer of technology from HDLs is a critical input.

CONCLUSIONS

While the working groups attacked orthogonal areas of the domain of interchange, there are interlocking dependencies among all areas. For example, design synthesis and measurement and hardware description languages have meaning only when they are tied together. This situation requires that the interchange of ideas can not be performed by specialists in different areas (represented, say, by the five working groups), but by a team looking the entire problem of managing complexity in design. Because the software engineering community has been grappling with more complex designs than the VLSI engineering community, it would be natural to expect transfer from the software engineering domain. From the preceding discussion, however, there are potential areas of transfer from the VLSI arena. Finally, because of the ultimate goal of designing a system that includes both hardware and software, cooperation -- if not unification -- between the disciplines is inevitable.

A COMPARISON OF DESIGN STRATEGIES FOR

SOFTWARE AND FOR VLSI

Connie U. Smith and John A. Dallen
Duke VLSI Research Laboratory
Duke University
Durham, N.C. 27706

Abstract

A framework is presented and a comparison is made of the design processes for VLSI and computer software. An assessment is then made of the current state of the art of the tools and methodologies used in each domain. Some insights are offered which indicate areas with high potential gains through future research on technology transfer.

1. Introduction

Until recently the fields of software design and digital circuit design have been distinctly segregated; the end products of the design process and the orientation and training of the designers have been very different. There are now, however, some compelling reasons for comparing and contrasting the two processes. Technological advances have dramatically increased the scope and complexity of circuit designs to the level of VLSI. A VLSI engineering discipline similar to that of software engineering is essential to manage both the design complexity and the larger development projects (large teams of designers required in order to realize the new potential). Likewise, software engineers can benefit from the fresh perspective of VLSI designers.

There are good reasons for drawing analogies between the VLSI and software design processes. All design methodologies, irrespective of the discipline, embody similar developmental stages. A conceptual design is transformed into a physical reality by gradually refining the implementation details. The design is tested and evaluated to verify that it meets the design objectives or requirements. But there are additional similarities when comparing software and VLSI design. In particular, the products both are computer-related objects. Frequently used software functions are now being implemented in silicon; the tools and languages used in design are strikingly similar; and many software developers are now attracted to the new VLSI domain. The evaluation of design quality during the early development stages has become an increasingly important consideration in both domains. The quality of the resulting products is often inter-related, notably so for performance characteristics.

Therefore, by comparing software and VLSI design processes one can make an assessment of the current state of the art with respect to their evolution and the relative maturity of the methodologies used in the design stages. In order to make the comparison, both design processes are mapped onto a similar structure to graphically depict both past and current design methods. The comparison reveals the similar trends in the development of design tools and methodologies. It also indicates some areas with high potential gains from technology transfer and provides some useful insights into areas for future research in both domains.

2. Framework for Comparison

When considering the stages in a design process, a useful breakdown can be borrowed from Bláauw and Brooks' categori-zation of computer hardware design levels: architecture, implementation, and realization [BL81] These levels of abstraction are applicable to many design fields, including the two of concern here. The high level, architecture, embodies the basic design decisions for software and hardware systems.

For both VLSI and software engineering, the architecture level can be further stratified into three distinct layers. The highest layer is the requirements definition. It is ideally a precise statement of the (users') requirements that the system must satisfy, without regard to how it will be accomplished. Next is the system specification layer. This is a definition of the system proposed to satisfy the requirements. The next layer is the decomposition of the system. The system is partitioned into smaller units each of which may be designed and implemented separately.

In software design, the transition from the system specification to the decomposition layer usually changes the orientation from *systems* design to *program or procedure* design. Similarly, with VLSI the decomposition process progressively changes the orientation from abstract modules to specific hardware entities such as registers and logic units. For both VLSI and software engineering, concerns in this layer are with sequencing of events and are generally technology independent.

Intermediate to architecture and realization is the implementation level. In software engineering, it is here that decisions are made on data structures and algorithms to be used within programs and procedures, and how they will be translated into programming languages. A more distinct subdivision of this level would discriminate between design representations in macro languages and higher-level algorithmic languages. Implementation in VLSI encompasses the domain of clocked networks. Here, similar to software design, decisions are made which synthesize the design description into primitive circuit elements such as transistors. The clocked-network level can be further stratified into a clocked register/logic layer and a circuit layer.

The lowest levels of abstraction for VLSI and software engineering, while increasingly dissimilar in name and format of description, nevertheless retain closely analogous characteristics. These comprise the realization level. For software engineers, the assembly language layer includes primitive instructions and the relative positions of data items and code. The hardware instruction layer is the directly executable code and the end product of the software development endeavor. In VLSI, the realization level can be called the geometry level, where the final product is a description suitable as input to a chip fabrication process. Like the software assembly instruction layer, the flexible geometry layer of VLSI is where the design is described in terms of a planar topology. Normally, orientations of primitives are set as well as their relative positions; however, physical sizes and absolute locations are not yet fixed. The lowest layer in the design domain, also known as the layout or mask layer, is one in which all characteristics are set, except possibly scale.

It is not necessary that a design be explicitly expressed at every stratification. However, even the simplest designs must pass through descriptions within each general level of abstraction: architecture, implementation (clocked network), and realization (flexible geometry).

The design process cannot be completely characterized by levels of abstraction. At each level a description of a design can be considered a model that facilitates the expression and evaluation of properties of the design. These properties can be differentiated into behavioral, structural, and physical categories.

Within the category of behavioral properties, it is possible to further distinguish between functional and qualitative properties. Functional behavior properties address those aspects of a design which deal with its logical correctness at a given level of abstraction -- in other words, WHAT a design does.

Additional behavioral properties address the quality of the design. Here a designer is concerned with HOW WELL a design does, while doing what it does. Factors which must be considered are: testability, reliability, modifiability, efficiency, understandability, flexibility, complexity, and implementability.

In contrast, the structural category of model properties reflect the static organization of the design. It includes the hierarchical definition of components in terms of subcomponents and their connectivity. Finally, the physical model properties deal with the culmination of the design. For software, they include the executable form of the code, the internal representation of the data structures, and the mapping to their positions in the address space of the software. In VLSI, physical model properties address the actual layout of the design on a chip area.

This discrimination in model properties is important for both disciplines. However, physical considerations have become typically transparent to the software engineer.

The next step in the comparison of the design processes is the taxonomy of existing models. Charts 1 and 2 depict the software and VLSI domains, respectively, with the levels of abstraction vertically and the model properties horizontally. A cross-section of models are considered and included are primarily model description languages as opposed to modeling systems or tools. Each is placed on the chart according to the primary level of abstraction and model property that it addresses. The placement is derived by studying the primitives of the language and ascertaining the essence of the information contained within the primitive. If it is commonly applica-

Chart 1

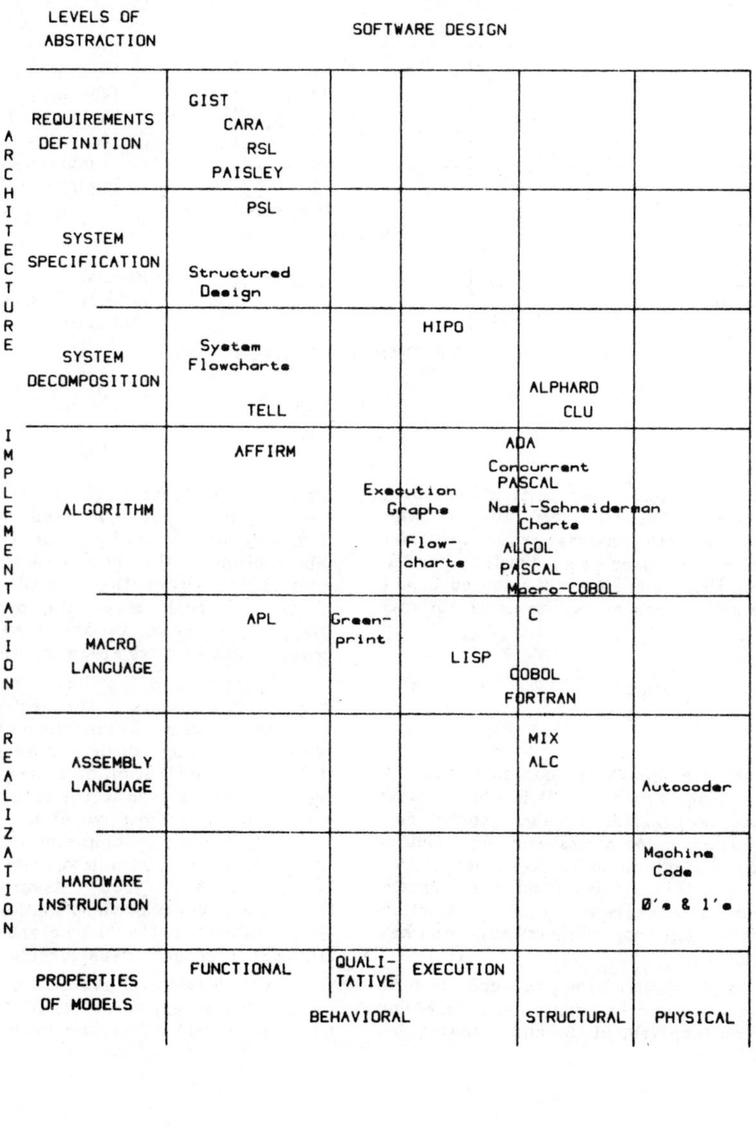

LEVELS OF ABSTRACTION — SOFTWARE DESIGN

		FUNCTIONAL	QUALITATIVE	EXECUTION	STRUCTURAL	PHYSICAL
ARCHITECTURE	REQUIREMENTS DEFINITION	GIST CARA RSL PAISLEY				
	SYSTEM SPECIFICATION	PSL Structured Design				
	SYSTEM DECOMPOSITION	System Flowcharts TELL		HIPO	ALPHARD CLU	
IMPLEMENTATION	ALGORITHM	AFFIRM	Execution Graphs Flow-charts		ADA Concurrent PASCAL Nasi-Schneiderman Charts ALGOL PASCAL Macro-COBOL	
	MACRO LANGUAGE	APL	Green-print	LISP	C COBOL FORTRAN	
REALIZATION	ASSEMBLY LANGUAGE				MIX ALC	Autocoder
	HARDWARE INSTRUCTION					Machine Code 0's & 1's
PROPERTIES OF MODELS		FUNCTIONAL	QUALITATIVE	EXECUTION	STRUCTURAL	PHYSICAL
			BEHAVIORAL			

161

Chart 2

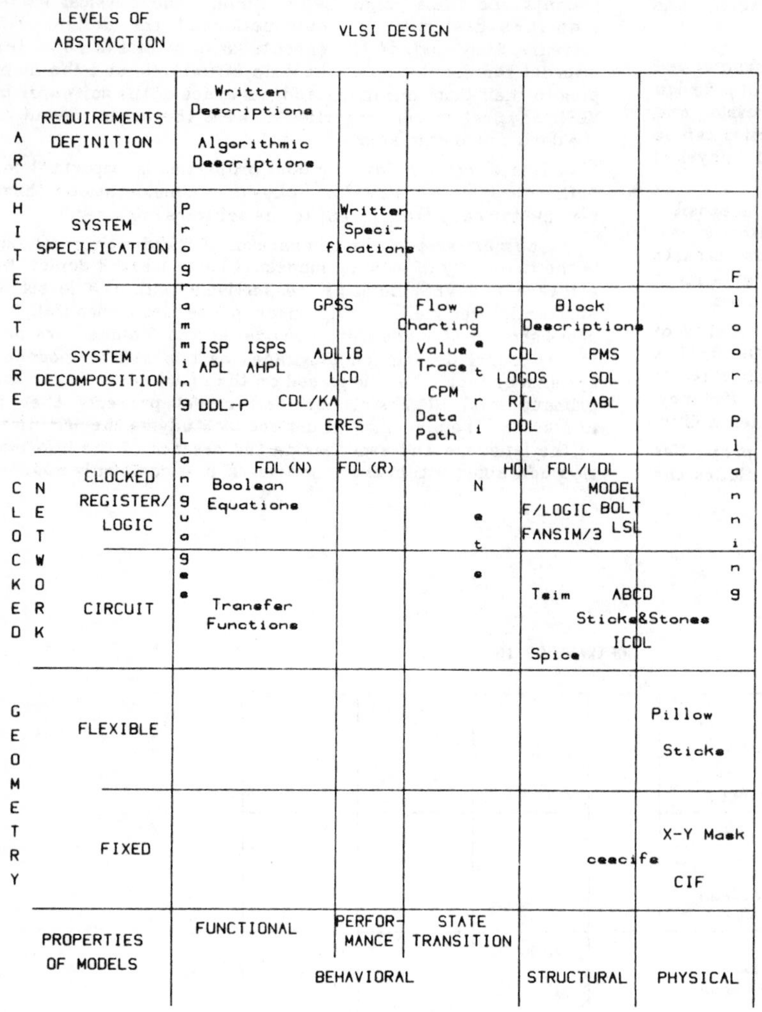

Chart 3. ELEMENTS OF DESIGN

LEVELS OF ABSTRACTION — VLSI DESIGN

		FUNCTIONAL	PERFORMANCE	STATE TRANSITION	STRUCTURAL	PHYSICAL
ARCHITECTURE	REQUIREMENTS DEFINITION	Written Descriptions, Algorithmic Descriptions				
	SYSTEM SPECIFICATION	Prog...	Written Specifications			Floor Plan
	SYSTEM DECOMPOSITION	GPSS, ISP ISPS, ADLIB, APL AHPL, LCD, DDL-P, CDL/KA, ERES		Flow Charting, Value Trace, CPM, Data Path	Block Description, CDL PMS, LOGOS SDL, RTL ABL, DDL	
CLOCKED NETWORK	CLOCKED REGISTER/LOGIC	FDL(N), Boolean Equations, FDL(R)		N	HDL FDL/LDL MODEL, F/LOGIC BOLT, FANSIM/3 LSL	Protocol / Planning
	CIRCUIT	Transfer Functions			Tsim ABCD, Sticks&Stones, Spice, ICDL	
GEOMETRY	FLEXIBLE					Pillow, Sticks
	FIXED					X-Y Mask, ceacife, CIF
	PROPERTIES OF MODELS	FUNCTIONAL	PERFORMANCE	STATE TRANSITION	STRUCTURAL	PHYSICAL
			BEHAVIORAL		STRUCTURAL	PHYSICAL

Chart 3. ELEMENTS OF DESIGN

PRINCIPLES OF DESIGN

- Hierarchical Decomposition
- Abstraction
- Hiding
- Localization
- Uniformity
- Regularity
- Completeness
- Confirmability
- Simplicity
- Symmetry

OBJECTIVES OF DESIGN

- Design Description
- Design Correctness
  > Feasibility
  > Equivalency
  > Consistency
  > Performance
- Design Quality
  > Testability
  > Reliability
  > Modifiability
  > Efficiency
  > Understandability
  > Flexibility
  > Complexity
  > Implementability

TEST AND EVALUATION OF DESIGN

- Proofs
- Analytic Analysis
- Simulation

---

ble to multiple levels or properties, its scope is indicated by arrows or boundary-lapping descriptions. While some languages can be considered to possess properties from several of the categories and can often be successfully used at several levels of abstraction, most are heavily oriented to one primary model property and to one or two levels of abstraction.

3. Comparison

3.1. Design processes

Having completed the framework, we can now begin to make comparison of the design processes. It is important to note that the design processes considered are for general, custom environments and are not limited by assuming a particular architecture or implementation technique. Examples of limited environments for VLSI are programmed logic arrays (PLA's) and standard cells; for software an example is Martin's "application development without programmers" approach in a data base environment [MA82].

Charts 1 and 2 are quite similar in appearance. In both disciplines, the design process can be seen as a progression from the top-left to the bottom-right of the chart, taking one or more routes through the various levels. At each level, a description language is used to represent the design. The difficulty lies in making the transitions from one level of abstraction to the next, and this mapping process, whether manual or automatic, constitutes the art and science of design. In both cases, the process is iterative in nature, requiring a return to design at higher levels of abstraction when problems arise at lower levels.

Not only are the design processes similar, but also the important elements of the design methodologies are common to both domains. These elements, shown in chart 3, include design principles, design objectives, and techniques for the testing and evaluation of a design. Design principles are proven techniques used in the formulation of a design which help to achieve the objective of the design. The objective of the design process is a completed description of the design (physical information at the lowest level of abstraction) which must be correct and "good". Assurance of correctness requires functional behavior information and assurance of quality requires metrics to characterize quality based on combinations of structural, behavioral, and physical properties.

Design test and evaluation procedures provide the information necessary to determine whether or not the objectives have been met. Test and evaluation techniques in the VLSI domain have been dominated by simulation methods. Analytic analysis techniques could theoretically provide more timely information on the status of a design than is usually possible with simulation. In the software domain, analytic techniques are being developed and used for evaluation. Testing is still largely conducted through repetitive execution of the software under varying conditions. Formal verification techniques are desirable in both domains, but are as yet impractical for very complex designs.

There are two notable differences in the two design processes depicted on charts 1 and 2. First, there is a considerable amount of model transparency in the software domain. That is, the transformation of designs from structural/algorithmic or macro language specifications into their machine instruction/physical form is typically transparent, due to the prevalence of automated tools such as compilers, linkers, and loaders. Second, the labor intensive efforts occur at different stages of the development process. In the custom VLSI domain, manual transformations are required in the lower-right portion of the chart. This is extremely labor intensive due to the complexity of the designs and the critical chip area considerations. In software, the labor intensive efforts occur between the conceptual/functional and algorithm/structural transformations.

Additional comparative information can be obtained through consideration of the evolution of the design process.

3.2. Evolution of design processes

The evolution of the design processes has many similarities. Initial breakthroughs were made in a "bottom-up" fashion. Tools and techniques first addressed the transformation of design representations in the lower-right corner of the charts. VLSI design tools have been physically oriented and based on descriptions at the geometry level. This state of the art is reflected in the prevalence of design tools which use CIF[Me80], X-Y Mask, and other low level descriptions as the primary building block. Then, design tools which used descriptions at the flexible geometry level were actively pursued, such as William's Sticks[Wi77] and Johannson's early form of Bristle Blocks[Jo79]. More recently, attempts are being made to use circuit level descriptions as the building blocks, exemplified by Rosenberg's ABCD[Ro82] and Cardelli and Plotkin's Sticks and Stones[Ca81]. In all cases of this bottom-up evolution, the orientation has been physical and structural.

The evolution of the software development process is similar to that of VLSI. In the 1950's attention was focused on physical properties of software at the assembly language and hardware instruction levels. Coding and memory layout were major concerns and quite time intensive activities. Subsequently, higher level languages such as FORTRAN and COBOL relieved many of the coding duties, but memory was still a primary concern. More recently, algorithmic languages such as ALGOL and Pascal have become the building blocks.

Early in the evolution of both disciplines, focus was (is) on time and space requirements. This was primarily due to physical constraints imposed by the state of the technology; both memory and chip area were limited. In the software domain, technological advances lessened the physical memory constraints and thus made automated (but less efficient) tools more tractable. Compilers, and later operating systems, had a dramatic effect on productivity and thus the scope of the designs that could feasibly be implemented. It appears that a similar state will soon be achieved in the VLSI domain.

It is interesting to note that there is considerable resistance among expert VLSI designers to the development and use of fully automated layout systems since they will be inherently less efficient than the custom layouts. Similar resistance was encountered when FORTRAN was first introduced. Extra attention was devoted to optimizing the code produced by FORTRAN compilers in order to mitigate this resistance. Such super-optimization has not been included in later versions of compilers, once initial acceptance of the tool was achieved.

Following the resolution of the hardware technology bottleneck in the software domain was a dramatic increase in the ambition and complexity of the systems designed. Software complexity has increased to the point where the system definition phase has now become crucial. A severe problem that arises as a result of this increased complexity is the testing, verification, and analysis of the resulting software. This problem has already been encountered in the VLSI domain and its severity is likely to increase due to the impending dramatic increase in VLSI complexity. The current technique of design verification via the extraction of behavioral descriptions from lower level physical descriptions will no longer be computationally feasible.

Paralleling the evolution of design processes originating at the lower levels have been attempts to extend system level techniques to VLSI design. The basis of these attempts has been through the adaptation of common register transfer level descriptions. Most of these descriptive languages are heavily oriented towards computer hardware design, such as ISP, CDL, AHPL, RTL and so on. Most of these languages are functionally oriented, however, requiring parallel design development in the structural and physical domains. An ISP description, for instance, is insufficient to represent the structure of a design, requiring use of a structural representation language such as PMS. The advantage of functional descriptions, of course, is that some analysis of a design is made early in the design process. Unfortunately, unless equivalence can be proven between the behavioral, structural, and physical models at any level of abstraction, final design verification and analysis must still rely on testing and evaluating lower level descriptions.

Bridging this gap from the architecture-behavior domain to the physical-geometry domain is the essence of the design problem. Ideal solutions include the search for the silicon compiler, the definition of some standard notation or algebra of design as is used in more established disciplines, and the invention of some universal description language appropriate for behavioral, structural and physical description at all levels of abstraction. On the other hand, most practical design systems existing today rely on a database approach to design in which several different descriptions are used and a great deal of human interaction is required to effect the mapping between levels. It is obvious from the literature, however, that the problems of design verification and analysis are getting worse and not better as the number of devices on a chip keeps growing.

4. Implications

What can we learn from this comparison of the two disciplines? First, it is apparent in the comparison that the design path taken from the functional/requirements definition level to the physical-geometry/machine level is much more linear in software design than in VLSI design. Currently, a custom VLSI designer must simultaneously use parallel languages in several domains during the process. This is rarely true in software. This can be seen in the frequency of dual language systems such as ADLIB and SDL at Stanford Univeristy [CO81], CDL and ABL at the University of Karlsruhe [HA77], and FDL/LDL at Nippon Electric Company in Japan [SA80]. This difference also reflects the fact that in software engineering the less profitable paths have been abandoned and the more profitable ones emulated. This winnowing process has just started in VLSI.

Also apparent is that VLSI designers may be able to predict, from the experience of software designers, future trends in the evolution of VLSI design tools. Just as memory layout became less important, perhaps as chip space becomes less critical, less concern for physical layout will be observed in VLSI design. Just as the higher-level programming languages have evolved as the basic building blocks of software engineering, so perhaps will higher-level switching network constructs (not necessarily logic gates) become the building blocks of VLSI design. The efficiencies that are currently gained by designing at the circuit level (and below) may eventually fall into disuse as has programming at the assembly language level. However, we should take note of the fact that the majority of industry software systems are still implemented in COBOL (and even FORTRAN) even though algorithmic languages are generally more suitable. Industry has become "locked in" due to the vast amount of existing code (and expertise) that must be used. The same could happen in the VLSI domain.

Less comforting conclusions can be postulated, unfortunately. Major problems in software engineering have yet to be solved, indicating that similar problems may thwart efforts in VLSI design. In particular, the process of design evolution from the architecture level to the clocked-network level has proved difficult to understand and control. Software compilers, it should be remembered, only map from the programming level to the machine level. The counterpart to the silicon compiler is an automatic program generator in the software domain. Early attempts at automatic program generators actually resulted in slightly higher level programming languages, such as RPG, which mapped to the next level of abstraction and then only in restricted application domains. Advances were made one step at a time rather than in quantum leaps. This bodes poorly for VLSI designer efforts to produce silicon compilers which map automatically from architecture-level descriptions to the geometry level. It suggests that the most fruitful research in the near term is in areas that will lead to automated tools for transforming clocked-network level descriptions into fixed geometry descriptions. If, on the other hand, effective system-level silicon compilers are found, perhaps software designers may be able to learn something from this.

Both disciplines face similar problems in the area of design verification and analysis. Reliance on simulation tools (test-runs in software) relegates the evaluation process to the late stages of the design process. The verification process is also slow and consumes a significant portion of the overall design effort.

If an analogy is to be drawn between the software and VLSI design processes, one must consider the issue of maintenance in software systems. Currently sixty percent of the cost of software systems is in the maintenance stage. What is the equivalent in the VLSI domain? Software maintenance consists of three primary activities: major enhancements, minor enhancements, and correction of latent errors. On the surface, it appears that there is no equivalent in the VLSI domain since chips are not "patched" once they are fabricated. However, software maintenance requires backtracking to an earlier step in the development process. The analogy in VLSI occurs when there is a need to construct a chip with slightly different functionality. It should be possible to return to an earlier design stage and to modify the previous design representation at that stage. Unfortunately the tools available currently limit the extent to which this can be done. The only feasible modifications at this time are minor enhancements (typically speed) and error corrections. Major enhancements to designs typically require an entire redesign. In order to significantly improve productivity, new tools are needed to facilitate modifiability.

Some of the differences in the design processes are due to the relative maturity of the disciplines and to the particular technology used for the design realization. Both affect the early focus of the tools and techniques developed to support design. Examination of some of the differences illuminate some areas for potential technology transfer to the other domain.

Areas from the VLSI domain with applicability to software engineering are: the use of the design principles of uniformity, regularity, and symmetry; increased emphasis on correctness and additional tools and techniques for assurance of correctness; and the use of integrated computer aid design systems. The most valuable areas from the software domain with applicability to VLSI in the near term are techniques for managing complexity and tools to support large, multi-designer projects.

There are several approaches that could be taken to manage large hardware projects. One is the use of libraries of existing designs. This, of course, is fruitful for designs of limited complexity and for ones with conventional architectures.

Another approach would be to divide design responsibility "horizontally". Here, one design team would, for instance work on clocking concerns, while another, perhaps, would be concerned with layout. Unfortunately, the complex interrelationship between these concerns would make such a breakdown difficult to effect in practice.

"Vertical" stratification of effort can be accomplished in several ways. For any particular design component, the synthesis operation (which is essentially a process in the structural domain) can be accomplished by one team, while a second team would be experts in design validation (primarily a concern within the behavioral domain). While obviously useful this division does not address the general problem of coping with complexity. Ultimately, a method must be found by which portions of a VLSI design can be semi-independently designed and tested by separate design teams.

To this end, the VLSI design process could be facilitated by a mythical silicon operating system (SOS). The goal of the SOS is to improve designer productivity by allowing large numbers of designers to "share" (or work on) the same chip without concern about the effect on other designers, relieving designers of concerns about physical limitations, and eliminating the need to re-implement commonly used functions. A primitive SOS can be constructed by providing capabilities for communication between the design entities or components, handling timing (synchronization) constraints, handling data flow onto and off of the chip, and assigning design entities to physical chip area.

The kernel of the SOS provides the handling of data flow onto and off of the chip. The physical constraint on the number of pins and the multiplexing of pin signals (if necessary) are encapsulated into the kernel. Pin assignments are made in the equivalent "file (data) manager" layer: the pin manager.

The kernel also contains communications and synchronization primitives. Communication between design entities can be handled either by direct connections (wires) between components or by a "mailbox" capability which temporarily stores output from one component until needed (requested) by another. Synchronization can be provided by the SOS when multiple components must be activated simultaneously or when one component must be activated when a specified state is reached. These capabilities relieve designers of a need to know the relative speed of design components.

Designers of components work with virtual real estate. With the recent technological trends, the number of devices within a single designer's real estate could easily equal or exceed the number of devices previously contained on an entire chip. There may, however, be constraints on the maximum amount of virtual chip area allocated to a design component and guidelines for its aspect ratio. The external interfaces are also defined, but the designer need not be concerned with the component's physical location, its position relative to components it interfaces with, or their relative speed. The chip area manager is responsible for assigning (placing) components to physical areas on the chip and the communication (routing) between components. Exceptional situations can be handled by allowing the option of assigning virtual chip areas to specific locations on the chip (a virtual=real analogy).

The silicon operating system is proposed as a development aid targeted towards the clocked network and geometry layers of abstraction and provides transparency between the structural and physical design properties. Its realization consists of both software support and chip components. The software system includes the outer "layers" of the SOS: the chip area manager, the pin manager, and communication/synchronization monitors. The chip components include the primitives necessary to carry out the OS kernel functions for multiplexing pin signals, providing signal buffering and synchronization logic, and common service functions (similar to operating system supervisor calls).

The use of an SOS, of course, results in a chip inherently less efficient than a custom-designed chip. It does, however, have many advantages. It has potential for significantly improving the productivity of designers and reducing the level of expertise required for designing chips of this type. It can provide support for novice designers and enable them to design chips that perform useful functions in a shorter period of time. It achieves these goals without constraining the architecture of the chip as in the case of PLA's and standard cells. Even though the efficiency of chips developed with an SOS would not be as good as that of custom-designed chips, it would facilitate the implementation of functions previously performed in software, thus there would be a net gain in performance. Critical constraints on chip area and performance unfortunately preclude the current use of an SOS; however, technological advances are rapidly being made and the SOS may be feasible in the near future. As in the software domain, it could offer greater potential for productivity gains than the automation of the design process itself as in silicon compilers.

5. Conclusions

A framework is established which facilitates the comparison of the VLSI and software engineering design processes. This comparison yields an assessment of the current state of the art of the methodologies and tools which support the design processes.

Great progress has been made in both domains, but many problems are as yet unresolved. In particular, designer productivity is a common problem. Additional tools are needed to support early life cycle activities in both domains. For VLSI, tools are also needed which provide additional transparency from the physical model properties and which provide support for large, multi-designer projects. For software, additional tools and techniques are needed for quality assurance which are applicable throughout the life cycle. Assurance of correctness is a key (unanswered) problem. These areas are prime targets for improvement through technology transfer.

The comparison and assessment process should not stop here. There are many additional areas within the two domains with high potential for improvement. This framework yields many insights into the two design processes. Additional frames should be established which use other elements of the design process as a basis. A thorough examination will illuminate additional solutions to unresolved problems.

References

[Bl81] G.A. Blaauw and F.P. Brooks, *Computer Architecture*, preliminary draft (1981).

[Ca81] Luca Cardelli and Gordon Plotkin, "An Algebraic Approach to VLSI Design," pp. 173-182 in *VLSI 81 Very Large Scale Integration*, ed. John P. Gray, Academic Press, Inc., New York (1981).

[Co81] W.E. Cory, "Symbolic Simulation for Functional Verification with ADLIB and SDL," Proc. 18th Design Automation Conference, 1981, pp. 82-89.

[Ha77] R.W. Hartenstein, *Fundamentals of Structured Hardware Design*, North-Holland Publishing Company, Netherlands, 1977.

[Jo79] D. Johannsen, "Bristle Blocks--A Silicon Compiler," in *Proc. of the 16th Design Automation Conference* (1979).

[Me80] Carver, Mead and Lynn Conway, in *Introduction to VLSI Design*, Addison-Wesley Publishing Company (1980).

[Ro82] J. Rosenberg and N. Weste, *A Better Circuit Description*, Technical Report 82-01, Microelectronics Center of North Carolina (1982).

[Sa80] T. Sasaki, A. Yamada, S. Kato, T. Nakazawa, K. Tomita, N. Nomizu, "MIXS - A Mixed Level Simulator for Large Digital System Logic Verification," Proc. 17th Design Automation Conference, 1980, pp. 626-633.

[Wi77] John D. Williams, *STICKS--A New Approach to LSI Design*, Master's Thesis, Massachusetts Institute of Technology (June 1977).

Formal Verification of VLSI Designs

Robert E. Shostak

Computer Science Laboratory
SRI International
333 Ravenswood Avenue
Menlo Park, CA 94025 USA

Abstract

We describe an approach to proof of correctness of hardware designs using program verification techniques. The approach is an adaptation of Floyd's method that works on circuit graphs rather than program flowgraphs. Our method may be viewed as a dual of Floyd's in which the roles of state and control are interchanged. An example is given that illustrates the application of the method to a simple VLSI circuit.

1 Introduction

While recent research in VLSI design methodology has given strong emphasis to means for simplifying the design of large systems, relatively little attention has been given to the problem of formal verification. The development of methods to ensure that a design is free of errors is especially important for the complex circuits made possible by very large scale integration. The high gate counts and gate-to-pin ratios of these circuits make traditional techniques, such as simulation and prototype testing, far more time-consuming and less apt to be effective.

This paper describes an approach to the problem using formal verification techniques. By "formal verification", we mean the mathematical proof that a design satisfies a given specification of its intended behavior. Formal verification techniques differ from testing in the important respect that they cover the entire domain of possible inputs rather than merely a representive test set.

Our approach is closely related to the assertional method described by Floyd [Flo 67] for the verification of sequential programs. Assertional methods depend on the annotation of the program to be verified with predicates that describe what must be true whenever control reaches the point in the program with which the predicate is associated. The proof of correctness rests on the application of an induction principle to demonstrate the truth of the predicates.

Our method may be viewed as a dual of Floyd's in which the roles of *state* and *control* are interchanged. Reflecting the duality, assertions that annotate the circuit graph to be verified describe local state at each point in time rather than global state at particular points in time. The Hoare axioms that characterize the behavior of primitive programming language constructs in Floyd's method are replaced here by *transfer predicates* that

describe the relation among inputs and outputs of circuit elements as functions of time. The method has been tested on a number of examples using the STP system [ShS 82] for deductive support[1].

The presentation of the method is organized as follows. Section 2 discusses the formal circuit model on which the proposed method is based. Sections 3 and 4 formally define correctness with respect to that model. The proof method itself is described in Section 5. Section 6 illustrates the method with the proof of correctness of a VLSI implementation of the Muller C-element. The concluding section discusses the cost effectiveness of the method.

A more detailed description of the method and a proof of its soundness are given in [Sho1 82].

2 The Circuit Model

A system to be verified is formally modeled as a graph whose nodes correspond to circuit elements and whose edges correspond to signal (or information) paths that connect these elements.

Associated with each circuit element is a set of *inputs* and a set of *outputs*. Each input and output has a formal *signal type* that represents the domain of values it may assume. A signal type may either represent some physical quantity, such as a voltage or current, or may be more abstract, as in the case of "array of integers" or "ordered pair of voltage, current". A circuit element is interpreted as forcing some relation among its inputs and outputs, considered as functions of time. Its behavior is formally modeled by a *transfer predicate* that expresses this relation.

A resistor of resistance r, for example, might be modeled as a circuit element with an input x of signal type $< voltage, current$ and an output y of the same type. The transfer predicate P_t might be given by

$$y_t^{current} = x_t^{current}$$
$$\wedge \quad y_t^{voltage} = x_t^{voltage} + r x_t^{current}$$

We define a *circuit graph* as a directed graph with a circuit element associated with each node. A node must have exactly one incoming edge corresponding to each input of the associated circuit element, and one outgoing edge corresponding to each

This work was supported in part by NSF Grant MCS-7904081, and by AFOSR Contract NAS1-15428

[1]STP is a mechanical verification system originally intended for software proof. It has been used in the design proof of the SIFT fault-tolerant operating system [ScM 82].

output. Moreover, the signal types of the input and output associated with the two ends of each edge must be identical.

As a convenient means of modeling inputs and outputs of the circuit as a whole, we allow dangling edges- we speak of a dangling edge with an initial node but no destination node as an *output edge*, and one with a destination node but no initial node as an *input edge*.

Roughly speaking, each nondangling edge represents a perfect connection between the circuit elements on either end. The connection is considered to be perfect in the sense of forcing the values of the input and output at each end to be equal. This assumption does not entail any loss of generality, of course, since imperfect transmission paths may be modeled as circuit elements. (Note that circuit element outputs that drive several inputs can be modeled in the same manner- one merely introduces a *junction* circuit element with one input and several outputs.) Each edge of a circuit graph may thus be viewed as representing a *signal* whose value is that of the input and output bridged by the edge.

3 The Meaning of Correctness

The aim of the method is to show that a circuit design operates in accordance with a mathematical characterization of its intended behavior. The characterization has three components: an *input specification*, which assigns an assertion (i.e., a formula in logic) to each input edge; an *output specification*, which assigns one to each output edge; and an *initial condition* specification, which assigns assertions to arbitrary edges of the graph. Initial conditions are useful to capture initial state information, such as the initial settings of registers. Each input, output, and initial condition assertion is a predicate that characterizes the corresponding signal as a function of time.

Intuitively, *correctness* means that if the circuit inputs satisfy the input specification, if the initial condition assertions are assumed to hold, and if each circuit element operates in faithfulness to its transfer characteristic, then the circuit outputs are guaranteed to satisfy the output specification.

4 Proving Correctness

The method of proof may be viewed as a dual of Floyd's method [Flo 67] for proving the correctness of sequential programs. Floyd's method entails the association of assertions with certain points in the flowgraph of a program in such a way that each loop of the flowgraph is "cut" (i.e., intercepted) by an assertion. Each assertion captures a property of the program state (defined by the instantaneous values of the variables) that must hold each time the flow of control reaches the point in the flowgraph with which the assertion is associated. The essence of the proof strategy is to show that the program semantics along any execution path from an assertion point A to an assertion point B are such as to guarantee that if the assertion at A holds just prior to execution of the path, then the one at B must hold just afterwards. Once this has been established for each straight-line execution path connecting two assertion points, it automatically follows by an induction argument that program inputs satisfying the assertion associated with the entry point must produce outputs (given that the program terminates) satis-

fying the exit assertions.

The differences between Floyd's method and our technique owe chiefly to two distinctions between program flow graphs and circuit graphs. First, circuit graph semantics do not depend on any notion of flow of control. Second, circuit state is associated with the collective condition of localized signals, rather than that of global variables. These differences may be viewed in terms of a duality between state and control: circuit *state* is associated with particular localities, whereas circuit *control* is global; for program graphs, exactly the reverse is true.

Like Floyd's method, our approach depends on the association of assertions with a subset of the edges in the graph. These include the input and output assertions, together with a set of additional assertions (called *loop assertions*) sufficient to cut each cycle of the graph exactly once. Reflecting the duality, these assertions characterize particular signals at arbitrary points in time rather than arbitrary signals (program variables) at particular points in time.

The crux of the proof strategy is to show through an induction argument that each assertion must hold at each time t, assuming that the input and initial condition assertions hold. The induction is carried out simultaneously over *time* and over the *structure* of the graph.

Once the circuit graph is annotated with assertions, the proof of correctness proceeds in three stages. First, a kind of path analysis is carried out, resulting in a set of acyclic subgraphs of the original graph. Second, a set of mathematical formulas called *verification conditions* is derived, one from each subgraph. Finally, the verification conditions are each proved, either manually or using a semi-automatic theorem proving program.

The path analysis phase produces an acyclic subgraph for each noninput edge e of the graph that is labeled by an assertion. The subgraph for e is "rooted" at the initial node for e, and is formed by tracing backwards from this root, branching at nodes along the way with more than one incoming edge. Incoming edges labeled by assertions, however, are not traversed, so that the backwards trace terminates at nodes all of whose inputs edges are labeled by assertions. These edges are left dangling in the subgraph, and are referred to as the *inputs* of the subgraph. Note that, since each loop of the original graph must be cut by an assertion, the tracing process must terminate and the resulting subgraph must be acyclic.

The *verification condition* for the subgraph generated from an edge e with noninput assertion A_t is constructed in the following way.

First, for each node n in the subgraph, let p_t^n denote the associated transfer predicate, expressed in terms of the signals that label the inputs and outputs of that node. Let P_t denote the conjunction of the p_t^n's. Next, let D_t denote the conjunction of all assertions labeling dangling inputs of the subgraph other than e itself. Finally, let I_t denote the conjunction of all initial condition assertions.

Then the verification condition is given by the formula

$$\forall t \in T\,(P_t \wedge I_t \wedge D_t) \quad \supset \quad \forall t \in T\,[(\forall u < t\ A_u) \supset A_t]$$

The formula states that if the transfer predicates, initial conditions, and assertions labeling subgraph inputs other than c hold at all times t, and if A holds at all times *prior* to t, then A must also hold at time t.

The last step in the process, and the most difficult one, is the proof of the verification conditions. As in software verification, the size and complexity of verification conditions arising from even simple systems dictates the use of automatic or semi-automatic proof techniques.

5 A Sample Proof

Figure 1a. shows an abstract representation of Muller's *C-element*, also known as a *rendezvous* circuit [Mil 65]. The C-element is a logic circuit invented by D. Muller during the 1950's as part of a speed-independent digital design discipline. Speed independent circuits have more recently been used in connection with self-timed VLSI designs [Sei 79].

The operation of the C-element is easily stated. The device has two binary input signals (a and b) and one binary output signal (c). The output becomes 1 whenever both inputs become 1; it becomes 0 whenever both inputs become 0. Otherwise, the output remains in its previous condition. Formally, we have:

$$c_{t+\delta} = \text{if } (a_t = b_t) \text{ then } a_t \text{ else } c_t$$

Here, δ is a positive constant that reflects propagation delay through the C-element.

The right half of Figure 1a. shows the schematic diagram of an nMOS implementation of the C-element given by Seitz in [MeC 80]. Figure 1b. shows a corresponding circuit graph. The signals that label the graph are of two types. The inputs and outputs (a, b, and c) and signals l^1 through l^6 are of type *logic level*. The values of this type are just the logic levels 0 and 1. The remaining signals are all of type *pull-down*. The values of type pull-down are the logic level 0 and a special tri-state (high-impedance) value *hi-z*.

The circuit elements of the graph are of five kinds, representing *ground*, *pull-down transistors*, *pull-up transistors*, *pull-down wire junctions*, and *signal splitters*. Table 1 gives the signal types and the transfer predicate for each type of circuit element.

The ground circuit element, for example, has no inputs, and one output of type pull-down; it merely forces its output to 0 at all times.

The pull-down transistor has a pull-down input s (for *source*), a logic-level input g (for *gate*), and a pull-down output d (for *drain*.) The operation is similar to that of a switch: if the gate input is high, the source signal is passed through; otherwise the output is forced to the *hi-z* state.

The pull-down junction, with two pull-down inputs and one pull-down output, captures the effect of "wire-or'ing" two pull-down signals together. Its output is low if and only if one of its inputs is low.

The signal splitter (used to split off the output signal c) provides fan-out but otherwise has no effect.

Finally, the pull-up transistor, with one pull-down input and one logic-level output, converts a pull-down signal to a logic level; 0 is mapped to 0, and *hi-z* is mapped to 1. In addition, a propagation delay of ϵ is introduced.

The specification with respect to which we wish to prove correctness is as follows. First, as no particular assumptions are made about the input signals a and b, the corresponding input assertions are just *true*. Because no assumptions need be made about the initial condition of any signal, no initial condition assertions are specified. Finally, the output assertion ψ_t associated with signal c is given by

$$c_{t+2\epsilon} = \text{if } (a_t = b_t) \text{ then } a_t \text{ else } c_t$$

Note that the parameter δ has been particularized to 2ϵ, where, once again, ϵ is one pull-up delay.

As the graph has only one directed cycle, a single loop assertion suffices. In principle, the assertion can be placed on any edge of the cycle. The signal l^6 has been chosen in this instance. Since l^6 must equal the output c, an appropriate loop assertion ω is easily formulated:

$$l^6_{t+2\epsilon} = \text{if } (a_t = b_t) \text{ then } a_t \text{ else } l^6_t$$

The path analysis process gives rise to two subgraphs: one for the edge labeled l^6, and one for the output edge.

It is easy to see that the first of these includes every node in the graph, and has dangling input edges corresponding to a, b, and l^6 itself. The conjunction P_t for this subgraph thus contains the transfer predicate instance corresponding to each node, and the conjunction D_t is just the formula *true*.

The subgraph generated for the output edge, on the other hand, contains a single node (the one at the output) with one dangling input edge corresponding to l^6. The conjunction D_t is thus composed of the single loop assertion ω.

The formulation of the corresponding verification conditions and their proofs are given in detail in [Sho1 82]. The first verification condition is quite lengthy (more than a page of syntax), since it contains as a subformula the transfer predicate instance for each circuit node in the graph. Its proof using the STP automatic theorem-prover required nearly four minutes of CPU time on the Foonly F2 computer. The second verification condition is substantially simpler, and required only 7 seconds of CPU time.

5.1 Conclusions

At present, formal verification is an extremely expensive technology, in terms both of man and machine resources. Its application to software systems, for example, has been estimated to cost on the order of a thousand dollars per line of code. In the foreseeable future, we expect its use to be confined to applications in which reliability is a foremost concern. Such applications include those (such as avionics and nuclear power control) in which human life is at stake, as well as commercial applications in which a large investment is made in a single design. It should also be noted that research in formal verification methods, and their application to hardware design in particular, is in its infancy. One can reasonably expect such methods to become increasingly viable (and their use increasing necessary) in the coming years.

6 References

[Bir 74] Birman, A.,"On Proving Correctness of Microprograms", IBM J. Research and Development, vol.14, no. 3, May 1974, pp. 250-266.

[Flo 67] Floyd, R. W., "Assigning Meanings to Programs", Proc. Amer. Math. Soc. Symp. in Applied Math. 19 (1967), pp. 19-31.

[Fos 81] Foster, M. J., "Syntax-Directed Verification of Circuit Function", VLSI Systems and Computations, H. Kung, B. Sproul, G. Steele, ed., Computer Science Press, Carnegie-Mellon University, 1981, pp. 203-212

[Gor 81] Gordon, M., "Two Papers on Modelling and Verifying Hardware", Proc. VLSI 81 International Conference, Edinburgh, Scotland, August 1981

[MeC 80] Mead, C., L. Conway, Introduction to VLSI Systems, Addison-Wesley, Philipines, 1980

[Mil 65] Miller, R., Switching Theory, vol. 2., Wiley, New York, 1965

[ScM 82] Schwartz, R.L., P.M. Melliar-Smith, "Formal Specification and Mechanical Verification of SIFT: A Fault-tolerant Flight Control System", TR CSL-133, SRI International, Menlo Park California, January 1982

[Sei 79] Seitz, Charles L., "Self-timed VLSI Systems", Proc. Caltech Conference on VLSI, January 1979

[Sho 82] Shostak, R. E., "Deciding Combinations of Theories", Proc. Sixth Conference on Automated Deduction, Courant Institute, New York, June 1982.

[Sho1 82] Shostak, R. E., "Formal Verification of Circuit Designs", Technical Report CSL-134, Computer Science Laboratory, SRI International, Menlo Park, May 1982

[ShS 82] Shostak, R. E., R. L. Schwartz, P. M. Melliar-Smith, "STP: A Mechanized Logic for Specification and Verification", Proc. Sixth Conference on Automated Deduction, Courant Institute, New York, June 1982

Table 1
TRANSFER PREDICATES FOR CIRCUIT ELEMENT TYPES

ELEMENT TYPE	SIGNAL TYPES	TRANSFER PREDICATE
GROUND	PULL-DOWN x (OUTPUT)	$x_t = 0$
PULL-DOWN TRANSISTOR	PULL-DOWN s (INPUT) LOGIC-LEVEL g (INPUT) PULL-DOWN d (OUTPUT)	$d_t =$ IF $g_t = 1$ THEN s_t ELSE hi – z
PULL-DOWN JUNCTION	PULL-DOWN x (INPUT) PULL-DOWN y (INPUT) PULL-DOWN z (OUTPUT)	$z_t =$ IF $(x_t = 0 \vee y_t = 0)$ THEN 0 ELSE hi – z
PULL-UP TRANSISTOR	PULL-DOWN s (INPUT) LOGIC-LEVEL g (OUTPUT)	$g_{t+\epsilon} =$ IF $s_t = 0$ THEN 0 ELSE 1
SIGNAL SPLITTER	LOGIC-LEVEL x (INPUT) LOGIC-LEVEL y (OUTPUT) LOGIC-LEVEL z (OUTPUT)	$y_t = x_t \quad z_t = x_t$

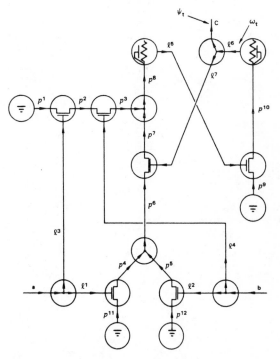

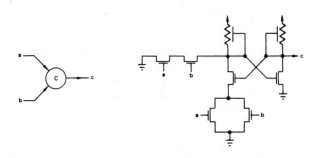

(a) MULLER C-ELEMENT AND NMOS REALIZATION

(b) CIRCUIT GRAPH FOR C-ELEMENT

FIGURE 1

Part IV: List of Working Groups

WORKING GROUP 1
DESIGN METHODOLOGY

Howard Baller
Hughes Aircraft Co.
P.O. Box 92426 (R1/C328)
Los Angeles, CA 90009

L. A. Belady
IBM (VAL)
Old Orchard Road
Armonk, NY 10504

John A. Dallen
Dept. of Computer Sciences
Duke University
Durham, NC 27706

Gerald Estrin
Computer Science Dept.
UCLA
Los Angeles, CA 90024

Randolph Franklin
E.C.S.E. Dept.
Rensselear Polytechnic Inst.
Troy, NY 12181

Chu S. Jhon
Electrical & Computer Engineering
University of Iowa
Iowa City, IA 52242

John Newkirk
AEL 205
Stanford University
Stanford, CA 94062

Bernard Witt
Univ. of North Carolina (and IBM)
Dept. of Computer Science
New West Hall 035A
Chapel Hill, NC 27514

WORKING GROUP 2
DESIGN SYNTESIS & MEASUREMENT

R. Cuykendall
CALTECH/JPL 171-209
4800 Oak Grove Drive
Pasadena, CA 91109

Anton Domic
Lincoln Lab
P.O. Box 73
Lexington, MA 02173

W. H. Joyner
IBM T. J. Watson Research Center
Yorktown Heights, NY 10598

Steve Johnson
Bell Labs
Murray Hill, NJ 07974

Steve Kelem
The Aerospace Corp. M1-102
P.O. Box 92957
Los Angeles, CA 90009

Dennis McBride
IBM Research Center
Yorktown Heights, NY 10598

Jack Mostow
USC-ISI
4676 Admiralty Way
Marina del Rey, CA 90291

G. Saucier
Lab IMAG
P.B. 53
38041 Grenoble, France

John Savage
Dept. of Computer Science
Brown University
Providence, RI 02912

WORKING GROUP 3
VERIFICATION & TESTING

Zen Kishimoto
GTE Labs
40 Sylvan Road
Waltham, MA 02254

Daniel Lubzens
Mircoelectronics Research Ctr.
Technion
Haifa, Israel

Edward F. Miller, Jr.
Software Research Associates
580 Market Street
San Francisco, CA 94104

Bill Overman
Aerospace Corp.
Los Angeles, CA 90009

Vijay Pitchumani
Syracuse University
Electrical & Computer Engr. Dept.
111 Link Hall
Syracuse, NY 13210

Rick Ramseyer
Honeywell, Inc.
Systems & Research Center
2600 Ridgeway Parkway
Minneapolis, MN 55413

Jean-Claude Rault
Agence De L'Informatique
Tour Fiat - Cedex 16
92084 Paris-La Defense
France

Rob Shostak, E1386
SRI International
Menlo Park, CA 94025

Larry Welsch
Bell Labs
Crawfords Corner Road
Holmdel, NJ 07733

Kwok Wu
Bell Labs, Rm. 2C426
Murray Hill, NJ 07928

WORKING GROUP 4
DESIGN ENVIRONMENT

Duane A. Adams
DARPA/IPTO
1400 Wilson Boulevard
Arlington, VA 22209

Randy H. Katz
Computer Science Dept.
Univ. of Wisconsin-Madison
Madison, WI 53706

Jacob Katzenelson
Dept. of E.E.
Technion-Israel
Institute of Tech.
Haifa, Israel

John Kellum
Honeywell, Inc.
2600 Ridgeway Parkway
MN17-2352
Minneapolis, MN 55408

Jock Rader
Hughes Aircraft Co.
P.O. Box 92426 (R8/4040)
Los Angeles, CA 90009

Steven P. Riess
Department of Computer Science
Box 1910
Brown University
Providence, RI 02906

Walt Scacchi
Computer Science Dept.
University of Southern California
Los Angeles, CA 90089-0782

Gilles Serrero
IMAG Laboratory - BP53X
38041 Grenoble Cedex
France

P. A. Subrahmanyam
Dept. of Computer Science
University of Utah
Salt Lake City, UT 84112

Jack Thomas
Aerojet Electro Systems
Box 296 B170/8427
Azusa, CA 91702

Gerard M. Baudet
Brown University
Computer Science Department
Box 1910
Providence, RI   02912

Mel Cutler
The Aerospace Corp.
P.O. Box 92957
MI/102
Los Angeles, CA   90009

Marc Davio
Philips Research Laboratory
Ave. van Becelaere, 2, Box 8
Brussels, Belgium   B1170

Surrendra Dudani
Honeywell
2600 Ridgeway Parkway, N.E.
MN17-2352
Minneapolis, MN   55403

A. Peskin
Building 515
Brookhaven National Labs
Upton, NY   11973

Franz J. Rammig
University of Dortmund
Abt. Inf. I
Postfach 500500
D-4600 Dortmund 50
West Germany

Author Index

Baller, H.H.	. . . .	3
Balzer, B.	. . . .	126
Baudet, G.M.	. . . .	64
Cutler, M.	. . . .	64, 157
Cuykendall, R.	. . . .	6, 97
Dallen, J.A.	. . . .	85, 160
Davio, M.	. . . .	64
Davis, A.M.	. . . .	75
Domic, A.	. . . .	6
Franklin, W.R.	. . . .	86
Hirschhorn, S.	. . . .	75
Johnson, S.C.	. . . .	6
Joyner, W.H.	. . . .	6
Joyner, W.H., Jr.	. . . .	134
Katz, R.	. . . .	50
Katz, R.H.	. . . .	135
Kelem, S.	. . . .	6
Kishimoto, Z.	. . . . . .	10, 140
Lubzens, D.	. . . .	10
McBride, D.	. . . .	6
Miller, E.	. . . .	10
Mostow, J.	. . . . 6, 117, 126
Overman, W.	. . . .	10
Peskin, A.M.	. . . .	64
Pitchumani, V.	. . . .	10, 138
Rammig, F.J.	. . . .	64, 112
Ramseyer, R.	. . . .	10
Rault, J.-C.	. . . .	10
Saucier, G.	. . . .	6, 107
Savage, J.E.	. . . .	6
Scacchi, W.	. . . .	50, 99
Serrero, G.	. . . .	107
Shostak, R.E.	. . . .	166
Smith, C.U.	. . . .	85, 160
Son, K.	. . . .	140
Stabler, E.P.	. . . .	138
Subrahmanyam, P.	. . . .	50
Subrahmanyam, P.A.	. . . . . .	90
Thomas, J.S.	. . . .	149